Wildflowers

OF THE **NORTHERN** AND **CENTRAL**
MOUNTAINS OF **NEW MEXICO**

Wildflowers

OF THE NORTHERN AND CENTRAL MOUNTAINS OF NEW MEXICO

Sangre de Cristo, Jemez, Sandia, and Manzano

Larry J. Littlefield & Pearl M. Burns

University of New Mexico Press • Albuquerque

Library of Congress Cataloging-in-Publication Data

Littlefield, Larry J.
 Wildflowers of the northern and central mountains of New Mexico : Sangre de Cristo,
Jemez, Sandia, and Manzano / Larry J. Littlefield and Pearl M. Burns. — First edition.
   pages cm
 Includes bibliographical references and index.
 ISBN 978-0-8263-5547-8 (pbk. : alk. paper) — ISBN 978-0-8263-5548-5 (electronic)
 1. Wild flowers—New Mexico—Identification. 2. Wild flowers—Sangre de Cristo
Mountains (Colo. and N.M.)—Identification. 3. Wild flowers—New Mexico—Jemez
Mountains—Identification. 4. Wild flowers—New Mexico—Sandia Mountains—
Identification. 5. Wild flowers—New Mexico—Manzano Mountains—Identification. I.
Burns, Pearl M. II. Title.
 QK176.L585 2015
 582.1309789—dc23
                                              2014013882

Cover photographs by Larry J. Littlefield
Interior photographs by Larry J. Littlefield and Pearl M. Burns unless otherwise noted.
Designed by Catherine Leonardo
Composed in Bell Gothic Std.
Display is Adobe Garamond Pro

Dedicated to the memory of Robert DeWitt Ivey (1923–2013), an outstanding teacher, scholar, artist, naturalist, and true gentleman. Through his guidance and five editions of *Flowering Plants in New Mexico* and other publications, DeWitt Ivey made New Mexicans more knowledgeable and more aware of the flora of our state.

CONTENTS

INTRODUCTION

Wildflowers of the Northern and Central Mountains of New Mexico is intended for wildflower enthusiasts, hikers, amateur botanists, and others interested in the more common flora of New Mexico's Sangre de Cristo, Jemez, Sandia, and Manzano Mountains, as well as neighboring mountains, including the Manzanita, San Pedro, Ortiz, and other lower-elevation mountains in central portions of New Mexico. The book includes color photographs, visual descriptions, and related biological and ethnobotanical discussions of the plants. Unless otherwise noted, all plants in the book are indigenous to North America, most to the semiarid Southwest. Included are common wildflowers and shrubs that bloom at different times, from early spring to late autumn, at elevations from ca. 5,500 ft. (1,664 m) to ca. 11,500 ft. (3,505 m) above sea level. Areas and plants in the alpine tundra above the tree line are not included. The examples of traditional uses of plants by Native Americans are primarily from tribes in New Mexico and Arizona.

Figures and accompanying text for each plant are grouped first by flower color, then alphabetically by family common name, then alphabetically by scientific name. See Elpel (2006) for well-illustrated, easy-to-follow descriptions of plant families. Plant descriptions are based on general field characteristics observable with the unaided eye. Whenever possible, descriptions are in nontechnical terms. Illustrated and text glossaries are provided for technical botanical terms used. All units of measure are English. Photographs and descriptions of flowers, other botanical organs, and various stages of development are included. Readers are referred to the references section for works containing more detailed descriptions; information about geographic distribution and basic biology; and traditional nutritional, medicinal, and ceremonial uses of the plants included. References in bold type are the ones that we used most often in writing this book.

Please note: plant flower colors and their intensities are often inconsistent. Variations in intensity or shades of color can result from genetic differences, time of day, environmental effects, the elevation at which the plant is growing, stage of flower maturity, or other reasons. *Flowers of pink, purple, blue, and lavender color are especially subject to wide variations in color and intensity.* For this reason, the words "to lavender" have been added to the Pink, Purple, and Blue Flowers color bars in those chapters, as these colors often shade into lavender. If you are uncertain about a flower's color, please refer to more than one color group for identification. Elevations given for the location of individual species are approximate at best. Plants with a more northern location are often found growing at lower elevations than plants that grow farther south. In addition to elevation effects, plants may be found growing outside the ranges stated in this book, depending on soil moisture, sun exposure, and other environmental factors.

The Sangre de Cristo Mountains extend southward from the Colorado border to approximately Bernal, some 50 miles east-southeast of Santa Fe. These mountains are the southernmost extent of the Rocky Mountains in North America and are the most striking visual topographic feature of northern New Mexico. They span an area approximately 120 miles north to south and 120 miles east to west. Of the four mountain ranges included in this book, the Rockies are by far the oldest, having been formed some 35–70 million years ago by massive compressional forces from the west as major tectonic plates collided, producing massive uplifts and crumpling of the earth's crust, with 10,000–20,000 ft. of uplift and associated folds and faults. Elevations within the Sangre de Cristos range from 5,590 ft. (1,704 m) near Española to that of New Mexico's highest mountain, Wheeler Peak (13,161 ft. (4,011 m), northeast of Taos (Price 2010).

The Sandia, Manzano (Spanish, "apple"), and Manzanita (Spanish, "little apple") Mountains are the most significant topographic feature of central New Mexico, extending approximately 60 miles (96 km) north to south and up to 15 miles (24 km) west to east, with a range of elevation from about 5,500 ft. (1,676 m) to 10,678 ft. (3,255 m) above sea level. The Manzanita Mountains, with an elevation lower than either the Manzanos or Sandias, extend for several miles south of Tijeras Canyon, the commonly designated boundary between the Sandias to the north and the Manzanitas and Manzanos to the south.

The Manzanitas and Manzanos are often referred to simply as the Manzano Mountains (Sivinski 2007).

The Sandias, Manzanitas, and Manzanos share basically the same geologic history, having been formed by rifting and uplift where the earth's crust was subjected to thinning and splitting apart to form a long, narrow fissure, or "rift," some 20–25 million years ago. That fissure, the Rio Grande Rift, extends today from southern Colorado into Texas and Mexico, forming a series of basins through which the Rio Grande flows southward. As the rift widened over a period of several million years, the earth's crust along the eastern edge of the rift gradually lifted upward, similar to a hinged trap door. That uplift exposed the present abrupt west face of the Sandia Mountains, the area toward the Rio Grande, and, to a lesser extent, the western parts of the Manzanitas and Manzanos. The more gently sloping east side of the mountains includes geologically "young" (300–65 million years old) sedimentary limestone and sandstone—"young," that is, compared to the 1.4 billion–year-old Sandia granite that comprises most of the exposed western face of the mountains (Price 2010). These limestone layers atop the underlying granite can be clearly seen along the crest of the Sandias when viewed from the west.

The Jemez Mountains, west of the southern reaches of the Sangre de Cristos, were formed neither by collision nor by separation of tectonic plates but rather by volcanic activity over the past 15 million years. More recently (1.6–1.2 million years ago), volcanic activity resulted in the Valles Caldera. Accompanying that cataclysmic volcanic activity, vast deposits of Bandelier ash-flow tuff were deposited atop more ancient sandstone and limestone, now clearly visible in canyon walls along the Jemez River and other areas of the Jemez Mountains. Even more recent volcanic activity (50,000–60,000 years ago) formed Battleship Rock north of Jemez Springs (Price 2010).

The rocks of all these mountains represent environments and time periods that encompass some 1.4 billion years and possess significant differences in chemical composition. Differences in chemical composition, physical properties (including permeability, hardness, texture, crystal size), whether the layers are flat-lying or folded, and other characteristics all contribute to the surface soils that eventually form upon degradation of the underlying bedrock, be it igneous, metamorphic, or sedimentary in origin (Hunt 1972). Additionally, topographic properties, primarily elevation and precipitation at different elevations of the mountains, greatly influence what plants occur where they do.

Despite the differing ecological and geological histories of these neighboring mountain ranges, they share a great commonality in wildflower occurrence. The large number and variety of plants in this relatively small region of convergence reflect the juxtaposition of regions that contain five major types of vegetation identified by Martin and Hutchins (1980) (Plate 1): (a) the **Rocky Mountain Ecoregion**, with its montane forests, prevalent in higher elevations of the Sangre de Cristo, Jemez, Sandia, and Manzano Mountains, including the ponderosa pine, mixed conifer, and spruce-fir zones (see Plate 2), up to but not including the alpine zone, the latter often being largely above the tree line and not included in this book; (b) the **Great Plains Grasslands Ecoregion** (adjoining the east faces of the Sangre de Cristo, Sandia, and Manzano Mountains); (c) the **Great Basin Grasslands Ecoregion** of the Colorado Plateau (adjoining the western faces of the Jemez and Sangre de Cristo Mountains); and (d) the **Chihauhauan Desert Ecoregion**, extending north from Mexico. At lower elevations of montane forests in all the above-mentioned mountains is the belt of encircling (e) **Piñon Pine–Juniper Woodlands** (Plate 2, the piñon pine–juniper zone) that form a transition zone between vegetation types of the higher mountains and the adjacent grasslands or Chihuahuan Desert influence regions (Dunmire 2012; Martin and Hutchins 1980). Plate 1 also shows the approximate area encompassed by this book, outlined in green, extending from approximately Mountainair (at the south end of the Manzanos) northward to the Colorado border and eastward from Valles Caldera in the Jemez Mountains to the Pecos River valley and Mora.

The predominate types of plant communities that occur at different elevations within ecoregions are referred to as **Life Zones** (Plate 2), named commonly by tree species characteristic of the respective zones. Some herbaceous wildflower species are more restricted to certain elevation ranges and Life Zones than other species; some occur across all elevations and Life Zones within the ecoregion. Plate 2 shows an approximation of elevations at which the Life Zones occur in the northern and central mountains of New Mexico. In both regions, the transition between Life Zones and the characteristic species therein is a gradual, not a distinct, change. As one travels from south to north in north central New Mexico, specific Life Zones are found to occur

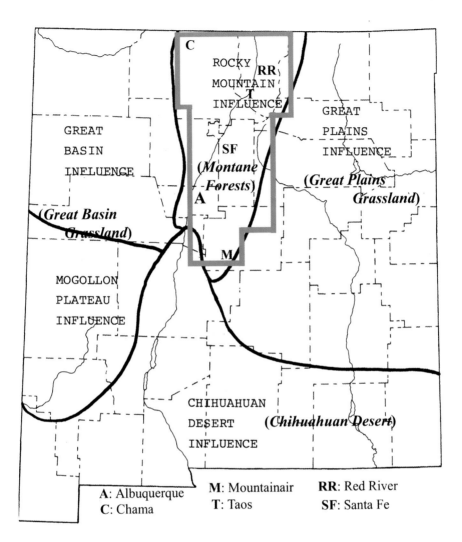

PLATE 1. Four major geographical/ecological regions (Great Plains Grassland, Montane Forests, Great Plains Grassland, and Chihuahuan Desert), all with different vegetational compositions, converge in north central New Mexico, providing the wide range of plant species present in the northern and central areas of the state. This New Mexico state map, from Martin and Hutchins (1980), shows their designations of five geographic ecoregion influences in the state in standard type; the corresponding four designations by Dunmire (2012) in italics; and, outlined in green, the area in which the plants included in this book were photographed. Map reproduced by permission of J. Cramer Verlag, distributed by Lubrecht & Cramer Ltd and Koeltz Scientific Books.

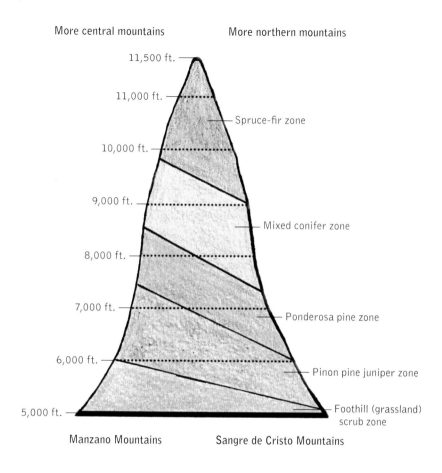

More central mountains   More northern mountains

11,500 ft.

11,000 ft.

    Spruce-fir zone

10,000 ft.

9,000 ft.

    Mixed conifer zone

8,000 ft.

7,000 ft.

    Ponderosa pine zone

6,000 ft.

    Pinon pine juniper zone

5,000 ft.   Foothill (grassland) scrub zone

Manzano Mountains   Sangre de Cristo Mountains

PLATE 2. Approximate elevations of different Life Zones in the mountains of central and northern New Mexico, ranging from about 5,000 to 11,500 ft. The average elevation for each Life Zone, going from left to right in the figure, *decreases* from south to north as elevation and annual moisture typically *increase*. The transition between adjacent Life Zones and the presence of species characteristic of those zones change gradually, not abruptly. Adapted from Dodson and Dunmire (2007) and Littlefield and Burns (2011). Note that elevation levels of the respective Life Zones in Plate 2 and the elevations and Life Zones stated in descriptions of individual plants in this book are *approximations at best* and take into account differences in latitude, elevation (as one moves from south to north in Plate 2), direction of the facing slopes of mountains (especially north vs. south or, for the Sandias, the west or east slopes), localized availability of moisture, and other factors where the plants are growing and were recorded.

at progressively lower elevations and are related to the reduced temperature and increased precipitation the farther one travels north (Plate 2).

The convention used by Moerman (1998), including his occasional use of individual Pueblo Indian tribe names rather than the language group names, is followed in this book. Three languages (**Tanoan**, **Keresan**, and **Zuni**) are spoken among the nineteen New Mexico Pueblo Indian tribes (Sando 1976). The **Tanoan** language includes three dialects: **Tiwa**, **Tewa**, and **Towa**. In this book, the name of the language or dialect group to which each Pueblo Indian tribe belongs is used more often than the name of the pueblo. For example, the Tiwa-speaking pueblos (Taos, Picuris, Sandia, and Isleta Pueblos) are typically referred to as "Tiwa"; the Tewa-speaking pueblos (Okhay Owingeh [San Juan], Santa Clara, San Ildefonso, Nambe, Tesuque, and Pojoaque Pueblos) are all referred to as "Tewa"; the Towa dialect is spoken only by Walatowa (Jemez) Pueblo. The **Keresan** language is spoken, with a few differences, by Acoma, Cochiti, Laguna, San Felipe, Santa Ana, Kewa (Santo Domingo), and Zia Pueblos; they are all referred to as "Keres." However, Moerman (1998) sometimes refers to Acoma and Laguna as "Western Keres," in which instances his reference is followed here. The **Zuni** language is spoken only by the Zuni Pueblo. Non-Pueblo Indian tribes, such as the Apache, Hopi, and Navajo, are referred to by their respective names.

We gratefully acknowledge the many valuable contributions made by others to the preparation of this book, including especially Timothy Lowrey and Phil Tonne, University of New Mexico; Patrick Alexander, New Mexico State University; Gene Jercinovic, Carolyn Dodson, Jim McGrath, and Robert Sivinski for their help in identifying plants; those who contributed photographs for the book and gave permission for their use: Linda Butler, Judy Dain, Kelly Dix, Jane Jeffords, and Gerald Simnacher; Jean Payne for countless hours of proofreading the manuscript; Adair Peterson for her meticulous drawings for the Illustrated Glossary; Annie Littlefield for hours of computer advice and assistance; and Jane Aubele for help in understanding the geology of the regions included. I am also grateful for; assistance and much support from Julie, David, and Sarah Littlefield; Louis Romero; Sally and Robert Lowder; Richard Frederiksen; Patricia Gegick; Robert Julyan; Walter Kleweno; Charles Metzger; Robert Parmeter, Valles Caldera National Preserve; Jeff Harris, U.S. Forest Service; Gerald Sussman; Donald Turton; Vince Case, Paul Mauermann, Rosie Norlander, and Chris Modelski of the

Sandia Mountain Natural History Center; the New Mexico Museum of Natural History and Science for extensive use of the Biosciences Reference Library; and fellow volunteers of the Trails Maintenance Team of the Friends of the Sandia Mountains (FOSM), U.S. Forest Service. Although we have received invaluable help from many others, the authors are solely responsible for any errors in this book.

BANANA YUCCA
Yucca baccata
(Datil Yucca)
Agave Family, Agavaceae

Native perennial, usually stemless, from thick roots on rocky soil in foothill scrub to ponderosa pine forest, 5,000–7,500 ft. **Leaves** basally clustered, lanceolate, rigid, spine tipped, up to 3 ft. long, 1¼–2 in. wide, concave upper surface with whitish, curled fibers along edges. **Flower stalk** not apparent until flowering; extends up to 2 ft., bearing densely clustered, drooping, white flowers on short stalks. **Flowers** have 6 overlapping petal-like segments 2–4 in. long; waxy; white, cream, or purple tinged. **Fruit:** a fleshy, cylindrical capsule, rounded at ends, resembling a small green banana, 3–7 in. long; does not split open upon maturity. **Blooms** mid-June to late July only once every few years. Used by numerous southwestern Native American tribes. Fruits used for food (fresh, dried, baked, or ground for use in cakes); leaves and leaf fibers for sandals, mats, baskets; leaf slivers for paintbrushes; large roots for soap and shampoo.

SOAPWEED YUCCA *Yucca intermedia*
(Narrowleaf or Plains Yucca) *(Y. baileyi* var. *intermedia, Y. glauca)*
Agave Family, Agavaceae

Usually stemless perennial in foothill scrub and piñon-juniper woodland, 4,000–7,000 ft. Similar in appearance to banana yucca except for leaf width, shape of flowers, and fruits that split open when mature. **Leaves** basally clustered, 12–26 in. long, ¼–⅜ in. wide; flat upper surface, convex lower surface; loose fibers along edges less prominent than those in banana yucca. **Flowers** bell shaped, white to cream, up to 2 in. long, borne along stalk that extends well beyond height of leaves in contrast to the stout, shorter stalk of banana yucca. Outer petals tinged with pink. **Fruit:** a small capsule 1¼–2½ in. long, splits open longitudinally when mature. **Blooms** mid-May to late June. Used by many southwestern tribes in much the same manner as banana yucca.

WESTERN YARROW   *Achillea millefolium*

Aster Family, Asteraceae

Erect perennial 1–2½ ft. tall; common in open meadows, moist areas, and along roadsides in ponderosa pine up to spruce-fir forest, 6,000–10,000 ft. **Leaves** alternate, strongly aromatic, 2–6 in. long, 1½ in. wide, soft, rather flat, feathery, divided repeatedly into fern-like segments. **Flower clusters** flattish to dome shaped, ca. 1½–2½ in. across, containing many small, stalked flower heads, each up to ½ in. diameter, consisting of a small center of 10–40 tiny **disk flowers** surrounded by 2–6 white- or pink-petaled **ray flowers**, each with blunt to rounded, sometimes notched tips. **Blooms** May into September. Used widely by Southwestern tribes and Hispanic settlers as a medicine for toothaches, upset stomach, coughs, sores, skin rashes and burns and as a natural insect repellent.

PEARLY EVERLASTING

Anaphalis margaritacea

Aster Family, Asteraceae

Erect perennial in open woods, piñon pine–juniper woodland to spruce-fir forest, 7000–10,000 ft. **Stems** 8–20 in. tall, unbranched, covered with short, stiff woolly hairs. **Leaves** alternate; sessile; narrowly oblong to lanceolate; ca. ¾–4 in. long; greener above than the white, woolly lower surface. Male and female flowers are generally borne on separate plants, but some plants have both. **Flower heads** numerous, white, furry, berry-like, to ¼ in. across; **rays** absent; **disk** yellow. Involucre ca. ¼–⅓ in. high; the numerous ovate, pearly white phyllaries in several series appear somewhat as clustered ray flowers. The flowers last quite a long time on the plant as well as dried, hence the name "everlasting." **Blooms** mid-July to October. No report found for uses of this plant by southwestern tribes, but many eastern and Great Lakes tribes report large numbers of medicinal, ceremonial, and decorative uses. Lower-right and upper photos courtesy of Gerald Simnacher.

SMALL-LEAF PUSSYTOES
(Nuttall's Pussytoes)
Aster Family, Asteraceae

Antennaria parvifolia

Woolly perennial forming tight mats of gray foliage with short, sparsely leafed **stems** bearing white, fuzzy terminal flowers. In open areas of mixed conifer and spruce-fir forest, 7,000–10,000 ft. Spreads laterally by horizontal rooting stems to form dense mats of foliage. **Basal leaves** in dense rosettes, ½ –¾ in. long, hairy on both surfaces; **upper leaves,** alternate on flower stalks, much narrower. **Flower heads** rayless, ca. ½ in. long, at top of 4–10 in. unbranched flower stalks; head consists of several tufted, fuzzy clusters of **disk flowers**; white, sometimes with a faint pinkish cast around the periphery, arising from a bell-shaped involucre below. Male and female flowers borne on separate plants. **Blooms** May through August.

MAYWEED
Anthemis coluta
(Stinking Camomile, Dog Fennel)
Aster Family, Asteraceae

Perennial introduced from Europe, on open areas of hills and forests more common in northern mountains, piñon-juniper woodland to mixed conifer forest, 5,000–9,000 ft. So named for its somewhat unpleasant odor and its appearance, which is similar to the true chamomile plant, *Anthemis noblis*. **Stems** to ca. 20 in. high, usually branched, smooth. **Leaves** ca. ¾–2 in. long, sparsely hairy, profusely pinnatifid, the segments linear. **Flower heads** solitary at stem and branch ends, up to 1 in. across; **ray flowers** 10–18, sterile, white with linear creases, tips rounded; **disk flowers** fertile, yellow; pappus lacking. Involucre saucer shaped, ca. ⅛–¼ in. high; phyllaries lanceolate to oblong-lanceolate, tips prominently pointed, midribs greenish to yellowish. **Blooms** May to August.

RAGWEED SAGE

Artemisia franseroides

Aster Family, Asteraceae

Erect perennial up to 24 in. tall, widespread on moist open ground, shaded slopes in mountains, mixed conifer and spruce-fir forest, 8,000–10,000 ft. Stems erect, smooth to finely hairy. Leaves alternate, ca. ⅓–2¾ in. long, lower leaves twice pinnatifid, upper leaves once pinnatifid, both with the lower lobes linear or lanceolate, cleft or entire; upper leaf surface green, mostly smooth, lower surface with tangled white hairs. Flower heads numerous, yellowish white, finely hairy, ca. ¼ in. diameter, on short branches, borne in a panicle along upper portions of stem; ray flowers absent; 50–100 tiny disk flowers per head. Blooms August through September.

FRINGED SAGE   *Artemisia frigida*
(Estafiata)
Aster Family, Asteraceae

Aromatic perennial up to 16 in. tall, an "under shrub," almost herbaceous, on dry plains, stony hills, piñon-juniper woodland and ponderosa pine forest, 5,500–8,000 ft. Herbage with appressed hairs giving a grayish appearance. **Stems** often woody at base, reclining to ascending to erect, branching. **Leaves** soft, doubly pinnatifid, with linear segments. **Flower heads**, with rayless flowers only, borne in clusters along stems and branches; greenish white. **Blooms** mid-July into October. Decoction of leaves taken by Navajo for cough and the very soft leaves as a convenient substitute for toilet paper. Hopi used the plant to flavor corn when roasting; leaves were also chewed or made into a decoction for indigestion, flatulence, or biliousness.

LOUISIANA SAGE *Artemisia ludoviciana*
(White Sage)
Aster Family, Asteraceae

Erect perennial, member of a cluster of several closely related, structurally similar subspecies. Common 5,000 ft. and above in piñon-juniper woodland up to spruce-fir forest. The common name "Louisiana Sage" comes from early 1803 records of the plant's presence throughout most areas of the Louisiana Purchase. Known also as white sage due to the silver-white appearance of its finely pubescent leaves. **Stems** up to 3½ ft. tall, covered with woolly white hairs. **Leaves** alternate, oblong to linear, edges smooth, variously lobed, mostly toward the tip, or incised, ½–4 in. long. Foliage aromatic, especially when crushed. **Flower heads** on short stalks, or sessile, along upper ½–⅔ of stem, often nodding in loose clusters. Heads consist of yellowish-white, fertile **disk flowers** only; **ray flowers** absent. **Blooms** July through September. All species of sage were widely used by native tribes throughout the western United States, for example, as a tea for treatment of stomach problems; as a snuff for sinus attacks, nosebleed, and headaches; as an astringent for eczema; as a deodorant; in many more medicinal applications; and in purification and other rituals.

FALSE BONESET   *Brickellia eupatorioides* var. *chlorolepis*

Aster Family, Asteraceae

Perennial from deep taproot, on plains, disturbed sites, foothills scrub, and piñon pine–juniper woodland, 4,000–7,500 ft., essentially statewide. **Stems** 12–28 in. high, erect, branched toward the apex, purplish green, lightly hairy, often forming subshrub clusters 3–4 ft. across. **Leaves** mostly alternate, linear to oblong, to ca. 2½ in. long without teeth or lobes, smaller toward top, with glandular dots beneath. **Flower heads** solitary or in small clusters at stem and branch ends (lower-left photo). **Disk flowers** only, each with a forked, creamy white to pale yellow thread-like style protruding from the flower's center (lower-right photo). **Fruit:** single-seeded achenes with long, feathery pappus extension when mature, forming open spherical heads (top left photo). Involucre narrow, ca. ½ in. high, phyllaries finely hairy, streaked, loosely overlapping. **Blooms** July through September. Used by Navajo as cough medicine, taken in a root decoction. Upper-right photo courtesy of Linda Butler.

TASSEL FLOWER

Brickellia grandiflora

Aster Family, Asteraceae

Perennial, sometimes rigid at base. Widespread in canyons, dry hills, and rocky slopes in piñon-juniper woodland up to spruce-fir forest, 5,500–10,500 ft. Stems erect, branched above, 12–40 in. high, lightly hairy. Leaves alternate or opposite, triangular to nearly lanceolate, long point at tip, ¾–4 in. long, coarsely toothed, with small glandular dots beneath. Flower heads in small clusters on upper stem and branches, nodding, white, becoming yellowish white; disk flowers only, in clusters of 20–40, perfect. Pappus of 25–30 soft tassels arising from achenes in the disk. Involucre cylindrical, ca. ½ in. high, phyllaries linear. Blooms August into October. Dried leaves used by Western Keres in a salve for rheumatism, infusion taken for overeating and flatulence; by Navajo in a cold infusion for headache.

DIFFUSE KNAPWEED

Centaurea diffusa

Aster Family, Asteraceae

Annual or short-lived perennial originating in the Mediterranean region, as are all the more than 400 species of this genus, now widespread over much of the United States; a highly competitive weed, a threat to pastures and rangelands, commonly scattered on roadsides or waste areas in New Mexico in scrub grassland to piñon-juniper woodland, 5,000–7,000 ft. Stems erect, up to 24 in. tall with ascending branches, rough to the touch. Stem leaves small, deeply pinnatifid, white, woolly below, to 3½ in. long. Leaves toward the inflorescences reduced in size, narrow, not pinnatifid. Flower heads near branch tips, many, small, narrow; predominately ray flowers, white to purplish, to ca. ½ in. long. Involucre yellowish-white, ca. ½ in. high; outer bracts (phyllaries) stiff, sharp pointed, ca. ⅓ in. long, with stout, thread-like hairs along the margins (lower-right photo). Blooms July to September.

BABY ASTER
(White Aster)
Aster Family, Asteraceae

Chaetopappa ericoides
(*Leucelene ericoides*)

Small, much-branched perennial; herbage with stiff, flat-lying hairs; on dry, often rocky slopes throughout New Mexico, grassland scrub up to ponderosa pine forest, 3,500–7,500 ft. Stems up to 6 in. tall. Leaves alternate, to ca. ½ in. long, tapering to petiole, with stiff hairs along the smooth margins. Flower heads small, singly at branch and stem ends; ray flowers pistillate, fertile, white, ca. ¼ in. long; tips commonly curling down in the evening and straightening by midmorning; disk flowers perfect, fertile, yellow. Pappas of white bristles. Involucre cylindrical, becoming open-vase shaped when fully open; 3 series of overlapping, linear phyllaries (lower-right photo). Blooms May through July. Plant used by Navajo dried and pulverized as snuff or drops of cold infusion for "nose problems," leaves chewed for toothache, infusion of plant and sumac berries taken for kidney disease; pulverized plant applied by Zuni for pain from cold or rheumatism and rubbed on body for swellings.

13

COMMON HORSEWEED
(Canadian Horseweed, Marestail)
Aster Family, Asteraceae

Conyza canadensis

Erect, branched annual up to 4 ft. tall; herbage with stiff hairs, throughout New Mexico in moist or dry ground from plains up to ponderosa pine forest; 3,500–8,000 ft. Leaves alternate, linear, oblong, or oblanceolate; ¾–4 in. long; up to ½ in. wide; tapering to a point, margins smooth or with fine teeth. Flower heads many, in small panicles along upper stem; unopened flowers somewhat vase shaped; ray flowers inconspicuous; disk flower corollas very slender, white, radiating from the base; white pappus bristles ca. ⅛ in. or smaller. Blooms July through September. Hopi applied a poultice of rubbed leaves to temples for headache; crushed plant rubbed on skin for sunburn by Western Keres. Navajos' many uses included an aid for stomachache, a lotion for pimples, and a treatment for infants with prenatal infections.

COULTER'S DAISY

Erigeron coulteri

Aster Family, Asteraceae

Perennial in moist meadows and along streams common in more northern mountains, ponderosa pine to spruce-fir forests, 8,500–11,000 ft. **Stems** erect, 8–24 in. tall, leafy, herbage hairy. **Leaves** tulip-like, oblong to lanceolate or the lower ones sometimes oblanceolate, margins smooth, sometimes toothed, usually somewhat clasping at the base, up to 6 in. long. **Flower heads** solitary or few in a cluster, to 1½ in. across with 50 or more white to pale lavender **rays** ca. ¾ in. long, **disk** almost hemispheric, yellow. Involucre (lower-right photo) saucer shaped, ca. ¼ in. high, phyllaries narrowly lanceolate with pointed tips, viscid with black hairs. **Blooms** June to August.

15

TRAILING FLEABANE   *Erigeron flagellaris*

Aster Family, Asteraceae

Biennial, 4–10 in. high; one of the most common "many-petaled daisies" in meadows, open woods, foothill scrub, piñon-juniper, ponderosa pine, and mixed conifer forest, 5,500–9,500 ft. **Stems** slender, sparsely leafy, of two types; flowering stems erect, bearing a single flower head at the tip and sterile, prostrate stems trailing along the ground, rooting at their tips. Rooting stems can form dense, tangled masses. **Basal leaves** elongated, spatulate to oblanceolate, ⅜–1 in. long, smooth margin; **stem and branch leaves** similar shape but smaller and narrower. Young buds initially pink, turning white upon opening. **Flower heads** solitary, up to ca. 1¼ in. diameter; typically reddish pink prior to opening; **ray flowers** many, 50–100 or more, white, often pink underneath (lower-right photo); **disk flowers** yellow. Subtending involucre ca. ¼ in. high with linear to lanceolate phyllaries of almost equal size, green to purplish. **Blooms** late May into September. Used by Navajo as a chewed poultice applied to spider and snake bites and to stop bleeding, also as an eyewash for livestock.

MOUNTAIN WOOLLY WHITE
(Mountain White Ragweed, Newberry's Hymenopappus)
Aster Family, Asteraceae

Hymenopappus newberryi
(*Leucampyx newberryi*)

Perennial up to 24 in. tall, in open areas on wooded slopes often in more northern mountains, ponderosa pine and mixed conifer forests, 7,000–9,000 ft.; occurs only in Colorado and New Mexico. Stems from a basal cluster, single to several, branched toward the top. Leaves alternate, mostly clustered at the base but a few, much reduced upper-stem leaves; basal leaves up to 10 in. long, pinnately divided into narrow, linear, flattened segments. Eight to ten flower heads per stem, ca. ½ in. high with yellow to reddish-brown disk flowers and 8–10 white, ⅝–¾ in. long, broad ray flowers, 3-lobed at the tip. Involucres bowl shaped, phyllaries broad with silky hairs (lower-right photo). Blooms June to September. Used by Isleta both as an infusion taken for stomachache and as a dried powder applied to the stomach for the same.

COULTER'S HORSEWEED
(Woolwort)
Aster Family, Asteraceae

Laennecia coulteri

Erect annual up to 3 ft. tall, common in a variety of disturbed habitats, plains, valleys, foothills, and mountains, piñon-juniper woodland to ponderosa pine forest, 3,500–8,000 ft. Herbage densely, finely hairy. **Stems** single to branched near base. **Basal leaves** ovate, to 4 in. long, sharply toothed, pointed tips; **stem leaves** linear to oblong, to 2½ in. long, sessile, their bases clasping, coarsely toothed margins, uppermost leaves less coarsely toothed. **Flower heads** small, many in panicles, from stem base to top; **disk flowers** only, less than ½ in. high, fertile, white. Involucre vase shaped, phyllaries linear, tips pointed with greenish center and white margins with fine, white tangled hairs (lower-right photo). Pappus bristles white. **Blooms** May to October. Identification kindly provided by Robert Sivinski.

OX-EYE DAISY

Leucanthemum vulgare
(*Chrysanthemum leucanthemum*)

Aster Family, Asteraceae

Perennial herb introduced from Europe by early colonists, now widespread across the United States; in New Mexico at scattered locations in meadows on moist slopes, along roadsides, mostly in mountains, 5,500–8,000 ft. **Stems** up to ca. 32 in., smooth to slightly hairy, branched toward the top. **Leaves** alternate, considerable variation in leaf shape and size; **basal leaves** (lower-middle photo) clustered in a rosette, obovate to spatulate, ca. 1⅜–4 in. long, with petioles longer than blades, margins toothed to deeply cut; **stem leaves** upright, 3–5 in. long, narrowly lanceolate, margins entire to sharply toothed or lobed, not stalked (lower-left and lower-right photos). **Flower heads** daisy-like, mostly single on stem ends; yellow **disk flowers** and white **ray flowers** ⅜–¾ in. long. Involucres saucer to bowl shaped, phyllaries linear, brownish margins, unevenly toothed at the tip (upper-right photo). **Blooms** June to September.

BLACKFOOT DAISY   *Melampodium leucanthum*

Aster Family, Asteraceae

Low perennial up to 12 in. high; in dry hills and canyons in foothill scrub and piñon-juniper woodland, 5,000–6,500 ft. Stems slender, branched, covered with appressed hairs. Leaves opposite, narrow, broadest toward the base, petioles lacking, up to 2½ in. long, ¼ in. wide, margin mostly smooth, sometimes with wavy lobes. Flower heads on stalks up to 4 in. long; ray flowers white, perfect, ¼–½ in. long, often purple-veined beneath; disk flowers perfect, yellow; involucre bowl shaped with 2 series of phyllaries, the outer series bending outward near their tips. Blooms June into October.

HEATH ASTER
(White Prairie Aster)
Aster Family, Asteraceae

Symphotrichum falcatum var. *commutatum*
(*Aster falcatum* var. *commutatum*)

Common perennial in piñon-juniper woodland and ponderosa pine forest; in open fields; along trails, roadsides, and ditches in late summer and early fall, 5,000–7,500 ft. Stems erect, one to several, hairy, grayish brown to brown, up to 24 in. high. Leaves alternate, sessile, linear, 1¼–4¼ in. long, margin smooth, upper and lower surfaces with flat-lying stiff hairs. Many flower heads, single or in loose groups on leafy, flowering branches up to ca. 4 in. long. Involucres more or less spherical, up to ½ in. high; phyllaries in 3–4 series, tips rounded to pointed, down turned (middle photo). Fifteen to thirty-five ray flowers, white, sometimes blue or pink; disk flowers yellow, becoming brown. Blooms late July to late September. Ground blossoms mixed with yucca suds used by Zuni to wash newborn infants to make hair grow and give strength to the body.

EASTER DAISY
Townsendia exscapa

(Dwarf Townsend's Daisy, Easter Stemless Daisy)
Aster Family, Asteraceae

Dwarf, often tufted, nearly stemless perennial up to 2 in. tall, on mountain slopes, gravelly hills, piñon-juniper woodland, and ponderosa pine forest, 4,500–8,000 ft. **Leaves** often matted, very narrow, clustered at base, up to 2⅜ in. long and ⅛–¼ in. wide, sharply pointed, variously hairy, margins smooth. **Flower heads** sessile or short stalked, nestled among the elongated leaves, up to ca. 1–1½ in. diameter, ca. ½ in. long, pistillate; white **ray flowers** tinged with pink or lavender surround many tiny, yellow, perfect **disk flowers.** Involucre hemispheric, phyllaries numerous, overlapping, linear to lanceolate. Pappus of gray-white bristles of fruit achenes (lower-right photo). **Blooms** mid-April into June, one of the earliest-blooming wildflowers. Plant chewed or taken as an infusion by Navajo to ease birth delivery; also used in the "unraveling" or "untying" ceremony.

HIDDEN FLOWER
(Thicksepal Catseye, Thicksepal Cryptantha)
Borage Family, Boraginaceae

Cryptantha crassisepala

Short, compact annual; stems 2–6 in. high, erect to spreading, with many coarse hairs. On calcareous soil in dry plains and foothill scrub, 3,500–6,500 ft. Leaves alternate, ¾–1¼ in. long, oblanceolate, covered with stiff, coarse hairs having inflated, blister-like bases; no distinct petiole. Flowers nearly sessile in dense, hairy clusters along stem ends, typically along one side of stem. Prior to flower opening, stem tip is curved, giving a somewhat "fiddlehead" appearance. Corolla tubular, opening into 5 very small, white petals. Blooms late April through June. Used by Hopi for boils or other swellings, by Navajo as a lotion for itching, by Zuni as a hot infusion applied to limbs for fatigue, but considered a bad, poisonous weed by Keres.

BINDWEED HELIOTROPE
(Fragrant Heliotrope)
Borage Family, Boraginaceae

Heliotropium convolvulaceum

Annual on sandy hills, rangeland, widespread throughout New Mexico except in more northern and southwestern mountains. Hairiness of herbage gives the plant an overall grayish appearance. **Stems** up to ca. 10 in. high, branched from the base and above, prostrate or ascending, with straight, stiff, appressed hairs. **Leaves** alternate, petiolate, ¼–½ in. long, blade ovate to lanceolate, tips blunt to pointed, with stiff hairs above and below. **Flowers** attractive, white and sweet scented, in clusters at branch tips, pedicel not elongating with age. Corolla exceeding end of calyx, funnel form, ca. 1 in. across, much. **Blooms** July and August. Seed made into a mush and used as food by Navajo.

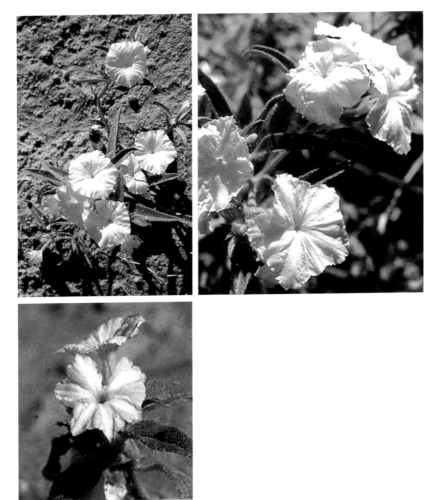

CUPSEEDED STICKSEED
(Spiny Sheepbur)
Borage Family, Boraginaceae

Lappula occidentalis var. *capulata*
(*L. redowskii*)

Erect annual up to 1½ ft. tall; common along roadsides, on dry slopes, or on disturbed sites; often on sandy ground in foothill scrub, piñon-juniper woodland to ponderosa pine forest, 4,500–8,000 ft. **Stems** branched above with short, stiff hairs. **Leaves** sessile, alternate, linear to lanceolate to oblong, ½–1½ in. long, with short, stiff hairs. **Flowers** perfect, numerous, very small, borne on short stalks in leaf axils, white to pale blue; 5 petals, tubular at base but opening widely, margins smooth; 5 stamens, not protruding. **Fruit** segmented into 4 spiny nutlets. Spiny nutlets easily entangle in wool, creating a problem for sheep ranchers; also cling to any passerby, facilitating the plant's dissemination. **Blooms** mid-April through August. Navajo applied a poultice of the plant to sores caused by insects and used as a lotion made from a cold infusion, for sores or swellings.

FENDLER'S BUCKBRUSH
(Mountain Lilac)
Buckthorn Family, Rhamnaceae

Ceanothus fendleri

Low, heavily branched shrub, mostly less than 3 ft. tall with branch tips sharply spined, thorn-like; in ponderosa pine to mixed conifer forest, 5,500–9,500 ft. **Leaves** alternate, on short petioles, narrowly elliptic to oblong, ⅜–1½ in. long, with 3 prominent veins running lengthwise from the base; hairy below; smooth margins. **Flowers** small, on stalks in dense clusters at stem and branch ends. Five petals, white, cup shaped, tapering to a narrow base; style 3-lobed, with stigma, and 5 greenish-brown stamens protruding beyond the petals (middle-left photo). **Fruit:** a small 3-lobed capsule, initially red, turning brown and dry when mature. **Blooms** entire summer from April through September, beginning soon after leaf initiation. Berries sweetened with sugar and used for food by Acoma, Laguna, and Keres; leaves chewed for sore mouth by Keres.

ANTELOPE SAGE
Eriogonum jamesii var. *jamesii*
(James' Wild Buckwheat)
Buckwheat Family, Polygonaceae

Low perennial, forming mats 4–12 in. high on dry, rocky slopes in piñon-juniper woodland up to rocky outcrops in mixed conifer forests, 6,000–9,000 ft. **Stems** ascending to erect, often rigid toward base, branched, covered with matted hairs. Flowering stems mostly leafless. **Leaves** mostly elliptic to ovate, narrowed to a wedge-shaped base, pointed to blunt at tip, 1¼–3¼ in. long, slightly hairy above, densely hairy beneath. Upper leaves smaller, restricted to base of stem branches. **Flowers** in small, stalked clusters subtended by leaf-like bracts at ends of flowering branches. Flowers up to 1¼ in. high, with a calyx of 6 creamy-white to yellowish-white, petal-like sepals, each typically light green toward the middle; petals absent (lower-left photo). Anthers and stigma extend well beyond sepals (upper-right photo). **Blooms** July through September. Roots soaked in water and used as an eyewash, fresh or dried roots eaten for stomachache or carried in mouth for sore tongue by Zuni. Navajo used decoction of whole plant as a contraceptive, also to ease labor pains.

EL VADO SPEARLEAF BUCKWHEAT *Eriogonum lonchophyllum*

Buckwheat Family, Polygonaceae

Perennial on dry ground in more northern mountains, sagebrush communities, grassland scrub to piñon pine–juniper woodland, 5,500–6,500 ft. Difficult to identify to species, as several varieties in the plant's natural range are defined largely on leaf size, shape, and distribution, as well as their spreading to subshrubby growth habit. Leafless flowering stems 12–24 in. tall, spreading to 2 ft., smooth, branched toward the top. Leaves basal, somewhat varied, essentially linear, nearly vertical, narrowly lanceolate, ¼ in. or less wide, surface often wrinkled (upper-middle photo), velvety to densely white-hairy below (upper-right photo) spreading to ascending and curved (middle-right photo). Flowers tiny, ¼ in. or less wide, in dense clusters at stem and branch ends; petals absent; 4 sepals, petal-like, white to pink; 6–9 stamens, anthers red; styles thread-like, extending beyond sepals (middle photo). Blooms June into October.

REDROOT BUCKWHEAT

Eriogonum racemosum

Buckwheat Family, Polygonaceae

Erect, stemless perennial in open areas of piñon-juniper woodland up to mixed conifer forest, 5,500 to 8,500 ft. Roots quite massive, reddish in color. **Leaves** basal, oblong to elliptic, up to 4 in. long, 1–1½ in. wide, on petioles of similar length; both surfaces with tangled, white woolly hairs, margins entire. Flower stalks 12–20 in. tall, leafless, woolly, 2 or 3 branched. **Flowers** sessile, in dense, bell-shaped clusters along upper portions of stalk. White to pink with slender, dark, lengthwise vein in each of the 6 small petal-like sepals. Petals absent. Nine elongated white stamens, each with a terminal pink anther (lower-right photo). **Blooms** July through September. Cold infusion of whole plants used by Navajo for blood poisoning or internal injuries, also for backaches and sideaches.

WRIGHT'S WILD BUCKWHEAT *Eriogonum wrightii*

Buckwheat Family, Polygonaceae

Perennial herb 8–16 in. tall, typically on rocky soil and dry slopes in foothill scrub and piñon-juniper woodland, 5,500–8,000 ft. **Stems** brittle; with tangled, woolly hairs; leafy toward base; much branched above with fewer leaves. **Leaves** lanceolate to elliptic to oblanceolate, pointed at tip and base, up to 1 in. long, ¼ in. wide, wooly hairs above and beneath. **Flowers** clustered into small groups within a sessile, woolly base; numerous clusters along upper stem. Flowers less than ¼ in. long, consisting of 6 pinkish-white, petal-like sepals, each with prominent, greenish midvein. Petals absent. Anthers and stigma extending beyond the sepals. **Blooms** July through August. Used by Navajo as an emetic.

SILVER LACE VINE
(Climbing Knotweed, Mile-a-Minute Vine)
Buckwheat Family, Polygonaceae

Polygonum baldschuanicum
(*Fallopia aubertii, F. baldschuanicum*)

Ornamental introduced from Asia, well adapted to central and northern New Mexico up to ca. 9,000 ft.; a vigorously climbing, dense, perennial, deciduous vine on disturbed riparian sites in sun to partially shaded nonriparian areas; sometimes planted along fences. **Stems** woody, smooth, wiry, twining, up to 10 ft. long or more, extending both horizontally and vertically. **Leaves** dark green, petiolate, blade ca. 1–4 in. long, 2½–2¾ in. wide, ovate to somewhat arrowhead shaped, margins entire to slightly undulate. **Flowers** on pedicels in whorls of 3 or more in inflorescences 1½–4 in. long. Sepals and petals white, greenish-white to pinkish. **Fruit:** 3-winged, teardrop-shaped samara (lower-right photo). Beware planting silver lace vine as an ornamental unless it will be vigorously pruned and contained to the area intended. The common name "mile-a-minute vine" is quite appropriate.

BANEBERRY

Actaea rubra

Buttercup Family, Ranunculaceae

Large, bush-like, perennial, up to ca. 3 ft. tall in higher, moist areas of ponderosa pine to spruce-fir forest, above 7,500 ft. **Leaves** alternate, divided into 3 leaflets, each leaflet palmately 3-lobed. Overall leaf length, including petiole, 6–14 in. **Flowers** small, white, borne in a dense "bottle brush" cluster at stem end; 3–5 sepals, early deciduous; 4–10 petals, small, spatulate, ⅛ in. long or less; stamens many, extend well beyond petals. **Berries** bright red, occasionally white, glossy, in elliptical clusters at stem end; berries ¼–½ in. long. **Blooms** May to late July; red fruits prominent mid- to late August. No reports of use by southwestern Native American tribes; several northern and eastern woodland tribes used preparations from roots and leaves for colds and stomach pains and to increase milk flow of nursing mothers. The fruits are toxic.

NORTHERN ANEMONE
(Meadow Anemone, Windflower)
Buttercup Family, Ranunculaceae

Anemone canadensis

Erect perennial 8–24 in. tall, from slender rhizomes; usually found in woods and meadows, commonly along streams in canyon bottoms of ponderosa pine and mixed conifer forest, 7,000–8,500 ft. **Leaves** of two types; **basal leaves** 2–6 in. wide with long petioles, palmately 3–5 lobed, each lobe irregularly toothed and deeply veined; **stem leaves** similar but smaller, in 1 to 3 sessile, whorled sets, with 3 deep, irregularly and sharply toothed lobes. **Flowers** perfect, solitary on stalks from leaf whorls; petals absent; mostly 5 sepals, white, unequal, ⅜–¾ in. long, broadly rounded; pistils and stamens numerous (lower-right photo). **Blooms** early June through July. Although utilized medicinally by numerous northern tribes where the plant is more prevalent, no reports found of the plant's use by southwestern tribes.

WHITE MARSHMARIGOLD
(Elk's Lip)
Buttercup Family, Ranunculaceae

Caltha leptosepala
(*Psychrophilias leptosepala*)

Perennial up to 8 in. tall in wet meadows, seeps, boggy ground in high northern mountains, subalpine forest, 9,500–12,000 ft. **Stems** single, erect, smooth, bearing a single flower. **Leaves** 1⅝–3¼ in. long, mostly basal, petiolate, thick, glossy, ovate to heart shaped, notched at the base, palmately veined, margins with small, pointed, or rounded teeth. One **flower** per stalk, to 1¼ in. across with 6–12 white, petal-like sepals. Petals absent. **Blooms** June to August.

VIRGIN'S BOWER

Clematis ligusticifolia

Buttercup Family, Ranunculaceae

Perennial vining herb common on slopes and in canyon and forest edges throughout New Mexico, 4,000–7,500 ft. Stems trailing, often climbing over fences and other vegetation. Leaves opposite, pinnately compound, with 3–7 smooth, lanceolate, oblong or ovate, coarsely toothed or 3-lobed leaflets. Flowers unisexual with the male (staminate) and female (pistillate) flowers on separate plants, both borne in loose clusters on long, hairy stalks. Petals absent, but both with 4 white, petal-like sepals. Staminate flowers (upper photos) with numerous greenish-white stamens projecting almost to ends of sepals. Pistillate flowers (lower photos) with ovaries projecting into narrowly feather-like styles ca. 1–2 in. long (see also Rocky Mountain Clematis). Blooms May to September. Cold infusion of the plant used by Navajo as a lotion for backache or swollen arms.

PASQUEFLOWER
(American Pasqueflower)
Buttercup Family, Ranunculaceae

Pulsatilla patens ssp. *multifida*
(*Anemone patens*)

Erect, early-blooming, low-growing perennial occurring in open meadows and shaded ponderosa pine and mixed conifer forest, 7,000–10,000 ft. Usually several stems, 6–12 in. tall, entire herbage with long, easily visible, dense, silky hairs. Basal leaves (not shown in these photos) appear after flowering; 3–7 lobed petiolates, each lobe further divided into narrow segments; stem leaves slender, feather-like, sessile, ¾–2 in. long, in a single whorl initially around base of flower. Flower stalk continues to elongate, distancing the base of the flower from the leaf whorl (lower-left photo). Flowers perfect, solitary on stalk, 1½–3 in. across. Petals absent. Five to seven sepals, showy, petal-like, ¾–1½ in. long, lanceolate to ovate, pale blue to white, silky hairs on the back. Numerous yellow stamens surround a spherical cluster of feathery styles (lower-right photo). Blooms late March to early May. The common name ''pasqueflower'' comes from the Old French word for Easter, indicative of the approximate period of flowering.

FALSE BUGBANE

Buttercup Family, Ranunculaceae

Trautvetteria caroliniensis
(*T. grandis*)

Perennial from rhizomes in shaded, wooded seepage slopes, stream banks, bogs, in ponderosa pine to spruce-fir forest zones in more northern mountains, 8,000–11,500 ft. One to several **stems** up to 3 ft. tall, smooth, usually unbranched below inflorescence. **Basal leaves** large with petioles up to 20 in. long, blade ca. 4–12 in. wide, deeply palmate with lobe apices pointed. **Stem leaves** reduced toward stem apex. **Flowers** in a panicle inflorescence up to ca. 3 in. across, more or less flat topped (middle-right photo); individual flowers borne in clusters at ends of peduncles (middle-right photo). Sepals early deciduous, greenish white, 3–5; petals absent. The many white, flattened stamen filaments are the most conspicuous part of the plant's flower. **Fruit** a samara, tan, flat, papery when mature (lower-middle photo). **Blooms** June to August. Upper-left, upper-right, and lower-right photos courtesy of Jane Jeffords.

RED-OSIER DOGWOOD

Cornus sericea
(C. stolonifera)

Dogwood Family, Cornaceae

Deciduous, many-stemmed perennial shrub up to 8 ft. tall, in clusters 10 ft. or more across, in sunny, moist meadows, around streams and other sunny riparian areas more in northern mountains, from foothills to mixed conifer forest, 5,500–9,000 ft. Spreads by prostrate, rooting stems and lower branches. Bark of **stems** reddish brown to purplish red, becoming grayish white when mature. **Leaves** opposite, elliptic, pointed at ends, short petioled, 2–3¼ in. long, dark green, glossy, smooth on upper surface, finely haired beneath, imparting a dull, grayish-green appearance. **Flowers** with tiny white petals and sepals, to ca. ¼ in. across, in a terminal flat- topped, clustered inflorescence (cyme) 1–2½ in. across. **Fruit:** white, berry-like, ca. ¼ in. diameter, in clusters, maturing to bluish white. **Blooms** late May into July. Sometimes mistaken for willow before leaves emerge in spring. Very few uses reported by southwestern tribes—as a ceremonial emetic by Navajo and for bows and arrows by Jemez—but scores of uses, including food (berries), smoking (leaves), cordage and a dye source (stem bark), medicinal, and more by numerous tribes in more moist eastern and northern regions where the plant is widespread.

TOOTHED POINSETTIA

Euphorbia Family, Euphorbiaceae

Euphorbia davidii
(*E. dentata, Poinsettia dentata*)

Erect annual in canyon bottoms and on disturbed soils in foothill scrub up to ponderosa pine forest, 6,000–8,000 ft. Characteristic of all euphorbias, the plant contains a milky, latex-like sap. **Stem** 5–12 in. tall, usually branched. **Leaves** mostly opposite, ½–2½ in. long, on petioles; largely ovate to lanceolate with distinct, lightly to coarsely toothed margins and irregularly shaped, reddish-brown blotches of various sizes sometimes along the midrib area. **Flowers** greenish white in small, congested clusters at stem and branch ends; pistillate and staminate flowers separate but both situated in a cup-like involucre with small greenish-white lobes containing a pistillate flower surrounded by several staminate flowers; sepals and petals absent. **Fruit** a somewhat cylindrical, greenish-white to brownish-red, 3-segmented body ca. ³⁄₁₆ in. diameter below the flower (upper-left and lower-right photos). At maturity, the fruit splits open longitudinally and forcibly ejects seeds several feet. **Blooms** July into September. Close relatives of toothed poinsettia include the beautiful Christmas poinsettia and leafy spurge, an introduced noxious weed injurious to cattle that vigorously invades rangelands of the northern plains states.

39

STEMLESS EVENING PRIMROSE
(Tufted Evening Primrose)
Evening Primrose Family, Onagraceae

Oenothera caespitosa

Stemless perennial growing in tufts 2–5 in. high on open slopes and in arroyos and disturbed sites in foothill scrub, piñon-juniper woodland, and ponderosa pine forest, 4,000–7,000 ft. The hypanthium (upper-left photo), an elongated basal portion of the flower, may often be mistaken for the stem. Leaves clustered at ground level; mostly lanceolate up to 4 in. long, usually wavy-lobed or merely toothed. Flowers fragrant, initially white, drying and pink with age. Ovary near the basal cluster of leaves, with the 2–4 in. long hypanthium extending upward to the sepals and petals. Four sepals, bent downward after flower opens. Four petals, showy, white, somewhat triangular, 1–1½ in. long. Petals open in the evening, remain open all night, allowing pollination by moths; the following day they turn red and close. Fruit an ovoid capsule ¾–1¼ in. long at base of the hypanthium. Blooms mid-May into July. Used by Hopi as treatment for sore eyes and toothache and by Navajo as a poultice for large swellings.

PINK EVENING PRIMROSE
(Cutleaf Evening Primrose)
Evening Primrose Family, Onagraceae

Oenothera coronopifolia

Erect perennial common in exposed areas of foothill scrub up to ponderosa pine forest, 5,000–8,000 ft. **Stems** sometimes branched, mostly finely hairy, up to 10 in. tall. The common names "cutleaf" and "combleaf" primrose refer to the alternate, oblong to lanceolate, deeply pinnately divided **leaves**, 4–8 in. long with narrow lobes. Lower leaves smaller, also with wavy-toothed margins. **Flowers** nodding in the bud stage, borne singly at end of a 4–12 in. long, finely haired hypanthium arising from ovary in the leaf axils; see Stemless Evening Primrose. Four sepals, pinkish red, bent downward after flowers open (lower photo). After the flower opens, the four ¼–½ in. long white petals become pink with age. Eight yellowish, elongated stamens radiate from center of flower. Four larger, greenish stigmas with an elongated cross configuration extend above the stamens. Members of the evening primrose family typically open in afternoon or evening, facilitating pollination by nocturnal moths. **Blooms** early June into August. Used traditionally by Navajo and Zuni for treatment of large swellings.

SICKLETOP LOUSEWORT *Pedicularis racemosa*

Figwort Family, Scrophulariaceae

Perennial in damp woods, bogs, and wet meadows of northern mountains in mixed conifer and spruce-fir forests, 9,000–11,500 ft. **Stems** up to 20 in. tall, slender, leafy, erect
or ascending in clumps from woody roots. **Leaves** well distributed along the stems,
alternate, petioles absent, 1¼–3 in. long, lanceolate to linear, margins finely toothed.
Flowers borne singly in a short, loose raceme at stem apex, each subtended by 2 small,
leaf-like bracts in the leaf axil. Calyx deeply divided, with pointed tips. Corolla white
to purplish pink, ca. ½–⅝ in. long, the hooded upper lip ("galea," comprising the two,
coalesced upper petals) strongly arched and curved downward, tapering to a slender,
down-curved beak that often touches the prominent, shallowly 3-lobed lower lip, which
is about the same length as the upper lip (upper-right and middle-left photos). **Blooms**
July and August.

GREEN GENTIAN
(Monument Plant; Deer's Ears)
Gentian Family, Gentianaceae

Frasera speciosa
(*Swertia radiata*)

Large, erect, perennial, usually on partially shaded open slopes, in mixed conifer and spruce-fir forest, 7,500–10,500 ft., requiring several years for growth of basal leaves to produce and store sufficient nutrients in the roots to initiate formation of the thick flowering stems. **Stem** single, 2–7 ft. tall, with an overall slender cone shape of stem and leaves (upper-middle photo). **Basal leaves** (upper-left photo) in a low, 1–1½ ft.-high cluster, 4–12 in. long, oblong to ovate; individual leaves resemble deer ears. **Stem leaves** sessile, lanceolate to linear, smaller than basal leaves. **Flowers** on short stalks in leaf axils along most of stem length. Four petals, each 1–1½ in. wide, greenish white with purple dots and pointed tip. Four sepals, greenish white, narrow, beneath and extending beyond the petals. Ovary green, distinct, conical, at the center. Eight large, densely but finely haired, yellowish-green anthers extend outward from beneath the ovary and above the petals (lower-right photo). **Blooms** mid-June through August. After flowering and seed production the plant dies; dry stalks persist throughout the winter.

RICHARDSON'S GERANIUM   *Geranium richardsonii*

Geranium Family, Geraniaceae

Perennial, in partially shaded, moist, ponderosa pine, mixed conifer, and spruce-fir forests, 7,000–11,000 ft.; often among purple geranium and other vegetation. Stems single or few, in clusters, ascending or spreading, much branched, 16–32 in. long with short, soft, hairs. Leaves opposite, with long petioles, leaf pentagonal in outline, up to 4 in. wide, palmately 5-lobed with coarsely toothed or lobed margins. Flowers prominent, ca. ¼–1 in. wide, solitary or in loose clusters on purplish flower stalk. Five petals, spreading, flat, oblong, white to pink with purplish veins. Five sepals, greenish white, tips pointed, shorter than petals, less prominent than in purple geranium. Ten stamens, radiating outward; anthers tan to tannish-gold (middle-right photo). Styles united into a column with 5 curled stigmas (middle-left photo). Seed pod slender, elongated, ca. 1½ in. long (lower-right photo), similar to purple geranium. Blooms June through September. Paste made from crushed roots used by Keres for treatment of sores.

TRUMPET GOOSEBERRY   *Ribes leptanthum*

Gooseberry Family, Grossulariaceae

Branched shrub up to 6 ft. high. Common in wooded and riparian areas and in canyons, from foothill scrub to ponderosa pine forest, 6,500–8,500 ft. **Stems** slender with gray to brown bark and 1 or 3 stout spines up to ¾ in. long at nodes (middle-left photo). **Leaves** alternate, on petioles, averaging less than ¾ in. wide at maturity. Palmately 5-lobed, the lobes incised or toothed. **Flowers** white, 1–3 per group, perfect, subtended by a bract on short stalk. Floral tube cylindric, ca. ¼ in. long; 5 short sepals curved backward at their apex; corolla elongated, with 5 white petals fused ca. half their length; petals and sepals finely, softly hairy (right-upper photo). **Fruit:** a globose berry ⅛–¼ in. diameter, usually smooth, color progressing from green to red to black with maturity. **Blooms** early May into June. Berries eaten fresh by Jemez, Isleta, and Apache; fruit made into pressed cakes by Apache for use during winter.

WOLF CURRANT

Ribes wolfii

Gooseberry Family, Grossulariaceae

Spreading to erect shrub up to 6 ft. high, widespread in central and northern mountains, piñon-juniper woodland to spruce-fir forest, 7,500–11,500 ft. **Stems** spineless, young twigs with fine hairs. **Leaves** alternate on short, spur-like branches, often in clusters of 3, petioles ca. ½–2 in. long, blades almost round in outline, ca. ¾–3 in. long, 3–5 lobed, veins markedly impressed above, raised beneath, margins rounded or with sharp teeth. **Flowers** perfect, in dense clusters on erect stalks from leaf axils. Floral cup glandular, saucer shaped, finely hairy, tipped by 5 spreading sepals and 5 white, erect, obovate petals; 5 stamens. **Fruit:** berries up to ca. ⅓ in. diameter with many gland-tipped hairs. **Blooms** May into June. Fruit eaten fresh and used to make jelly by Apache, also ground, dried, and pressed into cakes for storage.

FOUR-WINGED SALTBUSH
Atriplex canescens

Goosefoot Family, Chenopodiaceae

Erect, highly branched shrub up to 8 ft. tall; typically on open, dry alkaline soils in foothill scrub and piñon-juniper woodland, 5,000–7,000 ft. **Leaves** alternate or in fascicles; blades oblong to lance shaped, ½–2 in. long, rough surfaced, smooth margin, gray green (upper- and lower-left photos). Dioecious plant with **staminate** and **pistillate flowers** on separate plants (upper-right photo: staminate plant, left; pistillate plant, right). **Staminate flowers** in small, globular clusters, cream colored to yellow; not present in these photos. **Pistillate flowers** and immature fruits (lower-middle photo) borne in panicles 2–10 in. long. **Mature fruit** (two lower-right photos), with a pair of two-winged bracts extending laterally from the center axis of the fruit, giving it a "four wing" appearance. **Blooms** May to September. Provides forage for deer, pronghorns, sheep, and cattle; seeds consumed by birds and rodents. Well suited for revegetating saline sites, mine spoils, roadsides, and other disturbed, alkaline soil sites. Numerous uses by many southwestern Native American tribes, including leaves and new shoots made into yellow dye, seed ground into flour, numerous dermatological uses, and ashes of burned foliage used as leavening agent for bread.

WINTERFAT

Krascheninnikovia lanata
(Ceratoides lanata)

Goosefoot Family, Chenopodiaceae

Low, erect perennial shrub or shrublet, woody at base, up to ca. 24 in. tall, covered with star-shaped hairs mixed with long, soft, unbranched white-gray hairs, on plains and foothills, 5,000–7,000 ft., often on dry clay, chalky, saline, or alkaline soils. Commonly in large clusters with many erect stems, branched near the base. Leaves alternate, linear or narrowly lanceolate, sessile or with short petioles, ca. ½–2 in. long, covered with hairs. Flowers in dense, finely haired, cottony clusters along upper ⅓–½ of the stem. Anatomy of the small unisexual flowers, on the same or different plants, is essentially impossible to discern in the field. Blooms July into October. Winterfat has high forage value for grazing and browsing animals. Hopi used powdered roots as a dressing to treat burns, a decoction of leaves for fever; used by Navajo as an antihemorrhagic for blood spitting, a cold infusion taken for *Datura* poisoning, considered a good winter forage for sheep; used by Tewa in ceremonials to produce steam.

POINTLEAF MANZANITA   *Arctostaphylos pungens*

Heath Family, Ericaceae

Erect or spreading shrub up to 6 ft. tall. More common in southwestern New Mexico, extending into the Jemez Mountains, 5,000–8,000 ft., on dry slopes and in sandy soils, in piñon pine, juniper, and oak forests. **Stem** bark smooth to scaly, reddish brown. **Leaves** elliptic to lanceolate, pointed at the tip, ¾–1¾ in. long, light green to bluish green. **Flowers** in drooping clusters, white to pinkish white, each with an inverted urn appearance; corolla lobes fused, recurved at their tips (lower-left photo). Prominent single style and stigma extending well beyond the ovary (lower-right photo). **Fruit:** globose, smooth, lustrous, red, up to ½ in. diameter. **Blooms** April and May. Dried leaves smoked in ceremonies by Cochiti; leaves used as a ceremonial emetic by Navajo.

BEARBERRY
(Kinnickinnick)
Heath Family, Ericaceae

Arctostaphylos uva-ursi

Abundant, perennial evergreen ground cover 4–6 in. high, in open coniferous forests, ponderosa pine to spruce-fir forest, 7,000–11,000 ft. in more northern mountains. **Stems** erect or trailing, up to 10 ft. long or more, shreddy barked, dark, reddish brown; branches often turning up at ends. **Leaves** firm, leathery, shiny green above, oval, ½–1¼ in. long. **Flowers** small, drooping, urn shaped, corolla white with pinkish-white tips, (middle-left photo). **Fruit:** scarlet **berries,** ¼–⅜ in. diameter, present in autumn. **Blooms** May to July. No specific reports of use by southwestern tribes, but scores of uses reported by more northern tribes, into Alaska. Berries eaten fresh or sun dried for winter use, juice drunk as a beverage; numerous medicinal uses; also a major food source for bears. The common name "kinnickinnick" is an American Indian word for tobacco, as the leaves were dried and smoked by some tribes.

SIDEBELLS
(One-Sided Wintergreen)
Heath Family, Ericaceae

Orthilia secunda
(*Ramischia secunda*)

Low perennial usually in shaded understory of mixed conifer and spruce-fir forests, 8,000–9,500 ft. True **stems** lacking; flowering stalks (scapes) ca. 3–7 in. tall. **Leaves** in basal clusters, petiolate, bright green, glossy, ovate to oval, ca. ⅜–1⅝ in. long, pointed to rounded at tip. Leaves remain green throughout the winter, hence the common name "wintergreen." Six to twenty **flowers**, greenish white, ca. ¼ in. long, nodding, all turned to one side of upper portion of scape; 5 petals; 1 prominent, fused style with cap-like stigma extending beyond petals (two lower-left photos). **Fruit:** a 5-lobed capsule, wider than it is high, hanging somewhat downward. **Blooms** June through August.

RED ELDERBERRY *Sambucus racemosa* var. *microbotrys*

Honeysuckle Family, Caprifoliaceae

Stout perennial shrub common between 8,000 and 10,500 ft. in mixed conifer and spruce-fir forest. Size varies up to 3–4 ft. wide, 6–7 ft. tall. **Leaves** opposite, pinnately divided into five to seven 2½–5 in. long leaflets with pointed tips and coarsely toothed edges. **Flower heads** white to cream, borne in dense hemispheric to pyramidal clusters at stem ends, 1¾–3 in. diameter at their base. Heads finely divided into smaller branches, each bearing large numbers of tiny, white **flowers**; 5 sepals, 5 petals, and 5 stamens with tan anthers radiating beyond the petals (middle-right photo). Each flower head produces a cluster of red berry **fruits. Blooms** June to early July; red berries prominent in August. Although stems, roots, and leaves are sometimes considered toxic, berries are eaten by bears and birds. Several varieties and subspecies of *S. racemosa* have been used medicinally and for food by many Native American tribes and other populations.

SNOWBERRY

Honeysuckle Family, Caprifoliaceae

Symphoricarpos rotundifolius
(*S. albus, S. oreophilus, S. utahensis*)

Shrub, widespread on wooded slopes in ponderosa pine to spruce-fir forest, 7,000–11,000 ft. **Stems** erect, up to 4 ft. long, much branched, often bending to horizontal; young twigs smooth. **Leaves** opposite, oval, ½–1½ in. long; smooth to toothed margin, pointed tip. **Flowers** hanging downward in 8–10 pairs on short stalks, yellowish red prior to opening, white to whitish pink when open; corolla funnel to tubular shape, 5 fused petals, ½–¾ in. long, opening into 5 lobes at the ends; lobes up to ⅓ the length of the corolla tube. **Fruit:** white, hanging downward, singly or in pairs, oval to elliptic, ⅓–½ in. long. **Blooms** May into August. No reported uses by southwestern tribes, but used extensively by more northern tribes for medicines, the shoots for making small bird arrows and fish arrows, and fruits as food, although some tribes considered them poisonous.

FENDLERBUSH

Fendlera rupicola

Hydrangea Family, Hydrangeaceae

Highly branched shrub up to 6 ft. tall, common on cliffs and rocky slopes in piñon-juniper woodland and ponderosa pine forest between 5,500 and 8,000 ft. Bark longitudinally grooved, shreddy, grey. **Leaves** thickish, opposite or clustered, nearly sessile, smooth margins, lanceolate to oblong, ½–1½ in. long, narrow (⅓ in. or less wide). Upper surface smooth, lower surface variably hairy. **Flowers** borne singly or in clusters of 2 or 3. Four light green, pointed, clearly visible sepals extend outward between narrow base of the petals. Petals white; lower half constricted to form a narrow, stalk-like base; upper half ovate to diamond shaped; ca. ¾ in. long, ¼–½ in. wide. **Fruit:** an acorn-like capsule (upper-left photo) pointed at tip, ⅜–⅝ in. long, initially white, turning yellowish green upon maturity. **Blooms** late April into June. An important wood for Ancestral Pueblo Indians for making arrow shafts, points, awls, and planting sticks. Stems straight, smooth, nontapered; hardened when heated by fire.

CLIFFBUSH
(Waxflower)
Hydrangea Family, Hydrangeaceae

Jamesia americana

Much-branched, woody shrub; younger branches with reddish peeling bark. Adapted to wide range of habitats between 7,000 and 10,000 ft., from piñon-juniper woodland to spruce-fir forest, on rocky outcrops and canyon sides and streams where stems reach 6–7 ft. or only 1–2 ft. when growing from fissures in solid rock of vertical cliffs. Leaves opposite, on hairy petioles, ovate to elliptical, ¾–3¾ in. long, crinkly, bright green above, white and woolly below, veins prominent, margins toothed. Five to twenty flowers in dense, prominent, opening clusters at branch tips; 5 sepals, hairy; 5 petals, white, ¼–½ in. long; 10 stamens. Fruit: an ovoid capsule ca. ¼ in. long. Blooms May and June. Fruit and seeds occasionally eaten fresh by Apache.

LITTLELEAF MOCK ORANGE   *Philadelphus microphyllus*

Hydrangea Family, Hydrangeaceae

Branched woody shrub in rock outcrops and on steep slopes in ponderosa pine to spruce-fir forest, 7,000–9,500 ft. **Stems** up to 6½ ft. tall; young branches with flat-lying hairs, older dark red, bark peeling, gray underneath. **Leaves** opposite, on short petioles, ovate to elliptical to oblong, ½–1 in. long, smooth margin. Lightly to densely hairy below with 3 main longitudinal veins. **Flowers** perfect, usually solitary, on short, hairy stalks at branch ends. Floral cup hemispheric, hairy, topped by 4 broad-based, pointed-tip sepals (lower-left photo). Four petals, oblong, ca. ¼–½ in. long, white, somewhat ragged appearance at rounded apex. **Fruit:** an ovoid, pointed capsule (lower-right photo) ca. ¼ in. long; produces a sweet fragrance similar to that of orange blossoms when flowering. **Blooms** in June. Fruit used as food by Isleta.

DEATH CAMUS

Lily Family, Liliaceae

Anticlea elegans
(*Zygadenus elegans*)

Erect perennial from bulbs, in partially shaded mixed conifer and spruce-fir forest, often under aspen, 8,500–11,000 ft. **Stems** unbranched, up to 24 in. tall, bluish green without hairs. **Leaves** few, grass-like, ⅛–⅜ in. wide, ca. 6–10 in. long, arising from base of plant. **Flowers** borne singly along upper portion of stem on usually ascending pedicels in a loose cluster; floral bract present at base of pedicel; 6 flower segments consist of fused sepals and petals, greenish white or tinged with yellow, ca. ¼–½ in. long, tapering toward the base, bearing greenish, kidney-shaped glands toward the base. Ovary a conical structure extending outward from floral segments; 6 yellowish-gold anthers extending above tip of ovary (lower-left photo). **Blooms** July and August. Reportedly toxic to humans and livestock.

MARIPOSA LILY
(Gunnison's Mariposa Lily)
Lily Family, Liliaceae

Calochortus gunnisonii

Erect, delicate herb from a bulb, in mountain meadows and open ground in mixed conifer and spruce-fir forest, 7,000–11,000 ft. **Stems** unbranched, 4–12 in. tall. Two to four **leaves**, alternate, linear, grass-like; lowest leaves large, upper ones smaller. **Flowers** saucer shaped, showy, 1–3 in a cluster at the end of a slender stalk; 3 petals, white to light purple, ca. 1¼–1 ¾ in. long with a densely bearded, yellowish-purple to yellowish-green ring on the inner surface of the petals. Three sepals, lanceolate, shorter and narrower than the petals and present between the latter. Sepals greenish below, white to purplish above. Six stamens, surrounding the ovary, stigma with 3 elongated lobes. **Fruit:** a 3-angled, linear to oblong capsule (lower-right photo). **Blooms** mid-June into August. Bulbs eaten raw or gathered in the fall and boiled by Navajo; decoction of whole plant used to ease delivery of placenta and juice from leaf applied to pimples. Infusion of plant taken by Keres for swellings.

FALSE SOLOMON'S SEAL

Lily Family, Liliaceae

Maianthemum racemosum
(*Smilacina racemosa*)

Erect to arching perennial with unbranched stems, 8–24 in. tall, in partially shaded, mixed conifer, and spruce-fir forest, 8,000–11,000 ft. Leaves alternate, broadly lance-olate to ovate, 4–6 in. long, 2½–3 in. wide, with many parallel veins, sessile with leaf base clasping the stem. Flowers at stem end in a somewhat loose raceme cluster up to 4 in. long, with each flower borne on a short stalk; 6 tiny, white, petal-like segments per flower. Six stamens. Fruit: a tiny red berry with purplish dots. Blooms late May into July. Sometimes confused with Star Solomon's Seal, which often grows in the same or similar habitats. Stems of False Solomon's Seal somewhat more robust, taller, and bear longer clusters with a greater number of flowers than Star Solomon's Seal. The leaves are also much wider. Used as a root decoction for internal pain by Navajo, who also used the berries for food and cooked leafy shoots as a flavoring for meat.

STAR SOLOMON'S SEAL
(Star Flower)
Lily Family, Liliaceae

Maianthemum stellatum
(*Smilacina stellata*)

Erect to arching perennial from rhizomes, in shaded ponderosa pine to spruce-fir forest, 7,000–11,000 ft. **Stems** unbranched, 8–20 in. tall, with a slight zig-zag bend at each node (lower-right photo). **Leaves** alternate, on opposite sides of stems, lanceolate with base clasping the stem; 2–6 in. long, ¾–2 in. wide, with many parallel veins. Five to ten **flowers** in a loose raceme at top of stem, each flower borne on a short stalk. Six petal-like sepals, white, all alike, together forming an essentially flat, 6-pointed star ca. ¼ in. wide. Six stamens. **Fruit:** a round berry, nearly black when mature. **Blooms** late May into July. Navajo used a decoction of the plant for internal pains; used by numerous eastern tribes to stimulate the stomach and cleanse the system.

TWISTED STALK *Streptopus amplexifolius*

Lily Family, Liliaceae

Perennial to 2 ft. tall in shaded ravines and damp woods in more northern mountains and in ponderosa pine and mixed conifer forests, 8,000–9,500 ft. Herbage smooth. **Stems** from creeping rhizomes, branched, arching, flexuous. **Leaves** alternate, sessile with base clasping the stem, elliptic, to 4½ in. long, 2½ in. wide, ovate with pointed tips and parallel veins. **Flowers** solitary, ¼–½ in. long, hanging downward on a slender bent or twisted stalk from the leaf axil, hence the plant's common name. **Fruit:** red, globose to ellipsoid berry, ca. ½ in. long. **Blooms** July and August. Lower-right photo courtesy of Jane Jeffords.

CORN LILY
Veratum californicum

(False Hellebore)
Lily Family, Liliaceae

Stout perennial up to 7 ft. tall, commonly in diffuse clusters in moist mountain meadows and in ponderosa pine to spruce-fir forests, 8,000–12,000 ft. **Stems** erect, unbranched; lower portions smooth; upper portions with soft, short, woolly hairs. **Leaves** alternate, lanceolate to oval, 12–16 in. long with accordion-like folds, hairy beneath, clasping the stem at the base, veins conspicuous and parallel. **Flowers** small, in 20 in. long, branching, matted hairy clusters on upper portions of stem; 3 sepals, 3 petals, all white, ca. ½ in. long. **Fruit:** lobed capsules to ca. 1¼ in. long (middle photo). **Blooms** June through August. High alkaloid content of entire plant, especially roots and young shoots, makes the plant highly toxic to animals, including insects and birds. Despite that toxicity, some northern tribes used the plant to treat several dermatological problems and snakebite, even making a decoction that was taken internally by males and females as a contraceptive.

BLAZING STAR
(Desert Stickleaf, Adonis Blazing Star)
Loasa Family, Loasaceae

Mentzelia multiflora

Coarse, erect perennial, in full sun on dry, sandy, coarse soils in arroyos and roadcuts, mostly in the more central mountains, in foothill scrub to ponderosa pine forest, 4,500–8,000 ft. **Stems** whitish, to 3½ ft. tall, with peeling layers on lower portions, often branched above. **Leaves** alternate, lanceolate to oblanceolate, to 4 in. long, ¾ in. wide, deeply lobed to pinnatifid, wavy-toothed margins; both surfaces, especially the lower, covered with rough, barbed hairs that cause the leaves to stick tenaciously to clothing and animals. **Flowers** perfect, ca. 2 in. across, several at branch tips, opening only in late afternoon. Five sepals, narrow, pointed (upper-middle photo). Usually 10 petals, yellowish creamy white, ca. ½–1 in. long; many stamens in several series, 1 pistil, long, slender (lower-middle photo), petals readily detached, leaving top of the seed capsule exposed. **Fruit:** an elongated, bell-shaped capsule ½–1 in. high with spike-like appendages around the top, remnants of the sepals (lower-right photo). **Blooms** May through August. Used by Navajo as a dermatological aid to keep smallpox sores from splitting, as an eyewash, as an aid for abdominal swellings.

NORTHERN BEDSTRAW

Galium boreale

Madder Family, Rubiaceae

Erect, very leafy perennial, in meadows and openings in mixed conifer to spruce-fir forests, 7,500–11,000 ft. **Stems** 8–32 in. tall, 4-angled, edges smooth to rough. **Leaves** mostly smooth, in sessile whorls of 4, linear to narrowly lanceolate, pointed at tip, up to 2½ in. long, ½ in. wide, with 3 longitudinal veins, edges smooth. **Flowers** numerous, small, ca. ¼ in. diameter, borne on stalks in dense, terminal clusters. Sepals diminished or absent; 4 petal lobes, white; 4 stamens. **Fruit:** a pair of rounded, 1-seeded pods. **Blooms** June into September. European species are more aromatic and were traditionally used for mattress stuffing.

WILD HOLLYHOCK

Iliamna grandiflora

Mallow Family, Malvaceae

Erect, unbranched perennial from rhizomes, up to 40 in. tall; mostly in clearings, along roadsides, or in damp meadows in mixed conifer forest, 7,500–9,000 ft. Upper stems, lower leaf surfaces, and flower sepals hairy. Leaves alternate, petiolate. Lower leaves almost circular, 1½–6 in. wide, with shallow lobes; upper leaves palmately divided into 3–7 narrow segments; smooth to irregularly toothed margin. Flowers 1¼–2 in. diameter, stalked, in slender clusters at top of stem. Sepals united around base of petals. Five petals, showy, white or tinged with pink, constricted and densely hairy at the base. Numerous stamens closely surrounding the central style. Blooms late June through August.

CHEESEWEED
(Common Mallow)
Mallow Family, Malvaceae

Malva neglecta

Introduced low annual or perennial, common on waste ground, disturbed sites, and roadsides, from foothill scrub to mixed conifer forest, 4,000–8,500 ft. **Stems** creeping but pointing upward at the tip, to ca. 16 in. long, forming a somewhat dense cluster. **Leaves** alternate with long petioles, blades circular to kidney shaped with rounded teeth on margins, sometimes with shallow lobes. One to several **flowers**, perfect, stalked, from leaf axils. Five sepals, pointed, tapering to a point; 5 petals, white, tapered to a blunt to notched tip, with pink veins, about twice the length of the sepals. **Fruit:** small, button-like disk divided into ca. 15 segments, similar to a small cheese round, hence the plant's common name. **Blooms** May through September. A cold infusion of plant taken and used for injury or swelling by Navajo.

WHITE CHECKERMALLOW

Sidalcea candida

Mallow Family, Malvaceae

Erect unbranched perennial in damp meadows, near springs and stream sides in ponderosa pine and mixed conifer forest, 6,000–10,000 ft. **Stems** 20–40 in. high, smooth below, hairy in flower clusters. **Upper leaves** alternate on long petioles, palmately deeply divided into 3–7 narrow segments, smooth above, hairy beneath, prominently veined, margins smooth. **Lower leaves** almost circular in outline, with 5–7 palmately divided, shallow lobes with margins rounded to toothed. **Flowers** stalked from leaf axils, single or in groups of several; 5 sepals, tapering to a point (middle-right photo); 5 petals, distinct, up to 1 in. long, opening broadly; stamens numerous, united into a column around the style. **Blooms** May through September.

BROADLEAF MILKWEED
Asclepias latifolia

Milkweed Family, Asclepiadaceae

Erect perennial from deep rhizomes, in arroyos, open areas, and disturbed soil in foothill scrub and piñon-juniper woodland, 5,000–7,000 ft. **Stems** not branched, 8–30 in. tall with milky sap. **Leaves** opposite, sessile, with milky sap, grayish green, thick, broadly rounded to oval, 2½–5½ in. long, 2½–3 in. wide, blunt or shallowly notched at the apex, conspicuously veined. **Flowers** perfect, on short secondary stalks originating from a common point, forming a cluster in the leaf axils (upper-left photo). Five petals, small, greenish white, united at base, reflexed downward (lower-left photo). More visible are 5 rounded, sac-like structures ("hoods") radiating downward from the flower's center (upper-right and middle photos), surrounding the central, columnar, vase-shaped "corona." The hoods store copious amounts of nectar, fed upon by pollinators and other insects. The stigmas and anthers, out of sight inside the corona, are accessible to pollinators through slender vertical slits in the corona wall (middle inset photo). **Fruit:** an ovoid, pointed, capsule-like pod up to 3 in. long, ¾ in. diameter, plump, slightly ridged, on a recurved stem at its base (lower-middle photo). Splits lengthwise at maturity to release flat brown seeds attached to fine, silky threads that facilitate wind dissemination. **Blooms** mid-June into September. Ground leaf and stem powder inhaled by Isleta as a respiratory aid. Milkweed species, particularly the narrow-leafed species, generally toxic to livestock. All milkweeds provide a major nectar source for many insects and some are the only source of nutrition for caterpillar larvae of monarch butterflies.

HORSETAIL MILKWEED
Asclepias subverticilliata

(Whorled Milkweed, Poison Milkweed)
Milkweed Family, Asclepiadaceae

Perennial, widespread on disturbed areas of plains, valleys, grassland scrub to piñon-juniper woodland, 4,000–7,500 ft. Usually several stems, erect or spreading, mostly 12–36 in. tall, often with short, small-leafed, nonflowering branches, smooth or with short hairs near points of leaf attachment; herbage with milky sap. Leaves usually in whorls, sometimes opposite, narrow, mostly 1½–4½ in. long, petioles short. Flowers creamy white, perfect, stalked, in a clustered inflorescence at stem apices (left and upper-right photos). Five sepals hidden below the petals when the flower is fully open. Five petals, bending downward and curving outward near their tips (middle-right and lower-right photos). Five bowl-shaped "hoods," each with its upward-protruding "horn," surround the central, columnar, cylindrical vase–shaped "corona" (middle-right and lower-right photos). See Broadleaf Milkweed for more detailed description of milkweed flower anatomy. Fruit: narrow, cylindrical, upright pods 2–4 in. long, pointed toward tips (lower-middle photo). Blooms June into September. Toxic to humans and animals. All milkweeds provide a major nectar source for many pollinators and other insects.

WHITE MILKWORT   *Polygala alba*

Milkwort Family, Polygalaceae

Perennial, branched mostly at or near the base, in the more central mountains in dry plains to piñon-juniper woodland, 5,000–7,500 ft. **Stems** smooth, clustered, slender, 6–14 in. tall, sometimes branched, sparingly leafy above. **Leaves** alternate or whorled, linear to lanceloate, less than ⅛ in. wide, those at base wider than above, early deciduous. **Flowers** (lower-right photo) small, perfect, in a dense, many-flowered raceme, appearing spike-like, bilaterally symmetrical, on short stalks. Five sepals, outer 3 smaller, inner 2 (laterals) larger, petal-like. Three petals, united at the base, upper 2 similar, lower 1 conspicuous, longitudinally ridged, often with a fringed or lobed crest, often purplish. Eight stamens, filaments united into several tubes, often surrounded by the lower petal. **Fruit**: an elliptic capsule. **Blooms** late May through August.

DRAGONHEAD   *Dracocephalum parviflorum*

Mint Family, Lamiaceae

Erect annual, biennial, or short-lived perennial, 4–24 in. tall, occurring on moist, open slopes in ponderosa pine to spruce-fir forest, 7,000–11,000 ft. **Stems** 4-angled, usually with short, curled hairs. **Leaves** opposite on short petioles, lanceolate to oblong or elliptic, ¾–3½ in. long, ⅜–1¼ in. wide, lightly hairy below, margin coarsely toothed, teeth often spine tipped on upper leaves. **Flowers** perfect, small, barely visible in dense, whorled clusters at stem ends or in leaf axils, interspersed with many green, spiny-edged bracts. Corolla tubular, white to light pink to purple, extending beyond the tubular calyx (middle photo). **Blooms** June into September. Used by Navajo as an antidiarrheal for infants, as a cold infusion of leaves for an eyewash, and taken internally for fever and headaches.

HOREHOUND

Marrubium vulgare

Mint Family, Lamiaceae

Introduced perennial long revered in Europe for its medicinal uses, now widely distributed in North America. Occurs along roadsides and other open, disturbed sites in foothill scrub up to ponderosa pine forest, 5,000–7,500 ft. **Stems** stout, square, mostly erect, with woolly, white hairs. **Leaves** opposite, petiolate, paired from each stem node; distinctly rippled, broadly elliptical to almost round or fan shaped, ¾–2 in. long, margin with rounded teeth. **Flowers** perfect, very small, white, borne in dense globular aggregates surrounding the stem in leaf axils. Calyx of each flower in the inflorescence surrounds the fruit and develops a whorl of small, dry, hooked spines, forming a cluster of bur-like structures encircling the stems at leaf axils (lower-right photo). **Blooms** June through August. Decoction of plant used by Navajo for stomachache and influenza and as a gynecological aid before and after childbirth. Used historically and still today in cough syrup and candy.

CUTLEAF GERMANDER
(Lacy Germander)
Mint Family, Lamiaceae

Teucrium laciniatum

Leafy perennial with clumped, ascending, or spreading stems; restricted to open dry areas in foothill scrub to ponderosa pine forest, 4,000–8,000 ft. **Stems** finely hairy, densely leafy, branched at base, 2–6 in. tall. **Leaves** opposite, finely hairy, ½–1½ in. long, pinnately divided nearly to midvein, with 2–3 pairs of narrow, linear lobes, smooth margin. **Flowers** solitary, typically crowded near stem ends, subtended by leaf-like bracts. Five prominent white petals, the largest lower petal up to 1 in. long, lobed with pink lines. Large lower-lip petal also tongue-like with two pairs of side lobes. **Blooms** June through August.

FIELD BINDWEED   *Convolvulus arvensis*

Morning Glory Family, Convolvulaceae

Introduced from Europe several centuries ago; a deep-rooted, perennial vine, hard to eradicate, either trailing or climbing over other plants; widespread over much of the western United States. Common along roadsides and other exposed sites between 4,000 and 8,000 ft. Vines often 4–6 ft. long. **Leaves** alternate, ½–1½ in. long, with short petioles, generally triangular to arrowhead shaped with 2 pointed lobes at base. **Flowers** solitary, on stalks about same length as leaf petioles, corolla consisting of 5 fused petals, opening to ca. 1–1½ in. diameter, pinkish white to white, funnel shaped, lower sides of petals often more prominently pink (lower-right photo). **Blooms** May into September. Used by Navajo as a skin lotion for spider bites, as a cold infusion taken internally, and as a laxative. Parched seed used as food in times of need.

DODDER

Cuscuta sp.

Morning Glory Family, Convolvulaceae

Parasitic annual devoid of chlorophyll; attacks more than 100 species of broadleaf weeds and agricultural crops for its nutrition. Found mostly in scrub grassland and disturbed sites on sunny, west-facing foothills, 5,000–6,500 ft. **Stems** yellowish white to orange, thread-like, twining around (lower-left photo) and covering the host plant (upper photo) and sending small, nutrient-absorbing branches (haustoria) into the host plant; infections often extending over several to many square yards. **Leaves** absent or reduced to minute scales. **Flowers** tiny, numerous, white to pink, in small clusters scattered over the mass of prostrate stems, 5 petals with pointed tips; seeds produced in globular capsules; can remain viable many years in soil. Seeds germinate on soil surface; young plantlets develop a small, short-lived root system and 2–4 in. long, thread-like stalks that attach to host plants. Nutrients and water absorbed from the host's phloem tissue are then transported throughout and utilized by the parasitic dodder plant.

DRUMMOND'S ROCKCRESS

Mustard Family, Brassicaceae

Boechera drummondii
(Arabis drummondii)

Biennial or perennial in open meadows, rocky slopes, and woods in more northern mountains, ponderosa pine to mixed conifer forest, 7,000–9,000 ft. **Stems** 12–32 in. tall, leafy, erect, single, often in small clusters. **Stem leaves** to 1 in. long, upright, narrow, linear and lanceolate to oblong, quite closely appressed to stem, smooth; midvein prominent. **Basal leaves** narrowly oblanceolate, smooth or hairy. **Flowers** in small upright clusters toward tops of stems. Four petals, pinkish white, ca. ½ in. long, ¼ in. wide, tips rounded. **Fruit** (silique): slender, cylindrical pods, upright, to 3 in. long, smooth (lower-middle photo). **Blooms** May to September. Kindly identified by Robert Sivinski.

SHEPHERD'S PURSE

Capsella bursa-pastoris

Mustard Family, Brassicaceae

Introduced annual, on disturbed soils in piñon-juniper woodland, ponderosa pine, and mixed conifer forest, 6,000–9,000 ft. One to several slender **stems** from a basal rosette, 4–16 in. tall, erect, sparsely branched. **Basal rosette leaves** 1¼–4 in. long, deeply incised; **stem leaves** much smaller, mostly basal, alternate, sessile, with leaf base wrapped around stem. **Flowers** perfect, in loose clusters on short stalks at stem end. Individual flowers extremely small, with 4 white petals, rounded at the apex; 4 greenish stamens (middle-left photo). As stem elongates, apical flowers continue to form, with the earlier-formed fruits below, borne on elongated, slender stalks. **Fruit:** a smooth, heart-shaped pod ca. ½ in. long, divided into 2 compartments, with short, persistent style tip extending from notch in the apex. **Blooms** April into September.

SPECTACLE POD

Dimorphocarpa wislizenii
(Dithyrea wislizenii)

Mustard Family, Brassicaceae

Erect annual, common in sandy arroyos and open areas in foothill scrub and piñon-juniper woodland, 5,500–7,000 ft. Stems and leaves with woolly, star-shaped hairs that give the plant an overall gray cast. **Stems** 8–20 in. tall, sparsely branched. **Leaves** alternate, lanceolate, 1–5 in. long, ½–1¼ in. wide with wavy-toothed margins. **Flowers** white, in clusters at stem tip, each with four petals up to ½ in. long and a tapering base. Flowers borne on spreading stalks from stem. Four sepals, spreading; 6 stamens. As flowering progresses, the stem continues to elongate, with the unique, flattened, two-compartmented, spectacle-shaped **fruits** becoming prominent along the stem below the terminal flowers (middle-right photo); one seed per fruit compartment. **Blooms** May through September. Used by Navajo, Zuni, Apache, and Hopi as a salve or infusion for treating skin cuts, sores, rashes, insect bites, and sore throats.

PEPPERWEED
(Peppergrass)
Mustard Family, Brassicaceae

Lepidium alyssoides

Erect perennial in foothill scrub, piñon-juniper woodland, and ponderosa pine forest, 4,000–7,500 ft. Leaves and seeds have a pungent, peppery flavor. One to several **stems**, unbranched below flowers, branched above. **Basal leaves** smooth edged to pinnately lobed, less than 4 in. long; **stem leaves** alternate, narrow, lanceolate, tapering toward tip. Numerous **flowers** (upper-middle photo), small, in loose, stalked clusters at branch and stem ends. Four sepals, oblong or ovate, white; 4 petals, white, almost round; 6 stamens. **Fruit:** flat, elliptic to ovate, on short stalks; style projecting from the apex. **Blooms** June into September.

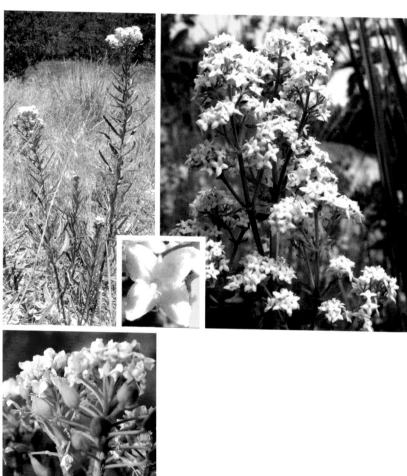

PERENNIAL PEPPERWEED
(Broadleaf Pepperweed)
Mustard Family, Brassicaceae

Lepidium latifolium

Erect perennial from rhizomes, forming clusters; native of southern Eurasia, now adapted to much of North America, declared a noxious, invasive weed in many western states. Widely distributed in New Mexico at many elevations, especially along moist roadsides. **Stems** smooth, branched, up to 3 or more ft. tall. **Leaves** alternate, upturned, lanceolate, bright green to gray green, margins entire to toothed; basal leaves oblong, to 12 in. long, petiolate; stem leaves smaller, sessile. **Flowers** small, in dense clusters on racemes at stem and branch ends. Sepals ovate, shorter than the 4 white, spatulate petals ca. ¼ in. wide. **Blooms** June through August. Roots have a hot, peppery taste similar to horseradish and have been used similarly as a condiment. Kindly identified by Timothy Lowrey, University of New Mexico.

VASEY'S TUMBLE-MUSTARD

Thelypodiopsis vaseyi

Mustard Family, Brassicaceae

Annual on open wooded slopes, canyons, ponderosa pine to mixed conifer forest zones, 7,000–9,000 ft. in more northern mountains. **Stems** smooth, 14–32 in. tall, branched in upper portions. Branches long, ascending to horizontal, widely spaced on stem. **Basal leaves** (soon withered) broadly ovate, ¾–3 in. long, on flattened, winged petiole. **Stem leaves** alternate, sessile, sparse, those on upper stem sessile (middle-right photo), larger toward lower portions of stem, margins entire or somewhat wavy (lower-right photo). **Flowers** in raceme clusters at stem and branch ends. Four sepals, spreading, whitish or purplish; 4 petals, white, obovate to spatulate with rounded ends, small, ca. ¹⁄₁₆ in. long, 8 yellow anthers. **Fruit:** a silique, ½–1 in. long, cylindrical, slender, erect to ascending, straight or curved, widely spaced along stem below flowers (upper-left photo). **Blooms** July through August. Kindly identified by Timothy Lowrey, University of New Mexico.

BEARGRASS

Nolina texana
(*N. greenei*)

Nolina Family, Nolinaceae

Large, native, dioecious perennial common in foothill scrub and piñon-juniper woodland, 6,500–7,500 ft.; not a true grass. Male and female flowers on separate plants. Many **leaves** in a dense cluster near the ground; narrow, wiry, curving, triangular in cross section; up to 3 ft. long; edges sometimes gently toothed. Many **female flowers**, white, borne in dense clusters along many branches from the main stalks (upper-right photo). Main stalks shorter than the leaves. **Male flowers** (upper-middle photo) pinkish white with anthers extending from the male flowers (lower-right photo); otherwise similar in appearance to female flowers. Many **fruits**, spherical, 3-lobed capsules ca. ¼ in. diameter; color progressing from green to olive to brown with maturity (lower-left photo). **Blooms** May into June. Many uses of leaves by many southwestern Native American tribes; important for weaving baskets and mats and as cordage for ropes, cords, and whips. Dried fruits ground into flour or put into dry gourd shells to make ceremonial rattles.

SPOTTED CORALROOT ORCHID   *Corallorhiza maculata*

Orchid Family, Orchidaceae

Erect, saprophytic plant devoid of chlorophyll, common on shady, mixed conifer forest floor, 8,000–10,000 ft. **Leaves** absent; several papery bracts partially wrap around the pale yellow to reddish-brown **stems**, 8–20 in. tall. Each stem may bear 10–30 perfect **flowers**, ½ in. long, on slender stalks along upper half of stem. Three sepals, opening to form elongated concave "wings" loosely surrounding the 3 petals; 2 smaller reddish-brown upper petals, 1 large, two-lobed, tongue-like petal, concave to flattened and bent downward; the latter white with purple to magenta dots. Mature **fruits** elliptic to obovate, drooping from stem, light tan to yellow, ca. ⅜ in. long (lower-right photo). **Blooms** late May into August. Dry, hard stems persist through the winter. The plant depends on specific saprophytic fungi that inhabit its root mass, extending out into soil and decaying leaf litter, there absorbing nutrients and translocating them back into the orchid. Infusion of the plant used by Navajo as a lotion for ringworm and other skin diseases.

RATTLESNAKE ORCHID

Goodyera oblongifolia

Orchid Family, Orchidaceae

Erect perennial 8–12 in. tall, in shaded understory of mixed conifer and spruce-fir forest, 8,000–9,500 ft. **Stems** from creeping rhizomes, single, leafless, densely glandular-hairy. **Leaves** in basal rosette, elliptic lanceolate, 1¼–2½ in. long, margin smooth; green with white area along midrib, often with white, net-like pattern between midrib and margins. Leaves persist for more than one year. The rosette of leaves precedes flowering by 3 years and persists for 1 or more years after flowering. Prior to opening, flowers at stem tip enclosed by green, papery bracts (lower-left photo). **Flowers** (right photo) occur mostly along one side of stem; perfect, small, white, clustered at stem end, each subtended by the green bract that previously enclosed the unopened flower; 3 sepals, finely hairy, white with a trace of green to greenish brown, ca. ⅓ in. long, tips curling somewhat backward; 3 petals, white. **Fruit:** an elliptic capsule ca. ½ in. long, finely hairy before mature and dry (lower-middle photo). **Blooms** July into September. Chewed by Navajo women as a gynecological aid before and at time of childbirth.

HOODED LADY'S TRESSES

Spiranthes romanzoffiana

Orchid Family, Orchidaceae

Perennial orchid up to 16 in. tall, more commonly 6–8 in., in moist to wet meadows, marshy ground, clearings, and along stream banks in northern mountains, mixed conifer, and spruce-fir forests, 7,500–10,000 ft. **Stems** single, stout, succulent, smooth or nearly so. Three to six **leaves**, mostly basal, smooth, lanceolate, to 7 in. long, ca. ½ in. wide. **Flowers** white, waxy, fragrant, tubular to ½ in. long; sepals and petals form a tight hood over the downward curving, spreading lip; lip white with pale green stripes in center, ca. ½ in. long. Flowers borne in a dense raceme up to 4 in. long. **Blooms** July to September.

WESTERN WATER HEMLOCK   *Cicuta maculata*

Parsley Family, Apiaceae

Coarse, extremely poisonous perennial along and in streams, edges of ponds, and other marshy habitats, central and northern mountains, piñon-juniper woodland, and ponderosa pine forest, 4,500–8,500 ft. **Stems** stout, smooth, to 6 ft. tall. **Leaves** compound, deeply pinnately divided, lanceolate, margins serrated with veins ending in gaps between the teeth (lower-left photo). Many **flowers** in a compound umbel borne on long pedicels to 6 in. long, which in turn branch to produce ¾–2½ in. long secondary pedicels, at the tips of which individual flowers are borne on short pedicels. At the base of each flower are 5 small, leaf-like bracts; each flower has 5 distinct white petals notched at their end; 5 stamens, white. **Blooms** June to September. *Do not touch the plant*, as its yellow, resiny toxin can enter through open wounds as well as by ingestion.

POISON HEMLOCK

Conium maculatum

Parsley Family, Apiaceae

Biennial introduced from Europe, widespread along ditches, streams, and low wet areas in weedy spots and waste ground, grassland scrub to ponderosa pine forest, 5,000–7,500 ft. **Stems** up to 9 ft. tall (6 ft. more commonly), stout, branched, purple spotted to blotched, especially toward the base (upper-left photo). **Leaves** alternate, repeatedly divided pinnately into coarsely toothed segments (lower-left photo). Lower leaves petiolate, blades 6–12 in. long, upper leaves smaller, sessile. **Flowers** white, tiny, 5 petals, narrowing toward the base, borne on tops of compound umbels 2–5 in. across (upper-right photo). **Fruit** (lower-right, larger photo): almost spherical, ca. ⅛ in. high, surface ridged. **Blooms** June to August. *Do not handle this plant.* Poisonous if ingested or through open wounds. Its toxin was the official state poison of ancient Athens and used for the execution of Socrates.

COW PARSNIP
Heracleum maximum

Parsley Family, Apiaceae

Stout, leafy perennial up to 6 ft. tall, herbage hairy, in marshy ground near streams or seeps, northern mountains, ponderosa pine and mixed conifer forests, 7,500–9,000 ft. This is the largest species of the parsley family in North America. **Stems** single, finely hairy to woolly above. **Leaves** large, up to 16 in. long, round in outline, pinnately lobed, the center lobe broader than the laterals, margins roughly serrated; petioles dilated, clasping the stem. Many **flowers**, at apices of stem or upper branches, borne in a compound umbel (see Western Water Hemlock for description of a compound umbel). Sepals small or absent, 5 petals, white; those at edge of umbel larger than those toward the center; ¼ in. long, cleft in the middle. **Fruit:** thin, round, paper-like samara containing the seed (left-middle photo). **Blooms** June to August. No reports of cow parsnip's use by southwestern tribes, but countless reports of uses for food (stalks, young leaves, and roots), both internal and dermatological medicines, and as a dye source by several northern tribes in more moist regions. Hollow stalks made into musical instruments by Cheyenne, played for romantic purposes at night.

OSHÁ
Ligusticum porteri
(Porter's Lovage)
Parsley Family, Apiaceae

Erect, aromatic perennial 2–4 ft. tall, widespread in partially shaded woods, piñon-juniper to mixed conifer and spruce-fir forests, 7,000–11,000 ft., more common in the higher elevations. **Stems** hollow, ridged, curved, much branched toward the top. **Basal leaves** fern-like, up to 24 in. long; smaller **stem leaves,** all deeply pinnately divided into primary segments, those segments further pinnately lobed, forming numerous saw-toothed leaflets. Base of leaf petioles wrap around the stem. **Flowers** in clusters in compound umbels (see Western Water Hemlock for description of compound umbels), with 11–24 secondary branches bearing short terminal pedicels, each bearing one flower. Petals small, white. **Fruit:** ovoid pods, ca. ¼ in. long, surface ridged. **Blooms** June into August. Historically widely used by Native Americans and Hispanic herbalists as root decoctions taken internally for body aches, various respiratory disorders, sore throats; dried tissue chewed for toothache relief. Caution—do not confuse this plant with its similar but poisonous hemlock relatives.

SWEET CICELY   *Osmorhiza depauperata*

Parsley Family, Apiaceae

Erect perennial in damp, shaded, mixed conifer and subalpine forests, 7,000–11,000 ft. **Stems** 6–24 in. tall, nearly hairless. **Leaves** alternate in groups of 3 with each group divided further into another group of 3 leaflets, each ¾–2 in. long, broadly lanceolate to ovate, coarsely toothed or incised, with a few stiff hairs on veins. Flower stalks elongate, extending beyond leaves. **Flowers** borne in an umbel. Individual flowers tiny, somewhat trumpet shaped with tips of white petals extending slightly beyond the much longer green sepals. **Fruits** ca. ½–⅝ in. long, at tips of elongated umbel branches (lower photo). Green when immature, with a pleasant licorice taste; black when mature with a narrow, arrowhead shape that often "burrows" into clothing and animal fur. **Blooms** May to August. Isleta boiled roots and stems to make a beverage.

RUSHY MILKVETCH   *Astragalus lonchocarpus*

Pea Family, Fabaceae

Perennial on sandy, gravelly, or rocky slopes in more northern mountains, scrub grassland to ponderosa pine forest, 5,000–8,000 ft. **Stems** erect to ascending, rush-like, 8–24 in. tall, leafless at base, typically clustered with previous year's dead growth around base of cluster. Herbage grayish green. **Leaves** on slender, long, soft rachis with 3–9 narrow, oblong to filiform leaflets 8–10 times longer than wide (middle photo). **Flowers** whitish cream, 5 petals, upper petal (banner) ½–¾ in. long, shallowly notched at apex, lower petal (keel) slightly shorter. **Fruit:** pod hanging downward, linear, somewhat flattened, up to ½ in. long, sometimes reddish tinged. **Blooms** May to June. Used by Navajo as an emetic and as a poultice applied to goiter.

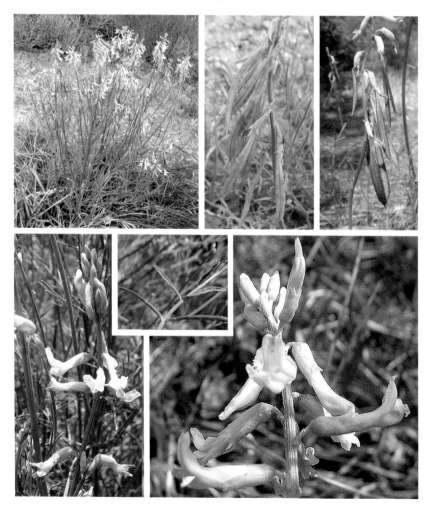

WHITE PRAIRIE CLOVER

Dalea candida

Pea Family, Fabaceae

Erect perennial, 1½–3¼ ft. high, common along roadsides and in plains, arroyos, old fields, and piñon-juniper woodland, 4,500–8,000 ft. One to several **stems**, simple or branched. **Leaves** smooth, bright green, pinnately compound with 5–9 oblong leaflets, each ½–1½ in. long. **Flowers** tiny, white, at tops of stems and branches in a dense, narrow, cylindrical spike ½–2½ in. long; flowers bloom from the bottom up on the spike. **Blooms** June into September. Navajo used raw roots as a food delicacy for women, children, and sheepherders; numerous medicinal uses, including relief of tooth and abdominal pain.

WILD LICORICE   *Glycyrrhiza lepidota*

Pea Family, Fabaceae

Aromatic perennial up to 3½ ft. tall, widespread across New Mexico along irrigation canals, roadside ditches, and similar moist ground, plains grasslands to piñon-juniper woodland, 3,500–6,500 ft. **Stems** from thick sweet roots, erect, single to several, smooth or lightly hairy. **Leaves** alternate, to 7 in. long, pinnately divided with 9–19 pinnate leaflets, lanceolate to oblong, smooth above. **Flowers** in dense clusters on long peduncles from upper leaf axils; calyx teeth, tubular, with 5 unequal teeth around base of the corolla; 5 petals, white, top one lanceolate ca. ⅓–⅔ in. long, bent backward, 2 lateral petals, 2 bottom petals fused into a keel between the laterals, similar to white locoweed. **Fruit:** reddish-brown oblong pods up to ⅝ in. long, covered with hooked prickles. **Blooms** in July. Used as an infusion by Keres, as a wash for chills, and as cough drops for singers and talkers. The commercial licorice plant, *G. glabra*, is widely used for medicines and candy.

WHITE PEAVINE
(Aspen Pea, Rocky Mountain Sweetpea)
Pea Family, Fabaceae

Lathyrus leucanthus
(*L. lanswertii* var. *leucanthus*)

Twining to erect perennial 8–24 in. high, in meadows and aspen glades in mixed conifer and spruce-fir forests, 7,000–11,000 ft. **Stems** angled, smooth or with long, soft hairs. **Leaves** alternate, 2–5½ in. long, prominently veined, pinnately divided into 4–12 ovate to elliptic leaflets, each ½–2½ in. long, up to ¾ in. wide, margins smooth. Central axis of leaf terminated by simple or branched tendrils. **Flowers** pea-like, up to 1 in. long in loose clusters of 2–5 on a short stalk arising from a longer ¾–4 in. stalk from the stem. Calyx bell shaped, up to ⅜ in. long, 5 toothed, the teeth shorter than the tube. Corolla: 5 petals, white to light pink. Top petal (banner) (lower-right photo) wider than long, ca. ½ in. long, bent backwards, often with pink streaks rising from the base, becoming yellow or yellowish brown with age; 2 lateral petals, slightly shorter; 2 bottom petals, fused, forming a keel between the laterals. **Fruit:** slender straight pods 1¼–2½ in. long (lower-left photo). **Blooms** June into September. Ripe pods dried, stored, later soaked and boiled when needed for food by Apache.

WHITE SWEETCLOVER

Melilotus albus

Pea Family, Fabaceae

Erect biennial up to 6 ft. tall, occurring along roadsides and in valley bottoms and open meadows, in areas of foothill scrub up to mixed conifer forest, 6,000–8,000 ft. **Stems** branched above, smooth to sparsely hairy. **Leaves** alternate on short petioles, with 3 narrowly oblong to elliptic leaflets, ⅜–1¼ in. long with finely serrate margins (upper-left photo). **Flowers** in long, loose, many-flowered clusters up to 4 in. long, from axils of upper leaves. Individual flowers on short stalks. Five petals, white; top petal longer than others, 2 lateral petals; bottom 2 petals fused to form a keel between laterals. **Fruits:** ellipsoid to ovoid, net-veined pods up to ¼ in. long. **Blooms** May until frost. Described as either a native or an introduced species from Eurasia, depending on the reference used.

WHITE LOCOWEED
(Silverleaf Locoweed)
Pea Family, Fabaceae

Oxytropis sericea

Perennial, widespread on open slopes, grassland scrub to subalpine forest, 6,500–10,000 ft. **Stems** lacking, but with scapes (leafless flower stalks) 6–10 in. tall. **Leaves** clumped, ca. 4–7 in. long, arising directly from root crown, odd-pinnate with 9–21 oblong to lanceolate, sometimes linear leaflets, each ca. ¼–1¼ in. long, with grayish or silvery appressed hairs (lower-middle photo). **Flowers** in elongate racemes that extend as new flowers develop at the tip. Individual flowers each subtended by a single lanceolate bract. Calyx tubular, 5 toothed. Corolla of 5 white petals; top petal ca. ¾–1 in. long, bent backward, 2 lateral petals somewhat shorter, dilated, each with a notched tip, 2 bottom petals fused into a keel having a narrow point. **Fruit:** small, erect, oblong pods tapering to a narrow point. **Blooms** April into July. Known to hybridize with purple locoweed, *Oxytropis lambertii*. White locoweed is generally toxic to grazing animals, as are all locoweeds, causing weight loss and abortion if large amounts are consumed.

SILKY SOPHORA
Sophora nuttalliana
(Nuttall's Sophora)
Pea Family, Fabaceae

Erect or ascending perennial to 14 in. tall, on dry field and plains, along roadsides, statewide, 4,000–7,000 ft. Herbage silvery, silky-pubescent, the hairs usually appressed. **Stems** 1 to several, branched. **Leaves** alternate, almost sessile, odd-pinnate with 13–21 obovate to oblanceolate leaflets, each up to ca. ½ in. long, 2–3 times longer than wide. Calyx tubular, purplish, with 5 mostly equal teeth. Five petals, top one to ca. ⅝ in. long, bent backward, 2 laterals and 2 bottom petals, the latter not fused into a keel as in many related species. **Fruit:** erect, fairly straight, cylindrical pods. **Blooms** April into June. Although the seeds of this plant are reportedly slightly toxic, the roots were chewed as a sweet delicacy by Acoma, Laguna, and San Felipe; Navajo used the plant as forage for sheep.

FENDLER'S SANDWORT

Eremogone fendleri
(*Arenaria fendleri*)

Pink Family, Caryophyllaceae

Perennial growing in tufts in soil often at the base of rocky debris in open, moist areas of piñon pine–juniper woodland to spruce-fir forest, 7,000–11,500 ft. **Stems** slender, arising in clusters, erect to ascending, branching limited, up to 12 in. tall, glandular-hairy in the inflorescence. **Leaves** opposite, sessile, narrowly slender, ca. ¾–2½ in. long. **Flowers** in widely spreading clusters; sepals taper to a long, slender point (lower-middle photo); 5 petals, distinct, obovate, ca. ⅛–⅓ in. long, tips rounded; 10 stamens on long filaments, anthers red, turning black (two lower-right photos). **Blooms** May to July. Navajo used powdered root as a snuff to cause sneezing for "congested nose."

TUBER STARWORT

Pseudostellaria jamesiana

Pink Family, Caryophyllaceae

Erect to ascending perennial 8–20 in. tall, occurring in moist canyon bottoms and shaded forests up to subalpine forest, 11,000 ft. **Stems** clumped, much branched, with glandular hairs above; 3–5 pairs of sessile, radiating leaves. **Leaves** opposite, 1¼–4 in. long, gradually pointed toward the tip, somewhat grass-like in appearance. **Upper stem leaves** shorter than those near base. **Flowers** ca. ½ in. diameter, borne singly at stem apex, 5 white petals, each V shaped, distinctly 2-lobed toward tip, often with distinct linear grooves (upper-right photo). Ten elongated stamens with brown, terminal anthers, the latter appearing somewhat as brown spots near the base of the white petals. **Blooms** May into July. Poultice applied to hailstone injuries by Navajo.

99

BOUNCINGBET
(Soapwort)
Pink Family, Caryophyllaceae

Saponaria officinalis

Perennial to 3 ft. tall in dense stands. Introduced as an ornamental from Europe, now naturalized throughout much of North America, including New Mexico. On waste ground, often along streams and roadsides, 4,000–7,500 ft. Stems sturdy, erect, smooth, branching above. Many leaves, opposite, lanceolate, sessile, smooth, to 5 in. long. Flowers in dense terminal clusters. Calyx tubular, long, prominent, up to ¾ in. long. Corolla to 1½ in. across, 5 separated petals, white to pale pink, somewhat elongated, notched at their tip. Fruit: an elongated, globular capsule. Blooms June to August.

WHITE CAMPION *Silene latifolia*
(White Catchfly, Bladder Campion)
Pink Family, Caryophyllaceae

Perennial introduced from Europe, grows from woody taproot on disturbed sites, meadows, open wooded areas, 7,000–9,000 ft., commonly in more northern mountains. Dioecious, with staminate and pistillate flowers on separate plants. **Stems** to 24 in. high or more, branched, finely hairy and glandular toward the top. **Leaves** bluish green, smooth, opposite, up to 20 pairs along the stem, lower ones petiolate, upper ones sessile; lanceolate with pointed tips, to 4 in. long, ca. ⅓ in. wide. **Flowers** overall similar in appearance, borne singly or in loose clusters on upper stalks and branches; both staminate and pistillate flowers have an inflated, tubular to bladder-like calyx topped with 5 white, flattened, deeply 2-lobed petals, ca. 1–1⅓ in. across. Staminate calyx inflated, with 10-nerved, purple ridges (upper-right and lower-left photos); pistillate calyx eventually more inflated with 20-nerved, purple ridges. **Fruit:** an ovate capsule with 1 compartment within the inflated calyx. **Blooms** June into August.

ENGLISH PLANTAIN
Plantago lanceolata

Plantain Family, Plantaginaceae

Stemless perennial introduced from Europe, now naturalized in North America, an abundant weed in lawns, golf courses, pastures, and disturbed sites. Common throughout New Mexico between 4,000 and 7,000 ft. **Leaves** basal, from the root crown, with some-what brownish hairs at the base, narrow, elliptic to lanceolate, to 8 in. long, distinctly parallel veined, margins entire. **Flowers** in a single spike at top of a flowering stalk (scape) 10–16 in. tall; spike ca. 1–2 in. high, dense with many minute, sessile, brownish white to white flowers. Flowers develop starting at the spike base, progressing upward. Sepals and petals small, ca. ⅛ in. long, difficult to clearly discern in the field. Best visual evidence of flowering are the long, thread-like stamens with large white terminal anthers radiating from the spike (lower-right photo). **Blooms** late May through September.

WOOLLY PLANTAIN

Plantago patagonica

Plantain Family, Plantaginaceae

Stemless, low-growing perennial 2–5 in. high; herbage with long wooly hairs, occurring in dry foothill scrub and piñon-juniper woodland, 5,000–7,000 ft. Leaves arising from a common base, linear to narrowly oblanceolate, ¾–6 in. long, usually with a pointed tip, smooth margin. Flowers at end of unbranched flower stalk in a dense, cylindrical spike 2–6 in. long. Individual flowers small, sessile, each subtended by a hairy bract (lower-right photo). Four petals, fused, with spreading lobes. Four stamens. Blooms late April into August. Used as ceremonial items by Hopi and Navajo, and as a medicine by Hopi, Western Keres, and Navajo for headaches, diarrhea, babies' colic, and to reduce appetite and prevent obesity.

DATURA
(Sacred Datura, Thornapple, Jimsonweed)
Potato Family, Solanaceae

Datura wrightii
(*D. metaloides*)

Large annual or perennial up to 4½ ft. tall with sprawling growth habit; **stems** branching. Favors disturbed sites or eroded arroyos in foothill scrub and piñon-juniper woodland up to 7,000 ft. **Leaves** ovate, up to 6 in. long, stalked, often with irregularly wavy, toothed margin. **Flowers** solitary, 6–8 in. long, funnel shaped, somewhat fragrant; 5 petals, basally fused, 5-toothed around apical ends. Five sepals, fused around base of corolla, 3–5 in. long. **Fruit:** globe shaped, nodding, ca. 1¾ in. diameter, covered with spines ca. ½ in. long, eventually woody. **Blooms** June to August. Toxic to humans and animals when ingested except in low concentrations, in which it was used by some southwestern tribes as a hallucinogen in many ceremonies, hence the common name "Sacred Datura" in some references. Used by Apache, Navajo, and Western Keres as a salve for treatment of skin wounds, swellings, snake and tarantula bites and for saddle sores on horses.

CUTLEAF NIGHTSHADE

Solanum trifolium

Potato Family, Solanaceae

Low-growing annual, widespread on plains, roadsides up to ponderosa pine forest, 3,500–9,000 ft. **Stems** highly branched from base, up to 20 in. long but only ca. 6–8 in. high, herbage smooth to slightly glandular-hairy, prickles absent. **Leaves** up to ca. 2 in. long, deeply pinnatifid with rounded sinuses between the segments, the latter mostly divergent, triangular, pointed; not all leaves compound. **Flowers** solitary, small, on pedicels from branches; corolla white, ca. ¼–½ in. across, 5 petals, broad, gently tapering toward tip, 5 anthers. **Fruit:** a globular berry, green or greenish black at maturity, ca. ⅓–⅝ in. diameter. **Blooms** May through September. Used as a starvation food by Acoma and Laguna and as a fertilizer for watermelon; Navajo soaked dried berries and planted with watermelon seed to increase productivity.

PYGMYFLOWER ROCK JASMINE *Androsace septentrionalis*
(Northern Fairy Candelabra)
Primrose Family, Primulaceae

Delicate, early-blooming, stemless annual with tiny flowers on slender stalks; in ponderosa pine to spruce-fir forest, 7,000–11,000 ft. **Leaves** simple, up to ca. 2½ in. long, aggregated in a dense basal rosette, toothed along the terminal margins. What appear as stems are individual **flower stalks** up to 10 in. long that branch at their tips as an umbel, forming numerous loosely spaced stalks, 1½–3 in. long, each producing a tiny white **flower** with 5 lobed petals less than ¼ in. long, fused at base. **Blooms** April through June. Decoction used by Navajo, taken before sweat bath for venereal diseases.

MOUNTAIN MAHOGANY
Cercocarpus montanus

(Palo Duro)

Rose Family, Rosaceae

Deciduous, perennial shrub to 6 ft. tall; on sunny slopes and dry hillsides and hills in piñon-juniper woodland to mixed conifer forest, 6,500–9,000 ft. **Branches** upright to branching; younger bark reddish, older bark gray brown. **Leaves** in bundles of 3–5 on short petioles. Simple, thin, ovate, ca. ¾–1½ in. long, rounded at tip, margins toothed toward apex. Parallel lateral veins extend from midvein. Green to grayish green above, paler and hairy beneath. **Flowers** small, solitary, brownish to yellowish white, somewhat flattened disks with spreading lobes, borne at the tips of ½–1½ in. long stalks bending downward from leaf axils. **Fruit:** an elongated capsule bearing a slender, curved, feather-like plume up to 3 in. long that remains attached to the fruit capsule, having a silvery cast from late summer into winter. **Blooms** May and June. The dense, tough wood provided Ancestral Pueblo Indians and Navajo with strong wood for cradleboards, bows, digging tools, and other implements. The red bark of roots was boiled and used by Keres, Navajo, and Hopi for making dyes for wool, leather, and baskets.

APACHE PLUME   *Fallugia paradoxa*

Rose Family, Rosaceae

Highly branched, perennial, deciduous shrub up to 10 ft. wide, 6 ft. high, often in dense stands in foothill scrub and piñon-juniper woodland, 5,000–7,500 ft., in coarse soils and arroyo bottoms. Young branches with white woolly hairs, older branches smooth, gray with peeling bark. Leaves alternate, in bundles on short lateral branches, pinnately divided into 3–7 short, linear-oblong lobes (upper-left photo). One to three flowers at branch ends, each with 5 showy, white, rounded petals ¼–¾ in. long. Each flower produces numerous tufted, feathery, white to light pink seed plumes ¾–2 in., formed from elongated stigmas. Blooms May into September. Straight, slender branches used by several Pueblo Indian tribes to make arrow shafts. Brushy branch ends used for rough brooms by Acoma and Walatowa.

WILD STRAWBERRY

Fragaria vesca
(F. americana)

Rose Family, Rosaceae

Low-growing perennial, 2–8 in. tall, in shady areas of ponderosa pine and mixed conifer forests, above 7,000 ft. Spreads by runners or stolons (prostrate rooting stems). Leaf petioles and flower stalks both arise from a basal crown. Petioles, leaves, stolons, and fruit are silky and hairy. **Leaves** on slender petioles 1¼–6 in. long, blades palmately divided into 3 coarsely toothed leaflets 1–2½ in. long. **Flowers** on stalks, in loose clusters of 3–10 with 5 white, narrow-based petals with 5 sepal-like bracts shorter than the petals. Twenty stamens, tipped with yellow-brown anthers. Many **fruits** (achenes) borne on the surface of a fleshy receptacle (middle-right photo), with one seed per achene. **Blooms** May into July. All species of wild strawberry used by Native American tribes throughout North America, including the Southwest, for food, both fresh and dried.

MOUNTAIN SPRAY
Holodiscus dumosus
(Rock Spirea)
Rose Family, Rosaceae

Densely branched shrub 2–6 ft. tall in mixed conifer and spruce-fir forests, 6,500–11,000 ft., common at Sandia Mountain crest. **Branches** slender, spreading, with peeling bark. **Leaves** alternate, petiolate, somewhat wedge shaped, coarsely toothed or lobed, ¾–2 in. long, hairy above and below. **Flowers** numerous, borne in loose clusters at branch ends; 5 cream-colored, elliptic to oval petals, tiny, ca. ⅛ in. long at most; 20 stamens, extending well beyond the petals; 5 pistils. Floral cup shallow. **Fruits:** spherical, hairy. **Blooms** June into August. Isleta steeped the leaves to make a beverage.

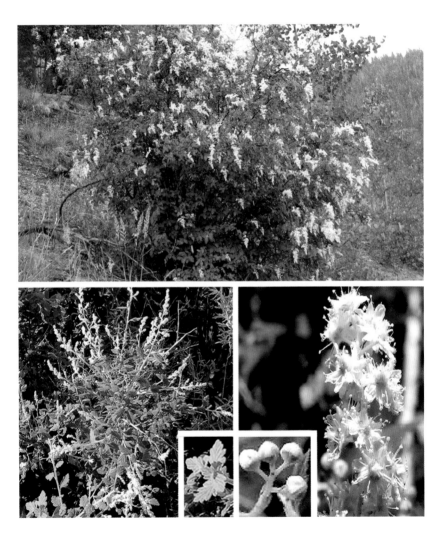

MOUNTAIN NINEBARK

Physocarpus monogynus

Rose Family, Rosaceae

Highly branched, deciduous shrub up to 3–4 ft. tall. On rocky outcrops, steep slopes, and open woods, 8,000–11,000 ft., in mixed conifer and spruce-fir forests. Common in the Sandias at and near the crest. **Stem** bark peeling, reddish brown, when young; when older, pale brown to gray brown (upper-right photos). **Leaves** alternate, simple, oval to round, ¾–1½ in. long, on petioles of about the same length; palmately lobed; veins prominent, margin regularly toothed; upper surface dull, dark green, paler below. **Flowers** small, ca. ¼–½ in. across, in dense round clusters at branch ends; 5 sepals, pink; 5 petals, white, almost round; 20–40 stamens extending beyond floral cup and petals, filaments white, anthers brown. **Blooms** June and July.

CHOKECHERRY
(Western Black Chokecherry)
Rose Family, Rosaceae

Prunus virginiana var. *melanocarpa*

Deciduous shrub to small tree 3–24 ft. tall, most commonly 10–15 ft., in moist canyon bottoms, stream banks, and riparian areas, central and northern mountains, piñon pine–juniper woodland and ponderosa pine forest, 6,000–8,000 ft. Younger branches reddish brown, older bark ashy gray. **Leaves** alternate, petiolate, ovate to elliptic, 1½–4 in. long, green above, paler below, margins finely toothed, mostly smooth. **Flowers** perfect, on stalks ca. ⅜ in. long, in dense clusters to 6 in. long, drooping, at branch ends (upper-right photo). Bell-shaped floral cups with 5 triangular to round sepals, 5 white petals, ovate to round. Twenty to thirty stamens with long filaments, 1 stigma and style. **Fruit:** small, globose, one-seeded cherry ¼–⅓ in. diameter, initially green, turning red, dark red to black when mature (the latter stages often difficult to find as this is a favored food for deer and other animals). **Blooms** April to June. Bark was made into a cough medicine by Western Keres, the fruit and seeds ground raw, patted into a cake, sun dried, and used for medicinal purposes. Fruits were used for food, either fresh or ground and dried for winter food, by Acoma, Apache, Cochiti, Western Keres, San Felipe, and Navajo. Isleta used the supple, straight-grained limbs to make bows.

CLIFFROSE
Purshia stansburiana

Rose Family, Rosaceae

Woody shrub found mostly in drier central and northwestern mountains, on rocky hills and canyon sides, 3,000–8,000 ft. **Stems** spreading to erect, to 9 ft. tall and to a similar width; highly and intricately branched, new year's branches are reddish. **Leaves** simple, generally alternate (but typically clustered at nodes), ¼–1 in. long, wedge shaped with 3–9 closely compacted lobes, thickened, green or gray green above, paler and dotted with white glands below. **Flowers** at ends of small side branches, creamy white to pale yellow, fragrant, ca. 1 in. across; 5 petals, creamy white; many stamens with deep yellow anthers in the center; 4–10 pistils with elongated, twisted, hairy styles and stigmas extending upward. **Fruit**: a slender, 1-seeded achene with an attached, elongated pinkish-white plume somewhat similar to that of the Apache plume. **Blooms** May and June. Navajo pounded leaves and stems and mixed with juniper to make tan to yellow-brown dye and also used shredded bark for bedding and pillows. Bark spun and woven into kilts for ceremonial priests; shredded bark from large stems used for cradleboard padding by Hopi.

113

RED RASPBERRY

Rubus idaeus var. *strigosis*

Rose Family, Rosaceae

Erect, perennial, sprawling shrub, widespread in dry to moist open woods, central and northern mountains, piñon-juniper woodland to subalpine forest, 7,000–10,000 ft. **Stems** woody, to 6 ft. long with stiff, slender, sharp bristles. **Leaves** alternate, on petioles with stiff hairs, pinnately divided, 3–5 lanceolate to ovate leaflets 1¼–2 in. long, margins toothed, mostly smooth above, short grayish hairs and prickly veins below. **Flowers** perfect, on prickly stalks arising from leaf axils with 1 or more flowers per cluster. Floral cup small, with 5 lanceolate sepals and 5 shorter petals, white, oblanceolate to spatulate (right photo, second from top). **Fruiting body** (inflorescence): a drupe ¼–⅓ in. wide, containing a cluster of numerous small, fleshy, one-seeded fruits around the hollow center, red. **Blooms** May into July.

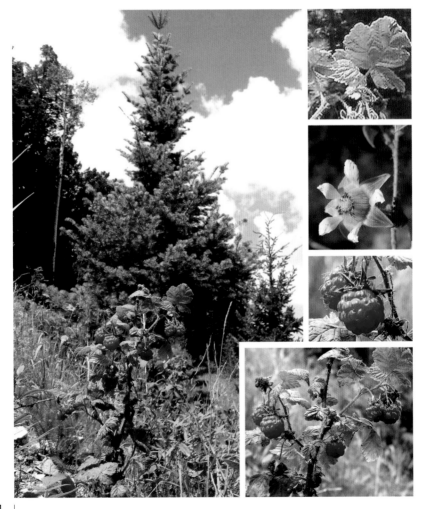

SPOTTED SAXIFRAGE   *Saxifraga bronchialis*

Saxifrage Family, Saxifragaceae

Perennial commonly on moist, rocky ledges, common in more northern mountains, ponderosa pine to subalpine forests, 7,000–12,000 ft. **Leaves** often forming a mat or dense carpet close to the ground, plus **flowering stems** to 6 in. tall, covering several square feet of area. Leaves mostly crowded at the base, narrowly oblong to lanceolate, sharply tipped with a fringe of tiny stiff hairs along margins (middle-right photo); stem leaves scattered and much reduced. **Flowers** in open, loose cluster on upper ends of flowering stems, with 5 short calyx lobes and 5 white, oblong to oval petals ¼ in. long with reddish and yellow spots, 5 prominent white stamens with hemispheric anthers. **Fruit:** small pods, ca. ¼–⅜ in. long. **Blooms** June to September.

COCKERELL'S STONECROP   *Sedum cockerellii*

Stonecrop Family, Crassulaceae

Perennial in rocky, often shady places in mountains, widespread, ponderosa pine forest to spruce-fir forest zones, 7,000–11,500 ft., herbage hairless. **Stems** 4–8 in. tall, leafy, erect. **Leaves** closely spaced on stems, alternate, sessile, succulent, flattened, linear to narrowly oblanceolate to obovate, ca. ¼–¾ in. long, margins smooth, tips rounded to gently pointed. **Flowers** in dense, branched clusters at stem ends (lower-left photo), subtended by small, leaf-like bracts (middle-right photo); usually 5 sepals; 5 petals, white, lanceolate, tips pointed. Ten stamens, 2 sets of 5, of different lengths, filaments white, anthers red, turning black. Usually 5 pistils, pink. **Blooms** July and August.

POISON IVY

Toxicodendron rydbergii

Sumac Family, Anacardiaceae

Deciduous, perennial shrub, 2–4 ft. high; restricted to open or partly sunny areas; typically near moist ditches, streams, or springs in ponderosa pine to mixed conifer forest; 6,000–8,500 ft. **Stems** sparingly branched, forming a thicket of mostly upright stems. **Leaves** alternate, palmately divided into three leaflets, each 2–4 in. long. Leaflets deep green, waxy, with variously serrated margins, turning brilliant red in autumn. Male and female **flowers** on separate plants in dense clusters, small, nondescript, creamy white; appear in late spring before or with the leaves. **Fruit:** a one-seeded, round berry produced in short-branched clusters on stems near the base of leaf petioles; initially green, turning yellowish white to white at maturity. Despite the effects the plant has on many people, several reports describe the use of other poison ivy species by eastern Native American tribes for treatment of sores, boils, and other skin eruptions. No reports found of uses by southwestern tribes.

CANADA VIOLET

Viola canadensis

Violet Family, Violaceae

Ascending to erect perennial, mostly 6–12 in. tall; common in shady, damp woods, mixed conifer and spruce-fir forest, 7,500–11,000 ft. One to several **stems**, finely hairy. **Leaves** both basal and on stems; **basal leaves** on 3–5 in. petioles, heart shaped, 1¼–4 in. long, ¾–3 in. wide, pointed at apex, margins with shallow, pointed to rounded teeth. **Stem leaves** alternate, otherwise similar to basal leaves. **Flowers** on ½–2 in. long stalks from upper leaf axils. Five petals, unequal size, white, with distinct violet to purple veins extending from the greenish-yellow base; lower petal with a terminal spur. Five stamens. **Blooms** early May to August.

NEW MEXICO SCORPIONWEED   *Phacelia neomexicana*

Waterleaf Family, Hydrophyllaceae

Robust annual up to 3 ft. tall, in open areas of ponderosa pine and mixed conifer forests, 7,000–9,000 ft. Herbage with gland-tipped hairs, somewhat tacky to the touch. **Stems** stout, sparsely branched except toward the tip. **Leaves** alternate, up to 3 in. long, irregularly pinnately lobed with each segment lobed; margins toothed. **Flowers** borne in dense, one-sided, coiled spikes at ends of upper branches; as flowers open from the base of the coil, the spike uncoils, forming a straight stalk bearing flowers along one side but remaining slightly coiled at the tip. Corolla of fused petals, funnel shaped, white to purple with 5 terminal lobes, having toothed margins; numerous bluish stamens and anthers extend beyond ends of petals (lower-right photo). **Blooms** May through August. Powdered roots mixed with water used by Zuni for skin rashes.

RAG-LEAF BAHIA
(Yellow Ragweed)
Aster Family, Asteraceae

Amauropsis dissecta
(*Bahia dissecta*)

Annual or biennial on gravelly soil, rocky hills, open areas, piñon-juniper woodland to mixed conifer forest, 5,500–9,000 ft. **Stems** solitary, branched, up to 40 in. tall. **Basal leaves** in a rosette; **stem leaves**, alternate, lightly hairy, smaller than basal leaves; two or three times pinnately divided or dissected, overall outline somewhat palm shaped. **Flower heads** small, numerous, clustered loosely at branch ends. Both **ray** and **disk flowers** fertile; rays up to ⅓ in. long. Involucres with 2 or 3 series of phyllaries (lower-right photo). **Blooms** August to October. Plant infusion used by Western Keres as both a cathartic and an emetic; decoction used by Navajo for menstrual pain, for arthritis, and as a contraceptive; powdered plant rubbed on affected parts for headache by Zuni.

BUR RAGWEED
(Annual Bur-Sage)
Aster Family, Asteraceae

Ambrosia acanthicarpa
(*Franseria acanthicarpa*)

Annual from taproots, to 2½ ft. tall, widespread in sandy, open ground from grasslands to ponderosa pine forest, 3,000–8,000 ft. **Stems** erect, branching from the base. **Leaves** mostly alternate, opposite below, petiolate to sessile, to 4 in. long, sometimes paler underneath, once or twice pinnately divided with margins irregular to deeply dentate. **Flowers** unisexual, with staminate and pistillate flowers separate on the same plant. As with other species in this genus, many greenish-yellow **staminate flowers** occur clustered in nodding **heads** along upper ends of stems and branches (upper-middle photo); green **pistillate heads** less numerous, with 1 floret per head in upper leaf axils, ca. ¼–½ in. long, forming a hairy, nut-like bur with 2 or 3 rows of curved, flattened, awl-shaped spines (lower-left photo). **Blooms** July to October. Ground root placed in tooth for toothache, and infusion of whole plant taken and used as a wash for obstructed menstruation by Zuni.

LEAFY ARNICA

Arnica chamissonis

Aster Family, Asteraceae

Erect perennial to ca. 3 ft. tall in wet meadows and other moist places, ponderosa pine to spruce-fir forest, 7,000–10,000 ft. in more northern mountains. **Stems** branched and with fine hairs only toward the top. **Leaves** opposite, lanceolate to oblanceolate, hairy, margins smooth or slightly toothed. Stem leaves in 4–10 pairs, sessile to ca. 12 in. long, ca. 3 in. wide; lower leaves narrowed to sheathing petioles at the base. Five to fifteen **flower heads** at stem and branch ends, 1¼–2 in. across, 10–16 **rays**, mostly pale yellow, ½–¾ in. long. Involucre bowl shaped, ca. ⅓–½ in. high, phyllaries hairy, lanceolate, tips blunt to soft pointed (middle-right photo). Pappas light brownish. **Blooms** June to August.

TARRAGON
(Wild Tarragon)
Aster Family, Asteraceae

Artemisia dracunculus

Erect perennial up to 4 ft. tall, on loose, dry, disturbed soil in open areas, 5,000–8,000 ft. in foothill scrub up to piñon pine forest. Many **stems**, typically reddish, smooth to finely hairy, not conspicuously aromatic. **Leaves** alternate, dark green, linear to lanceolate, up to 3 in. long, margins smooth, have an anise flavor when fresh. **Flower heads** small, whitish yellow, numerous, often drooping to upside down; **disk flowers** only, up to 60 per head, tightly clustered. Involucres with smooth to sparsely hairy phyllaries. **Blooms** July to September. Used by Navajo as a cold infusion for cuts and as a hair rinse to make hair long and soft.

DESERT MARIGOLD

Baileya multiradiata

Aster Family, Asteraceae

Annual; up to 24 in. tall; on sandy, gravelly areas and along roadsides; mostly in more central mountains, foothill scrub to piñon-juniper woodland, 4,000–6,000 ft. **Stems** single to a few; sparsely branched; with grayish, woolly hair. A few **leaves** on stems, mostly in a basal cluster, up to 3 in. long, broadly ovate, divided into broad lobes, those again divided or with rounded teeth. **Flower heads** solitary, at stem and branch ends, ca. 1½–2 in. diameter. **Ray** and **disk flowers** yellow, fertile; rays become bleached and tissue paper–like with age. Involucres almost masked by grayish, woolly hair. **Blooms** May into October. Plants rubbed under arms as deodorant by Western Keres; Jemez mixed the plant with clay when making adobe; plant was also used in plaster.

CHOCOLATE FLOWER
(Green Eyes)
Aster Family, Asteraceae

Berlandiera lyrata

Wooly perennial up to 16 in. tall, in grassy areas, rocky soils, or roadsides in foothill scrub to ponderosa pine forest, 4,000–7,500 ft. **Leaves** alternate, up to 6 in. long, each slender and deeply pinnately divided toward its base, with larger terminal end, serrated margin. Petioles often long on lower leaves. **Flower heads** on long stalks, up to 1½ in. diameter. **Ray flowers** usually less than 10, yellow, ½ in. or slightly longer; clearly separated from one another. **Disk flowers** dark reddish brown, turning greenish brown with age; distinct chocolate odor, especially early in the morning. Involucre below heads nearly flat, with numerous green, ovate phyllaries that persist after ray flowers have matured and disappeared, to form a green "collar" around the remaining disk flowers (middle-right photo). **Blooms** May through September. Acoma, Keres, and Laguna used flowers as a spice mixed with sausage; used by Keres as a sedative by inhaling smoke from dried, ground roots burned or placed on hot coals.

125

PALLID THISTLE
(Yellow Thistle)
Aster Family, Asteraceae

Cirsium parryi
(*C. pallidum*)

Perennial, 3–5 ft. high on rocky outcrops, meadows, and moist areas in mixed conifer and spruce-fir forests, 7,000–10,000 ft. **Stems** unbranched below flowers; with cobwebby, tangled hairs; very leafy. **Leaves** alternate, sessile, oblong to lanceolate; upper surface greenish without hairs; cobwebby hairs beneath, especially on midrib; irregularly toothed or shallow lobed along margin, each tooth or lobe with spined tip. **Flower heads** greenish yellow; **disk flowers** only; ca. 1 in. wide, clustered on ends of stems or branches with many small, spiny leaves. Involucre bulbous to urn shaped (lower-right photo), phyllaries in many series, each tapering to a spine tip, covered with cobwebby hairs. **Blooms** June into August. Seeds ground into flour used by Apache to make bread. Roots used by Western Keres as a diuretic.

ENGELMANN DAISY

Engelmannia peristenia
(*E. pinnatifida*)

Aster Family, Asteraceae

Hardy, drought-tolerant perennial, often in clusters, common along roadsides and in piñon pine–juniper woodlands, 5,000–7,500 ft. in the more central mountains. **Stems** rough with stiff hairs, sparsely branched. **Leaves** hairy (middle-right photo), 2–6 in. long, upper leaves sessile. **Flower heads** at ends of slender stems and branches; 8–10 rays, ca. ⅜–½ in. long; **ray flowers** fertile, **disk flowers** sterile, both yellow. Involucre hemispheric, phyllaries in 2 or 3 series (lower-middle and lower-left photos), linear. **Blooms** mid-June into September.

CHAMISA
(Rabbitbrush)
Aster Family, Asteraceae

Ericameria nauseosa
(*Chrysothamnus nauseosus* ssp. *bigelovii*)

Large, densely branched, somewhat rounded bush up to 5 ft. tall, 8–10 ft. wide, common in foothill scrub and piñon-juniper woodland, 5,000–6,500 ft. Easily recognized by its grey-green foliage, numerous upright branches arising from a clumped base, and masses of yellow-gold flowers. **Leaves** alternate, simple, wooly, linear, 1–3½ in. long. **Flower heads** yellow, feathery, in flat-topped or rounded masses at tips of branches. Inconspicuous **disk flowers** surrounded by many elongated, slender, curved to upright, yellow **ray flowers**. **Blooms** late summer into autumn. Many Native American tribes, including Navajo, Hopi, and Puebloans, used rabbitbrush in medicines, including a tea taken to break fever and promote sweating; as a source of natural dyes; and for making wicker mats, baskets, and arrow shafts from the peeled, straight stems.

YELLOW BLANKET FLOWER

Gaillardia pinnatifida

(Yellow Gaillardia)
Aster Family, Asteraceae

Perennial up to 24 in. tall, on roadsides and in sandy open spaces, foothill scrub, and piñon-juniper woodlands, 4,000–7,000 ft., typically in more central mountains. **Stems** arise from basal cluster, several, unbranched, with appressed hairs. **Leaves** mostly concentrated toward base of stems, alternate, up to 4 in. long, narrow, some deeply pinnately divided. **Flower heads** ca. 1½ in. diameter, single, on long stalks. **Disk flowers** reddish purple, fertile; **ray flowers** yellow, tipped with 3 teeth, sterile. Involucre somewhat flattened, with pointed phyllary tips extending ⅓–½ the length of the yellow rays. **Blooms** June through September. Infusion used as a diuretic for painful urination by Hopi. Western Keres rubbed the plant on mothers' breasts to wean infant; leaf infusion taken and a poultice of leaves applied for gout. A decoction used by Navajo for nausea and heartburn.

SHARPTOOTH GUMWEED

Grindelia hirsutula
(*G. acutifolia*)

Aster Family, Asteraceae

Perennial on dry slopes and roadsides, often in more northern mountains, 6,000–8,000 ft. **Stems** to 24 in. or more tall, smooth, somewhat reddish, branching above. **Leaves** alternate, mostly 4 or 5 times longer than wide, triangular to lanceolate; margins sharply serrated or dentate, mostly smooth, sometimes roughened on the margins; upper leaves somewhat clasping. **Flower heads** at stem and branch ends; **disk** yellow, ca. ½–1 in. across, initially masked by a clear to white resinous exudate; **rays** yellow, radiating to ca. 1¼ in. long, slightly wider toward the pointed tip. Involucre resinous, hemispheric, phyllaries short, cylindrical, awl shaped, definitely recurved. **Blooms** June to September.

CURLYCUP GUMWEED

Aster Family, Asteraceae

Grindelia squarrosa
(*G. nuda* var. *aphanactis*)

Erect biennial, common along roadsides, open plains, or slopes, in foothill scrub to ponderosa pine forest, 4,000–7,500 ft. **Stems** up to 16 in. tall, branched. **Leaves** alternate, firm, oblong, up to 3¼ in. long, usually at least 5 times as long as wide; margins smooth to wavy or toothed. **Flower heads** solitary on stems or branches; **disk flowers** only, up to 1 in. wide, bright yellow, initially masked by a clear to white resinous exudate. Prominent, hemispherical involucre beneath disk with many short, green, cylindrical, awl-shaped projections. **Blooms** July into September. Infusions of this plant used by Navajo to kill ants ingested by lambs, also poured into anthills to kill ants; the resinous exudate used to hold lacerated skin together until healed.

SNAKEWEED

Gutierrezia sarothrae

Aster Family, Asteraceae

Dense perennial producing a small, rounded, herbaceous sub-shrub. Common on roadsides and in disturbed sites in foothill scrub and piñon-juniper woodland in more central mountains, 5,000–7,500 ft. **Stems** 12–24 in. tall, often woody at their base. **Leaves** alternate, linear lanceolate or lanceolate, ¾–2 in. long, margins smooth. **Flower heads** small, numerous, in tight clusters, **ray** and **disk flowers** fertile; rays most prominent, 3–7 per head, golden yellow, less than ¼ in. long. **Blooms** late June into October. Used by Navajo as a source of yellow dye; several ceremonial uses by both Hopi and Navajo; also used as an infusion for coughs, colds, headaches, and intestinal and urinary disorders. When crushed, the turpentine-like odor released makes the plant inedible by livestock.

PARRY'S NODDING SUNFLOWER

Helianthella quinquenervis

Aster family, Asteraceae

Perennial from underground spreading rootstocks, widespread in mountains, meadows, and open areas, ponderosa pine to mixed conifer and spruce-fir forest zones, 7,000–11,500 ft. **Stems** stout to 4 ft. tall, simple or few branched, herbage smooth to sparsely hairy. **Leaves** numerous, glossy, almost leathery, mostly opposite, ovate lanceolate to oblong lanceolate, lower ones to 18 in. long, tapering to a narrow, petiole-like base, pointed at tip, upper leaves smaller, sessile. **Flowering heads** solitary, nodding on long peduncles; **rays** sterile, pale yellow, ca. 1–1½ in. long with ca. 5 prominent lengthwise veins; **disk flowers** fertile, yellow maturing to greenish yellow; dark, columnar achenes extend above (upper-right and middle-left photos). Involucre saucer shaped, almost flat, ¾–1¼ in. diameter, phyllaries hairy, in several overlapping series, outer ones leaf-like, all with pointed tips and ca. 5 prominent lengthwise veins. **Blooms** June through September.

ANNUAL SUNFLOWER

Helianthus annuus

Aster Family, Asteraceae

Coarse annual commonly 4–7 ft. tall, sometimes more; in foothill scrub to ponderosa pine forest, 4,000–7,500 ft. Often in large stands in open fields, along roadsides and in disturbed areas. **Stems** stiffly hairy, rough to the touch. **Leaves** mostly alternate, coarsely hairy, heart shaped to broadly lanceolate, up to 16 in. long, 12 in. wide, coarsely toothed on long petioles. **Flower heads** mostly single, large, up to 5 in. diameter; purplish-brown **disk flowers** in the center, ¾–2 in. diameter, surrounded by bright yellow **ray flowers**, 1–2 in. long. Flower heads subtended by flattened involucre (lower-right photo) with several series of pointed, ovate lanceolate, roughly hairy phyllaries. **Blooms** late June through September. Used by Apache and Navajo as a poultice of crushed plants applied to snakebites. Seed used for food by many southwestern tribes; outer seed coats boiled by Navajo to make dark red dye.

BLUEWEED
(Texas Blueweed)
Aster Family, Asteraceae

Helianthus ciliaris

Perennial; up to 30 in. tall; from woody, spreading rhizomes; often in damp, clayey, alkaline soils; from foothill scrub to ponderosa pine forests; 3,000–8,500 ft. **Stems** bluish green. **Leaves** mostly opposite, sessile, linear to lanceolate; up to 4 in. long, ca. ¾–1 in. wide; twisted; wavy, especially on the margins; entirely or shallowly lobed; prominent veins underneath. **Flower heads** single or a few on stalks; **disk** up to ¾ in. wide, almost hemispheric, reddish to purplish brown with gold, forked stamens. **Ray flowers** ca. ½ in. long or less, bright yellow, sterile. Involucre flat to hemispheric, phyllaries leaf-like, oblong, in several overlapping series, long hairs along their margins. **Blooms** mid-June into September. Can be an aggressive weed, more so in moist soils.

PRAIRIE SUNFLOWER

Helianthus petiolaris

Aster Family, Asteraceae

Annual, widespread throughout the state, including the northern and central mountains, in sunny, often sandy areas in arroyos and along roadsides, 4,000–8,000 ft. **Stems** erect to ca. 3 ft tall with appressed hairs, branching from near the base to upper portions. **Leaves** with stiff hairs, alternate, simple, on long petioles, oblong-lanceolate to lanceolate to triangular, up to 6 in. long, 3 in. wide, pointed at tip, margins entire to shallowly serrate. (Leaves are smaller and more lance shaped than annual sunflower, *Helianthus annuus*, and the maximum height is less). **Flower heads** mostly single on stalks, up to 2½–3 in. across; **disk flowers** fertile, reddish purple; **ray flowers** sterile, ca. ¾–1 in. long, yellow. Involucre flat to bowl shaped, phyllaries in several series, almost leaf-like, lanceolate with short stiff hairs. **Blooms** June into September. Dried rays ground and mixed with cornmeal by Hopi to make yellow face paint for women's basket dance.

SHOWY GOLDENEYE   *Heliomeris multiflora*
                                                    (*Viguiera multiflora*)
Aster Family, Asteraceae

Common, thin-stemmed perennial, a widespread component of the fall flora; along roadsides, in meadows and forest openings of piñon-juniper woodland to mixed conifer forest, 5,500–9,000 ft. **Stems** 20–40 in. tall with appressed or incurved hairs. **Leaves** both alternate and opposite; lanceolate to ovate lanceolate with stiff, flat-lying hairs; up to 3½ in. long, 1¼ in. wide; tips pointed; margins smooth. **Flower heads** numerous on slender stalks; 10–14 ray flowers, sterile, bright yellow, ½–¾ in. long. **Disk flowers** perfect, greenish yellow, numerous; disk up to ½ in. diameter. Involucre saucer shaped with 2 series of pointed phyllaries bent backwards at the tip (lower-right photo). **Blooms** mid-July into October.

137

MOUNTAIN OX-EYE

Heliopsis helianthoides
(*H. scabra*)

Aster Family, Asteraceae

Coarse perennial up to 36 in. tall, in open meadows and along mountain roadsides in central and north-central mountains, piñon-pine to mixed conifer forests, 7,000–9,000 ft. **Stems** upright, loosely branched, coarse to the touch. **Leaves** opposite, petiolate, base somewhat rounded, pointed at tip, up to 4 in. long, strongly veined, margins coarsely toothed, with small, stiff hairs on both surfaces (lower-left photo). Two axillary buds present at base of petioles produce a second set of smaller true leaves perpendicular to the first, larger leaves. **Flower heads** ca. 2½ in. wide, single, on stalks at stem and branch ends. **Disk** somewhat cone shaped, flowers fertile, yellow, becoming reddish orange. Ten or more **ray flowers**, fertile, distinctly veined below. Involucre up to ½ in. high, phyllaries in one series, tips rounded. Identification kindly provided by Timothy Lowrey, University of New Mexico.

HAIRY GOLDEN ASTER

Heterotheca villosa

Aster Family, Asteraceae

Perennial herb up to 24 in. tall, on dry trails, banks, and slopes in foothill scrub to rock outcrops in mixed conifer forest, 5,000–9,000 ft; a major contributor to fall colors in meadows and along roadsides. **Stems** erect, densely hairy. **Leaves** alternate, linear to oblong, without teeth or lobes, wavy, densely hairy, up to 2½ in. long, margins smooth; upper leaves sessile; lower leaves with petioles. **Flower heads** solitary, ¾–1½ in. wide, including rays. Both **disk** and **ray** flowers yellow. **Blooms** July into October. Used by Navajo and Cheyenne as a ceremonial medicine and a sweat lodge emetic, also as fodder for sheep.

WHITE RAGWEED

Hymenopappus filifolius

Aster Family, Asteraceae

Highly drought-tolerant perennial, on dry plains and in piñon-juniper woodlands, 5,000–6,500 ft in more central mountains. The name "white ragweed" comes from the slightly wooly hair covering stems and leaves. Several **stems**, much branched, up to 16 in. tall. **Leaves** alternate, clustered at the base, up to 5½ in. long, twice pinnately dissected into narrowly linear or thread-like segments. Stem leaves few, reduced. **Flower heads** yellow, on loose, apical stalks; heads ca. ½ in. high with elongated green to white bracts that enclose outer surface of involucre. **Disk flowers** perfect, tubular, 10–50 per head; style and stigma extend prominently from each disk flower. **Ray flowers** absent. The airborne pollen is a serious hay fever allergen. **Blooms** May into August. Zuni used a warm decoction of roots as an emetic and roots as chewing gum. Leaves boiled, rubbed with cornmeal, and baked into bread by Hopi.

ORANGE SNEEZEWEED

Aster Family, Asteraceae

Hymenoxys hoopeseii
(*Helenium hoopeseii, Dugaldia hoopeseii*)

Perennial up to 24 in. or more tall, often in large patches in open mountain meadows, ponderosa pine to spruce-fir forest, 7,000–11,000 ft., common in more northern mountains. **Leaves** alternate, basal leaves large, up to 12 in. long, broadest toward the tip, long tapering to a narrow base, usually clasping stem; upper leaves reduced. **Flower heads** solitary or few, stalked, orangish yellow, up to 2½ in. wide, **disk** ca. ¾ in. wide, dome shaped, **rays** up to 1¼ in. long, initially appearing as slender, in-curled extensions from base of head, later flat, notched at tip, eventually drooping. Involucre flat, phyllaries pointed at tip (lower-right photo). **Blooms** July into September. Important source of nectar for pollinating butterflies; toxic to sheep. Hopi used the plant as a source for dye and steeped it to make a tea.

PINGUE BITTERWEED
(Colorado Rubberweed)
Aster Family Asteraceae

Hymenoxys richardsonii var. *floribunda*

Perennial, 10–18 in. tall, widespread, piñon-juniper woodland to spruce-fir forest, 6,000–10,500 ft., often on rocky slopes and areas of rock outcrops. **Stems** with several to many branches, lightly hairy. **Leaves** alternate, both basal and stem, up to 6 in. long, very slender, almost thread-like, divided into 3–7 linear segments, smooth to lightly hairy. About 5 **flower heads** per stem, somewhat flattened initially. **Disk** flat, becoming dome shaped, yellow, disk flowers fertile. Five to ten **ray flowers**, fertile, ca. ¾ in. long, 3-lobed at tip, curling downward, lighter color with age. Involucre bell shaped to hemispheric; 2 series of lanceolate phyllaries. **Blooms** May to July. Toxic to sheep; avoided by most other foragers. Apparently not toxic to humans. Plant used as a chewing gum by Navajo; Zuni used a root infusion for stomachache and applied a poultice of chewed root to sores and rashes.

PRICKLY LETTUCE

Lactuca serriola var. *serriola*

Aster Family, Asteraceae

Tall biennial or annual, 20 in. to 6 ft. tall, on roadsides and disturbed sites in foothill scrub up to ponderosa pine forest, 5,500–7,500 ft. **Stems** with milky juice, single or branched above, leafy to the inflorescence, smooth or bristly toward base. **Leaves** alternate, sessile, and clasping or petiolate; to ca. 4 in. long; pinnately lobed into coarse, jagged segments with toothed margin; midrib prickly beneath. **Flowering heads** numerous, ca. ¾ in. diameter, single or in loose clusters; **ray flowers** only, yellow, multitoothed at ends. **Involucre** ca. ½–¾ in. long, essentially cylindrical with overlapping, lanceolate phyllaries (lower-right photo). **Blooms** July through September.

ANNUAL GOLDENWEED
(Slender Goldenweed)
Aster Family, Asteraceae

Xanthisma gracile
(*Haplopappus spinulosa*)

Tough, drought-resistant annual on roadsides and bare ground, in grassland scrub to piñon-juniper woodland, 5,000–7,500 ft. Herbage with stiff, flat-lying hairs giving a gray-green cast to the plant. **Stems** 4–12 in. high, highly branched. **Leaves** alternate, sessile, small, generally linear with finely toothed margin (lower-middle photo). **Flower heads** solitary or in small clusters at stem and branch ends, both **ray** and **disk flowers** yellow, rays ca. ⅓ in. long. Involucre cylindrical to hemispherical with numerous phyllaries in 4–6 series, tapering to a point. Pappus of fine, hair-like, white bristles. **Blooms** late May through September. Navajo used a cold infusion of the plant as an eyewash and as a lotion for pimples, boils, and sores; the plant was also used as a snuff to cause sneezing, clearing a congested nose.

DESERT DANDELION

Malacothrix fendleri

Aster Family, Asteraceae

Annual, with milky juice, to ca. 12 in. tall, on sandy or rocky slopes, dry plains surrounding mountains, foothill scrub and piñon-juniper woodland, 4,000–6,000 ft. in more central mountains. **Stems** smooth, lightly branched. **Leaves** mostly in basal rosette, up to 3½ in. long, margins coarsely triangularly toothed or lobed, petioles with woolly hairs near base, upper leaves few, smaller, smooth. **Flower heads** on stalks, single or in loose groups, ca. ¾–1¼ in. diameter; **disk flowers** absent; **ray flowers** fertile, bright yellow with purple below, ends blunt, toothed. Involucre bell shaped, ca. ¼–⅓ in. high, phyllaries in 2 series, the outer longer, radiating outward beneath the ray flowers, often purplish along the midrib. **Blooms** April into July. Navajo applied a poultice of leaves to sores and used a cold infusion as a wash for sore eyes.

RIGID GOLDENROD

Oligoneuron rigidum
(*Solidago rigida*)

Aster Family, Asteraceae

Perennial with stout **stems** 1–4 ft. tall with dense, short hairs, common in more northern mountains on open hills to low mountains, ponderosa pine forest, 4,500–8,500 ft. **Leaves** petiolate, thick, rigid, midvein prominent beneath (lower-left photo), margins entire to having gently rounded teeth. Basal leaves up to 12 in. long, oblanceolate to oval, upper leaves elliptic to oval, sessile, ca. 1¼–2 in. long, margins smooth. Numerous **flowering heads** in dense, upright clusters, **disk** and **ray flowers** yellow, ca. 6–10 rays. Involucre slender, bell shaped, ca. ¼–⅓ in. high with phyllaries in a few series, graduated or nearly equal length, papery at their base. **Blooms** August and September.

PARRY'S GOLDENROD

Oreochrysum parryi
(*Haplopappus parryi, Solidago parryi*)

Aster Family, Asteraceae

Erect perennial from rootstocks on wooded, open, mountain slopes, roadsides, riparian areas, ponderosa pine to spruce-fir forest, 8,000–11,500 ft. One to several stems, ca. 12–20 in. tall, unbranched, often purple toward the base (middle photo), herbage with soft, short hairs on upper portions. **Basal leaves** in a rosette, large, petiolate from stem base at ground line, oblanceolate to elliptic to spatulate, 1½–6 in. long, margins entire. **Stem leaves** prominent, alternate, sessile, becoming smaller upward, otherwise similar to basal leaves. Few to several **flower heads** in compact clusters of typically 3–6 at stem ends, **ray** and **disk flowers** present. Ray flowers 8–13, pale yellow, narrow, ¼ in. long with rounded ends. Involucre ca. ½ in. high, nearly as wide; phyllaries usually 3 ranked, oblong; some acute, outer phyllaries almost leaf-like. **Blooms** August into September.

LYRATE GROUNDSEL

Packera sanguisorboides
(*Senecio sanguisorboides*)

Aster Family, Asteraceae

Annual or biennial on moist slopes; in aspen glades; along seeps, springs, and stream banks in higher elevations of more northern mountains, mixed conifer to spruce-fir forest, 9,000–11,500. **Stems** 10–20 in. tall, smooth, branched, somewhat striate. **Leaves** mostly pinnately divided into wedge- or kidney-shaped, toothed divisions, with a wider terminal lobe, ca. ½–2 in. wide, lyre shaped; deeply lobed with a large terminal lobe and smaller lateral lobes. Basal and lower leaves (lower photo) petiolate; upper stem leaves sessile and clasping at the base. **Flower heads** erect, few to several per cluster; 8–10 **ray flowers**, yellow, sterile; **disk flowers** fertile, yellow. Involucre bell shaped, ca. ¼ in. high, 13–16 phyllaries, smooth, shiny, lanceolate. **Blooms** July to September.

PLAINS BAHIA
(Opposite-Leaf Bahia, False Bahia)
Aster Family, Asteraceae

Picardeniopsis oppositifolia
(*Bahia oppositifolia*)

Perennial to ca. 20 in. tall, on plains, grasslands, low hills, roadsides, edges of riparian areas, foothill scrub, and piñon-juniper woodland, 5,000–7,000 ft. Stems somewhat woody at base, much branched, finely and closely pubescent. Leaves mostly opposite; divided into 3–5 very narrow, linear to oblong segments; finely hairy; imparting a grayish cast; upper leaves sometimes entire. Usually several **flower heads** at tops of stem and upper branches, on short stalks ca. ¾–⅞ in. long. **Ray flowers** yellow, few, to ⅛ in. long, toothed at ends. **Disk flowers** prominent, in a somewhat flat array. Involucre ca. ¼ in. high, phyllaries usually in 2 series. **Blooms** June to September.

PAPER DAISY
(Woolly Paperflower)
Aster Family, Asteraceae

Psilostrophe tagetina var. *tagetina*

Perennial; up to 20 in. tall; tends to form hemispherical mounds; widespread on sandy plains and rocky, gravelly slopes; foothill scrub and piñon-juniper woodland; 4,000–7,000 ft. in more central mountains. **Stems** branching, with long, soft hairs. Basal leaves oblong to lanceolate spatulate, up to ⅜–½ in. long with woolly hairs, margins entire to pinnately lobed. **Stem leaves** alternate, sessile, oblong to lanceolate, often twisted, up to ⅜–⅞ in. long, very woolly, grayish green. **Flower heads** small, numerous, on short stalks; 3–5 **ray flowers**, mostly 3, perfect, largely horizontal when open, up to ca. ⅓ in. long, with 3 rounded lobes at ends; rays turn papery and color fades; rays remain attached when mature. **Disk flowers** yellow, fertile, in a dense cluster. Involucre ca. ¼–⅓ in. high, very woolly, phyllaries in 2 series. **Blooms** May into September. Flowers crushed and used to make a yellow dye or paint by Apache, Western Keres, and Zuni. Numerous medicinal uses by Navajo, including a strong infusion used for stomachache, coughs, and sore throat and a lotion for itching.

SHORT-RAYED CONEFLOWER
(Green Mexican Hat)
Aster Family, Asteraceae

Ratabida tagetes

Erect perennial up to 16 in. tall; often in clusters; widespread on plains, prairies, and foothills; in foothill scrub and piñon-juniper woodland, 5,000–7,500 ft. Stems branching, with stiff hairs. Leaves alternate, up to 2½ in. long; basal leaves entire to pinnately or twice divided; stem leaves pinnately divided into narrow, linear, hairy segments. Flower heads on stalks at stem and branch ends. Ray flowers yellow to reddish, up to ca. ½ in. long, sterile, drooping. Many disk flowers on a brown, subglobose disk ca. ½ in. high. Blooms mid-June through August. Strong infusion of leaves used for stomachache or as a cathartic, for colds and fever; root decoction used for "birth injuries" by Navajo. Western Keres used an infusion as a sedative for epileptic seizures.

151

BLACK-EYED SUSAN

Rudbeckia hirta

Aster Family, Asteraceae

Perennial or biennial up to 24 in. tall; on mountain meadows, open slopes, roadsides; often on moist ground; in more northern mountains; piñon-juniper woodland to mixed conifer forests, 7,000–9,500 ft. **Stems** single or branching; purple tinged; with stiff, spreading hairs. **Leaves** alternate, lanceolate, hairy, up to 6 in. long, lower leaves petiolate, upper leaves petiolate to sessile but not clasping, margins essentially entire. **Flower heads** up to 3 in. diameter, on long stalks. **Ray flowers** yellow, to 1 in. long, notched at tip, becoming reflexed with age; **disk flowers** raised, brownish or nearly black. **Involucre** ½–¾ in. high, phyllaries linear to lanceolate, spreading or reflexed, hairy. **Blooms** June to September.

CUTLEAF CONEFLOWER *Rudbeckia laciniata*

Aster Family, Asteraceae

Tall perennial common along streams in ponderosa pine and mixed conifer forests, 6,000–9,000 ft. **Stems** erect, up to 9 ft. tall; smooth, waxy. **Leaves** alternate; lower leaves often on long petioles, usually pinnately compound with 3–7 lance-shaped, coarsely toothed leaflets; upper leaves lobed, 3–5 sections; highest leaves often without lobes or with a few teeth. **Flower heads** large; showy; on long, mostly solitary stalks. **Disk flowers** fertile, greenish yellow, on an elongated conical extension up to 1¼ in. high; often an attractive source of pollen for bees; **ray flowers** nonfertile, 1¼–2 in. long, initially incurled lengthwise, later flattened, drooping downward. Involucre ca. ½–¾ in. high, phyllaries ca. 8–12 in 2 or 3 series, leaf-like, bending downward, smooth or lightly hairy. **Blooms** late June into September. Used by some Native American tribes as cooked spring salad, boiled, or fried with fat; young stems eaten like celery by San Felipe.

SANVITALIA
(Abert's Dome)
Aster Family, Asteraceae

Sanvitalia abertii

Branched annual up to 12 in. tall; on exposed, rocky slopes and canyons; typically in central mountains, foothill scrub, and piñon-juniper woodland, 4,000–7,500 ft. **Stems** slender, branching, purplish tinged, finely hairy. **Leaves** opposite, petiolate, linear lanceolate, to 3 in. long, ca. ⅓–⅜ in. wide, margins entire. **Flower heads** almost sessile, in axils of upper leaves of stems and branches. **Ray flowers** yellow, few, widely spaced, ca. ⅛ in. long, 2-toothed at ends, with greenish veins below. **Disk flowers** fertile, prominent, firm, greenish yellow, on the conical disk. Involucre phyllaries in 3 series, dry. **Blooms** July into September. Many uses by Navajo: plant chewed for mouth sores or toothache, poultice of chewed leaves applied to skin sores, chewed leaves swallowed for sore throat; decoction used for snakebite and for menstrual pain. The plant's scientific name is from the Italian Sanvitali family and the naturalist James William Abert, for whom the Abert squirrel is named.

VIPERGRASS
(False Salsify)
Aster Family, Asteraceae

Scorzonera lacinata

Introduced annual or biennial from a taproot, on disturbed sites and waste habitats; a somewhat recent introduction to New Mexico, 4,000–7,500 ft. **Stems** 4–12 in. tall, erect, one to several branches above the middle, with milky juice. Herbage smooth or with scattered tufts of long, soft, tangled hairs. **Basal** and **lower stem leaves** up to 8 in. long, deeply incised into very narrow, linear segments almost to the midrib with large open areas between segments. **Upper stem leaves** similar but smaller. **Flower heads** solitary on stems and branch tips; **ray flowers** only, yellow, perfect, fertile. Flowers open only in early morning, closing by midmorning. Involucre phyllaries pointed, of unequal length in several series. Tips of ray flowers barely extend beyond involucre. Pappus grayish white, plumose bristles, somewhat similar to that of salsify. **Blooms** mid-May into July.

CLASPING BUTTERWEED
(Alpine Groundsel)
Aster Family, Asteraceae

Senecio amplectens

Leafy perennial with **stems** to 2 ft. tall, single or loosely clustered, branching toward the top, in open ground and forest openings in more northern mountains, mixed conifer and spruce-fir forest zones, 9,500 ft. and higher. **Leaves** mostly lanceolate to elliptic to 6 in. long, margins sharply toothed; lower leaves tapering to a winged petiole; stem leaves sessile to somewhat clasping. **Flower heads** nodding slightly (lower-right photo); 12–20 **rays**, yellow, separated, unruly in appearance, ca. ¼–1 in. long, narrow, tips pointed; **disk flowers** yellow. Involucre broadly bell shaped, ca. ¾ in. high and as wide; phyllaries linear; tapering to pointed, often purplish tips with much smaller, purplish bractlets around the base. **Blooms** July and August.

NODDING GROUNDSEL
(Bigelow's Groundsel)
Aster Family, Asteraceae

Senecio bigelovii

Erect perennial occurring in mixed conifer and spruce-fir forests, 8,000–11,000 ft. Easily recognized by distinctive, nodding, yellow-green heads borne on branches arising from upper portions of leafy stems. **Stems** stiff, typically single, 1–3 ft. tall. **Leaves** alternate, with base clasping around stem, 4–8 in. long, linear to lanceolate, toothed margin. Lower leaves tapering to a winged base. **F lower heads** ca. ¾ in. long, hanging upside down in loose clusters on nodding stalks, cylindrical to bell-shaped involucre, wider toward base; **ray flowers** absent, fertile **disk flowers** only, yellow. Head, except for disk flowers, enclosed by elongated, pointed, parallel phyllaries. At maturity, the reddish-brown phyllaries flare open, exposing the soft pappus of tuft-like bristles of seeds. Blooms mid-July into September.

CUTLEAF GROUNDSEL   *Senecio eremophilis*

Aster Family, Asteraceae

Perennial herb common in mixed conifer and spruce-fir forests, 9,000–11,000 ft. One to several **stems** up to 2½ ft. tall, usually with woody base, leafy to the top. **Leaves** alternate, 1¼–4 in. long on short petioles, deeply pinnately lobed, finely hairy; apical portion narrows to acute tip; edges have coarse, irregular teeth. **Flower heads** erect, 2¾–4 in. high, on slender stalks; both **ray** and **disk flowers** bright yellow. Five to nine rays, fertile, up to ½ in. long, widely spaced; disk flowers sterile. Involucre narrowly bell shaped, ca. ¼ in. tall; phyllaries hairy, linear to lanceolate, ca. 13 in number, ca. ¼ in. long (upper-right photo). **Blooms** mid-June into September.

NOTCHLEAF GROUNDSEL
(Fendler's Groundsel)
Aster Family, Asteraceae

Senecio fendleri
(*Packera fendleri*)

Short perennial 4–10 in. tall, on open slopes in piñon-juniper woodland to rock outcrops in spruce-fir forest, 7,000–11,000 ft. One to several **stems**, wooly with soft tangled hairs when young, sparsely hairy when old. **Leaves** alternate, wooly, much less so with age. Basal and lower stem leaves petiolate up to 4 in. long, deeply lobed almost to the midrib; upper leaves sessile, linear to lanceolate, slightly lobed margins. **Flower heads** in loose, erect to spreading clusters at stem and branch ends; involucre short, bell shaped; about 13 phyllaries, linear, parallel, smooth to slightly woolly. **Ray flowers**, 7–12, yellow, ca. ¼ in. long, ends rounded. **Disk flowers** yellow. **Blooms** mid-June into August. Used by Navajo as a dermatological aid for frozen feet, as a poultice applied to pimples or sores, and as a strong decoction for a pediatric aid used in "birth injury."

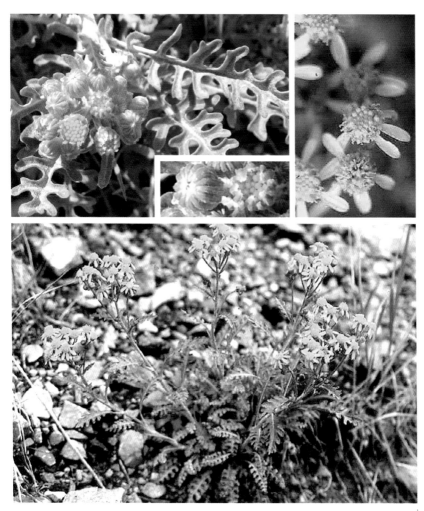

THREADLEAF GROUNDSEL   *Senecio flaccidus*

Aster Family, Asteraceae

Common perennial frequent on rocky or sandy slopes, sometimes in arroyos, in foothill scrub and piñon-juniper woodland, 5,000–7,500 ft. in more central mountains. Stems 16–45 in. tall, often in a cluster, woody at base, covered with soft, woolly hairs imparting a gray-green color. **Leaves** deeply divided pinnately, up to 5 in. long; reduced to pointed, elongated, cylindrical extensions from stem; often with several small, short, flexible, needle-like leaflets at base of leaves. **Flowering heads** numerous, with cylindrical to bell-shaped involucre beneath flower head. Typically 6–10 **ray flowers** per head, ½–¾ in. long, bright yellow. **Disk flowers** somewhat raised, orange yellow. **Blooms** July into October. Used by Navajo, Hopi, and some Puebloan tribes as a bedbug repellent and as a poultice or salve for various skin diseases, pimples, and sore muscles; plant tops used as a brush to remove spines from prickly pears and as a broom.

GOLDENROD   *Solidago* sp.

Aster Family, Asteraceae

Goldenrod is a native North American perennial that contains ca. 100 species, many difficult to distinguish individually. The unidentified species shown here is typical of some found in the Sandias and Manzanos between ca. 7,000 and 9,000 ft.; usually 1–3 ft. tall, with alternate **leaves** often smaller near the top. Numerous yellow **flower heads** contain both **ray** and **disk flowers** in somewhat loose clusters near top of **stem.** Goldenrods tolerate a wide range of soil textures and fertility; they often occur in abandoned fields, along roadsides, in disturbed forest understory, and similar open, dry, environments; fairly shade intolerant. Spread by seed, but after first year's growth, most reproduction and localized spread is by growth of extensive underground rhizomes. Contrary to popular belief, goldenrod is not an allergen causing hay fever; its sticky pollen is carried by pollinating insects and is not airborne. **Blooms** August into October. Many species of goldenrod were used by Native American tribes across North America as decoctions, infusions, or chewed leaves for fever, diarrhea, jaundice, wound dressing, bee stings, nosebleed, and more.

COMMON DANDELION   *Taraxacum officinale*

Aster Family, Asteraceae

Introduced perennial with milky juice, statewide, 3,000–10,000 ft.; common along roadsides and in meadows and lawns. **Stems** absent. **Leaves** all basal, oblanceolate in outline, deeply pinnatifid, up to 16 in. long, lobes triangular to lanceolate, often toothed and pointing toward leaf base, terminal lobe larger. Leaf base like a flattened, slightly winged petiole. **Flower heads** solitary at tip of flowering scape 8–20 in. high; **ray flowers** only, numerous, fertile; **disk flowers** absent. Involucre with outer phyllaries bending downward, shorter than inner phyllaries, both linear lanceolate (middle-left photo). Pappus of numerous slender, white bristles. **Blooms** March into October. All plant parts edible, variously as salads; dried roots roasted, ground, and used as a coffee substitute; and flowers used for making wine. Many nutritional and medicinal uses by tribes in other regions, but no reports found of uses by southwestern tribes.

PERKY SUE   *Tetraneuris argentea*

Aster Family, Asteraceae

Common perennial in open areas in foothill scrub and piñon-juniper and ponderosa pine forests, 5,000–7,500 ft. **Stems** simple or branched, 4–12 in. tall. **Leaves** few, alternate, mostly basal, up to 4 in. long, ⅓ in. wide, with soft, flat-lying hairs lending a silvery appearance. Upper leaves few, linear. **Flower heads** mostly single, with both **ray** and **disk flowers** bright yellow; rays ¼–½ in. long, notched along their tips and drooping with age, leaving a slightly raised circle of disk flowers surrounded by a peripheral ring of the ray flower remnants. Involucre bell shaped to hemispherical; phyllaries in 2 series (middle-right photo). **Blooms** April into October. Used as a lotion by Navajo for treatment of eczema and as a decoction for heartburn.

STIFF GREENTHREAD
(Indian Tea, Threadleaf)
Aster Family, Asteraceae

Thelesperma filifolium

Annual, up to 30 in. tall, on dry plains, hills; typically in central mountains, foothill scrub, and piñon-juniper woodland, 4,500–7,000 ft. **Stems** single or loosely branched, slender, smooth. **Leaves** opposite, not rigid, evenly distributed throughout; basal and stem leaves ca. 1 in. long, pinnately divided into narrow, thread-like segments. **Flower heads** showy, up to ca. 1½ in. wide with both **ray** and **disk flowers**, on long, mostly naked stalks (peduncles). About 8 ray flowers, ca. ½–¾ in. long, 3-lobed at apex. Disk flowers yellow to reddish brown to purplish brown. Involucre somewhat hemispheric, with 2 series of upward-curved, pointed phyllaries (lower-right photo); inner series united. **Blooms** mid-June to October. Steeped infusion of the plant boiled and used as a tea by Western Keres and Tewa.

COTA
(Greenthread, Hopi Tea)
Aster Family, Asteraceae

Thelesperma megapotamicum

Perennial up to 30 in. tall, widespread in plains, mesas, and grassland in more central mountains, foothill scrub, and piñon-juniper woodland, 4,000–7,500 ft. **Stems** arising from underground rhizomes, single or in clusters, slender branching with long internodes in upper half. **Leaves** opposite, ca. 1½–3½ in. long overall, once or twice divided into stiff, narrow, linear segments. **Flower heads** on long stalks, **ray flowers** absent, **disk flowers** yellow. Involucre (lower-right photo) with 2 series of phyllaries, inner series united, forming the "floral cup," outer series 4–6 slightly upward-curved projections ca. ¼, as long as the inner phyllaries. **Blooms** June into September. Boiled infusion of plant used to make tea by Navajo, Hopi, Apache, and Keres. The name "cota," originally used by Pueblo and other tribes, was adopted by Hispanics.

165

YELLOW SALSIFY
Tragopogon dubius

(Yellow Goat's Beard)
Aster Family, Asteraceae

Erect, introduced perennial up to 40 in. tall. Along roadsides and in meadows from foothill scrub up to ponderosa pine forest, 4,000–8,000 ft. **Stems** branched from base, hollow, with milky sap; single yellow flower head at top. **Leaves** few, alternate, up to 6 in. long, tapered, grass-like with bases wrapping around stem. Prior to opening, **flower heads** 1–1½ in. long, diameter larger at base, diminishing to pointed apex enclosed by yet unopened floral bracts (phyllaries). Open heads 1½–2 in. diameter; **ray flowers** only, bright yellow. Involucre: a single series of pointed, green bracts that radiate beyond ends of ray flowers once the head is open. Mature seeds extend from base of flower head, each terminating in numerous, pale-brown puffballs of feathery, webbed bristles that facilitate the seeds' wind dispersal. **Blooms** mid-June into September.

COWPEN DAISY
(Golden Crownbeard)
Aster Family, Asteraceae

Verbesina encelioides

Well-branched annual with grayish stems, 1–3 ft. tall, on disturbed soil and along roadsides, foothill scrub to ponderosa pine forest in more central mountains, 3,000–6,000 ft. **Leaves** mostly alternate, flat, triangular to ovate, to ca. 4 in. long with whitish hairs, especially beneath; margins usually coarsely toothed; borne on petioles winged at their base. Crushed leaves have a rather putrid smell, hence the common name. **Flower heads** 1½–2 in. wide, borne singly on stalks; **rays** yellow, ca. ½–1 in. long, 3-tipped at apex, surrounding yellow disk ca. ¾ in. wide. **Disk flowers** perfect, fertile, blooming from the disk periphery toward the center. Involucre somewhat flattened, in 2 series, with inner phyllaries about equal, spreading radially (upper-right photo). **Blooms** July through September. Infusion of the plant used by Hopi as a wash for fever or itch from spider bites; petals mixed with white clay used by Western Keres as a yellow dye for cotton.

ARIZONA MULE'S EARS

Wyethia arizonica

Aster Family, Asteraceae

Perennial on open or woody slopes in northern mountains, mixed conifer forest, 7,000–9,000 ft. **Stems** unbranched, purple, softly haired, coarse, to 16 in. tall. **Leaves** mostly basal, on softly haired purplish petioles (upper-right photo), oblong lanceolate up to ca. 16 in. long, more than 1¼–2 in. wide, tapering at both ends, margins entire, prominent midvein; upper leaves alternate, sometimes sessile, usually much smaller than basal leaves. **Flower heads** usually solitary, large, 2½ in. or more across, **rays** bright yellow, 1½–2 in. long, often in 2 series, fertile; **disk flowers** bisexual and fertile. Involucre with 2 or 3 series of 16–34 erect phyllaries, narrowing to awl-shaped tips. **Blooms** June to August.

ROCKY MOUNTAIN ZINNIA
Zinnia grandiflora
(Plains Zinnia, Desert Zinnia, Wild Zinnia)
Aster Family, Asteraceae

Low perennial to ca. 8 in. high in calcareous soils on open dry hillsides, mesas, and roadsides in foothill scrub and piñon-juniper woodlands, 3,000–6,500 ft. **Stems** diffusely branched, forming a rounded clump. Herbage with short, stiff hairs. **Leaves** grayish green, opposite, sessile, generally linear, up to 1 in. long, ⅛ in. wide, sometimes curled, margins entire. **Flower heads** solitary, 1–2 in. wide, at ends of branches. Three to six **ray flowers**, bright yellow, ovoid to elliptic, about as wide as long, ca. ⅜–¾ in., somewhat wrinkled along margins, becoming papery and remaining attached for several months. **Disk flowers** orange, becoming brown, extending upward above rays, finely hairy with a somewhat "ragged" appearance. Involucre cylindrical to bell shaped with several series of rounded-tip phyllaries. **Blooms** June through September. Used by Western Keres as a hot infusion drunk for kidney problems; yellow flowers ground with white clay as a yellow dye for wool; whole flowers rubbed into buckskin as a yellow dye or ground into a paste for a red body paint. Used by Navajo as a decoction of herbage for treatment of heartburn or stomachache, also as a ceremonial emetic; by Zuni as a poultice applied to bruises or a cold infusion for eyewash.

FENDLER'S BARBERRY
Berberis fendleri

Barberry Family, Berberidaceae

Woody perennial on open or partially shaded hillsides, sometimes in canyons or along streams, grassland scrub to ponderosa pine forest, 6,000–8,500 ft., common in northern mountains. **Stems** to 3 ft. tall, erect, smooth, shiny, bearing sharp spines at nodes (lower-middle photo). Second-year twigs a varnished reddish brown. **Leaves** alternate, sessile or on short petioles, elliptic to oblanceolate, ca. ¾–1½ in. long, up to ½ in. wide, margins smooth to lightly spiny and serrated. **Flowers** yellow; in a compact, downward-bending raceme on lateral branches and averaging fewer than 9 flowers per inflorescence. **Fruit:** scarlet berries (when mature), ca. ⅛–¼ in. long, 1 to 3 seeds. **Blooms** May to June. Berries used by Walatowa for food.

ALGERITA
(Red Barberry)
Barberry Family, Berberidaceae

Berberis haematocarpa

Erect woody shrub 3–6 ft. tall, common in the central mountains on dry and sandy slopes, from grassland scrub to piñon pine–juniper zone, 4,500–6,800 ft. An attractive native species, well-adapted to landscaping in the southwest. **Stems** woody without spines. **Leaves** grayish green, smooth, pinnately compound, usually with 5 leaflets, sometimes 3 or 7. Leaflets up to 2½ in. long, terminal leaflet commonly 2 or more times longer than lateral leaflets, margins sharply toothed and spine tipped. **Flowers** perfect, bright yellow, in loose clusters of 3–7 at branch ends; 6 sepals in 2 series; 6 petals, erect; 1 pistil. **Fruit:** a round, solid, juicy, purplish-red berry when mature, ca. ¼–⅓ in. diameter. **Blooms** April into June.

OREGON GRAPE
Berberis repens

(Creeping Mahonia)
Barberry Family, Berberidaceae

Perennial species occurring in dry, shady ponderosa pine and mixed conifer forests, 6,500–10,000 ft. Plants trailing and spreading close to the ground with smooth woody stems up to 8 in. tall. **Leaves** alternate, holly-like, pinnately compound; leaflets opposite, 3–7 per leaf, up to 3 in. long with 12–40 spine-tipped teeth along margins; upper surface bluish green, gray green below. Turn purple to red in autumn; remain on plant during winter. **Flowers** small, perfect, on short stalks in dense, many-flowered clusters, bright yellow. **Fruit:** a waxy, blue-black berry with a whitish bloom, ca. ¼ in. diameter. **Blooms** April into June.

CUTFLOWER PUCCOON
(Fringed Gromwell)
Borage Family, Boraginaceae

Lithospermum incisum

Perennial herb on foothill scrub and open, piñon-juniper slopes, 4,000–8,000 ft.; often with clustered, erect stems 4–24 in. tall with stiff, straight hairs erect or lying flat. Basal leaves deciduous prior to flowering; stem leaves alternate, sessile, linear to linear oblong, ¾–2½ in. long, less than ¼ in. wide. Flowers perfect, on short stalks in leafy clusters at stem end. Calyx divided into 5 green, narrow lobes. Corolla bright yellow, basally fused, trumpet shaped with 5 broadly opening, crinkly petal lobes with delicately fringed to rough-edged margin. Blooms April into June. Many medicinal uses by Navajo, including chewed plants for colds and coughs, as an oral contraceptive, infusion of pulverized seeds and roots as an eyewash and of roots alone to facilitate drying of the umbilical cord in infants.

WAYSIDE GROMWELL
(Many-Flowered Puccoon)
Borage Family, Boraginaceae

Lithospermum multiflorum

Perennial up to 24 in. tall, widespread in open, dry areas; mountain slopes; foothill scrub up to mixed conifer forest, 6,000–10,000 ft. Several **stems**, clumped, often branched at the top with spreading hairs and stiff hairs lying flat, especially below leaves. **Leaves** alternate, with 1½ in. or more between stem nodes, sessile, linear to narrowly lanceolate, ca. ¾–2½ in. long, becoming smaller toward the top, with stiff hairs lying flat above, more spreading below. **Flowers** yellow, numerous, in terminal clusters of 2–6, on short stalks, sometimes drooping. Calyx ca. ⅛–¼ in. long, opening into 5 narrow, hairy sepals. Corolla bright yellow, tubular funnel shape, ca. ⅝ in. long, opening into 5 petal lobes, rounded at tips. Five stamens, 1 style. **Blooms** June to September.

WINGED WILD BUCKWHEAT

Eriogonum alatum

Buckwheat Family, Polygonaceae

Perennial from thick taproots; the tallest buckwheat in New Mexico; widespread in dry, open areas in piñon-juniper woodland up to openings in mixed conifer forest, 5,500–9,000 ft. **Stems** 8–48 in. tall, hairy, often solitary with branching above. **Leaves** mostly basal, up to 4 in. long, narrow, wider toward ends, hairy, margins entire. Stem leaves alternate, few, similar, reduced above. **Flowers** small, yellow, borne in loose clusters at branch tips; leaf-like bracts subtend flowers. Seed borne in smooth, 3-angled, pendulose achenes (lower-right photo), each ¼ in. long with a thin, papery margin; brown when mature. **Blooms** June into September. Ground seed used for porridge by Navajo. Many medicinal uses by Navajo and Zuni, including a lotion for rashes; powdered root mixed with tallow as ointment for infant's sore navel; a cold infusion for sore gums, diarrhea, and bad cough; roots eaten as an emetic for stomachache.

BEARCORN   *Conopholis alpina* var. *mexicana*

Broomrape Family, Orobanchaceae

Native, parasitic plant common in piñon-juniper woodland to mixed conifer forest, 5,000–8,500 ft. **Stems** erect, stout, mostly underground. Stem portions above ground, 4–8 in. tall. **Leaves** rigid, brownish, overlapping, and scale-like, immediately below the flowers. **Flowers** reduced, sessile, tightly clustered around stem. The yellow color and compact structure of the closely spaced flowers on the thick stem resemble small ears of yellow corn. **Fruits:** numerous, small, single-chambered capsules (lower-left photo); upon maturity, dark brown, rigid walled, containing large numbers of tiny seeds. **Blooms** May to June. Mature plants maintain their overall structure and brown to black color until the following year or until eaten by bears, the plant's major means of dissemination. Thousands of the tiny seeds occur commonly in bear scat (lower-right photo), especially in years when production of acorns and other favored food is limited. Having no chlorophyll, bearcorn is a parasitic plant that obtains its nutrition by parasitizing roots of nearby oak trees.

FANLEAF BUTTERCUP
(Crowfoot)
Buttercup Family, Ranunculaceae

Ranunculus inamoenus

Erect perennial, 4–12 in. tall, occurring along streams and in damp meadows in pon-derosa pine forest up to understory of spruce-fir forest, 7,000–10,000 ft. **Stems** often solitary, smooth, hollow, sparingly branched. **Leaves** of 2 types: basal leaves on petioles up to 2 in. long, blades fan shaped, ca. ½–2 in. long and wide, somewhat 3-lobed, edges round to toothed and stem leaves alternate, sessile, divided into 3–5 linear, lanceolate lobes resembling a fan or a bird's foot; the two leaf shapes give the plant its two most common names. **Flowers** perfect, solitary or in loose clusters on several stalks; 5 greenish sepals; 5 petals, stout, glossy yellow, ⅛–¼ in. long. Numerous stamens aris-ing around base of the cylindrical flowering head, which bears numerous pistils over its surface. **Blooms** April into August. Roots used for food by Acoma, Keres, and Laguna.

DAGGER CHOLLA CACTUS
(Club Cholla)
Cactus Family, Cactaceae

Grusonia clavata
(*Opuntia clavata*)

Low cholla on sandy soils, 6,000–8,000 ft.; range limited to the central and southern New Mexico drainage areas of the Rio Grande and the Gila River; 3–4 in. high, forming mats to 3–6 ft. across. **Stem joints** short, club shaped to egg shaped, upright or nearly so, becoming woody in the first year. **Spines** arising from prominent areoles; 10–20 per cluster, mostly toward upper portions of stem joints, ca. 1 in. long, with 4–7 inner spines and 6–13 radial spines per cluster. Spines bright pink when growing, ashy gray to white and rough when mature; broader toward their base, rigid, mostly bending downward or straight, strongly flattened, the longest ones dagger shaped. Base of spine cluster with barbed hairs, yellowish white. **Flowers** yellow, small, to 2 in. wide, less in length. **Fruits:** elongated, club shaped or almost spindle shaped with a deep apical cup where floral parts have been shed; 1¼–2 in. long; when ripe, bright yellow, surface almost completely covered with many slender, white to straw-colored bristles. **Blooms** May into June.

PRICKLY PEAR CACTUS

Opuntia phaecantha

Cactus Family, Cactaceae

Common in piñon-juniper woodland and ponderosa pine forest, 6,000–8,000 ft.; generally branched, along the ground, forming clumps. **Stems** (pads) low, broadly egg shaped, 2¼–4 in. tall, 2½–3½ in. wide, fleshy, bright green when young, often fading somewhat when older. **Spines** rigid, up to 1½ in. long, often in clusters of three. **Flowers** yellow to greenish yellow, 2 in. across, 1½–2¼ in. high, located along outer edge of pads, at or near apical end of pad. **Fruits:** ("tunas") spherical to somewhat oval, ¾–1½ in. long and wide, initially yellow green, later turning deep red to dark purple in some species. **Blooms** May through June. Pads of several species of prickly pear cactus used by Keres, Acoma, Laguna, and Hopi for food after thorns removed; fruits as a source for red food dye; thorns as needles, for sewing and tattooing; liquid extract used for diarrhea; scorched stems split and applied to cuts and infections.

PUNCTUREVINE
(Goathead, Sandbur)
Caltrop Family, Zygophyllaceae

Tribulus terrestris

Annual prostrate weed, native of Mediterranean region, now naturalized in the southwest and other areas of North America. Common along roadsides and disturbed bare ground, below 7,000 ft. in foothill scrub and piñon-juniper woodland, more in central mountains. **Stems** trailing, 6 in.–5 ft. long. Entire plant, including leaves and flowers, less than ca. 2½ in. high. **Leaves** opposite, hairy, pinnately compound, with 4–8 pairs of oval leaflets ca. ¼–½ in. long. **Flowers** borne in leaf axils, yellow, sometimes orange, ⅓–½ in. wide, 5 petals. **Fruits:** hard, spined, star-shaped bodies that at maturity separate into 5 brownish-gray nutlets or burs, each bearing a pair of ¼ in. long spines. The hard, spiny burs injure livestock, puncture bicycle tires, are very painful to bare feet, and become embedded in fur and fabrics. The sharp burs facilitate the plant's spread over large areas by animals and vehicles. **Blooms** and produces seed from July into October.

HARTWEG'S SUNDROPS

Calylophus hartwegii ssp. *fendleri*

Evening Primrose Family, Onagraceae

Erect perennial along roadsides and in open meadows and piñon-juniper woodland, 5,000–7,500 ft. Several species and subspecies of sundrops occur in New Mexico. Stems spreading, 4–16 in. tall. Leaves alternate, ascending, linear to oblong, up to ¼ in. wide, margins smooth. Flowers form in upper leaf axils. Elongated, funnel-shaped corolla tube (hypanthium) below sepals and petals extends downward ca. ¾–2 in. to ovary. Unopened flowers enclosed in 4 yellow-orange sepals. Four petals, yellow, ¾–1½ in. long, somewhat crinkled, turning reddish orange after a day's blooming. Eight stamens, thread-like, yellow, unequal. Stigma yellowish green, more or less square, indented in the center, at tip of style (middle-right photo). Blooms June through August. Used by Navajo as a "life medicine" for internal bleeding.

HOOKER'S EVENING PRIMROSE

Oenothera elata ssp. *hirsutissima*
(*O. elata* ssp. *hookeri*)

Evening Primrose Family, Onagraceae

Erect perennial, 2–4 ft. tall, in canyon bottoms, along streams, road ditches, and other areas with sufficient soil moisture, in piñon-juniper woodland to mixed conifer forest, 6,000–9,000 ft. **Stems** unbranched, reddish, rough with small bumps and coarse hairs. **Leaves** alternate, numerous; lower leaves 2–5 in. long, lanceolate, progressively smaller toward top of stem. **Flowers** grouped near top of stem. Hypanthium, connecting base of sepals and petals to ovary below, ca. 1½ in. long; 4 sepals, reddish, ca. ¾ in. long, bent downward after flower opens; 4 petals, yellow, 2–3 in. across, tubular toward base, opening out into a bowl; become orange day after opening. Four stigmas, elongated, 4 linear lobes in an inflated cross configuration (lower-right photo). **Fruit:** slender, coarsely haired pod 1–2 in. long. **Blooms** mid-June into September. Used by Zuni as a poultice applied for rheumatism and joint swelling, similarly by Navajo for sores and mumps, and by Jemez as a good-luck charm when deer hunting.

WESTERN YELLOW PAINTBRUSH
Castilleja occidentalis

Figwort Family, Scrophulariaceae

Perennial up to ca. 8 in. tall, in moist meadows in more northern mountains, mixed conifer to subalpine forests, 9,000–13,000 ft. **Stems** leafy, unbranched, smooth or sometimes hairy below the inflorescence. **Leaves** alternate, sessile, narrow, linear lanceolate to 1½ in. long, margins entire. Terminal leaves (bracts) yellow, ovate to 1 in. long. **Flower** and bracts greenish yellow, purple tinged below. **Blooms** July and August. A semiparasite, as are all paintbrush plants.

DALMATIAN TOADFLAX

Linaria dalmatica

Figwort Family, Scrophulariaceae

Introduced, attractive but sometimes invasive perennial weed, typically in open, disturbed areas and along roadsides in piñon-juniper woodland and ponderosa pine forest, 6,500–8,000 ft. **Stems** erect up to 3 ft. tall. **Leaves** alternate, waxy, blue green, oval, with broad base, pointed toward tip; clasping stem at their base, smooth margin; up to 3 in. long toward stem base, becoming progressively smaller toward stem tip. Several yellow, snapdragon-like flowers borne in axils of upper leaves. **Flowers** large, prominent, irregular; corolla yellow, 2 lipped, ¾–1½ in. long with an elongated, straight spur extending backward; petals fused; upper two petals lobed and pointing upward; lower three bent downward. Five sepals, lanceolate with pointed tips around base of corolla. **Blooms** late spring to midsummer. The common name "toadflax" comes from the opening of the fused petals, similar in appearance to a toad's mouth, and the resemblance to the leaves of the closely related yellow toadflax, *L. vulgaris*, and common flax, *L. usitatissimum*.

BUTTER AND EGGS
(Yellow Toadflax)
Figwort Family, Scrophulariaceae

Linaria vulgaris

Introduced perennial noxious weed now widespread across North America, up to 12–36 in. tall, often on open, disturbed ground; in clearings; along roadsides; and on plains, 6,000–9,000 ft. **Stems** erect, unbranched, stiff, leafy, from lateral roots, often in dense clusters. Many **leaves**, sessile but not clasping, linear to lanceolate, to 1–2½ in. long. **Flowers** bilaterally symmetrical, tipped upward, in dense terminal raceme. Corolla yellow, ¾–1 in. long; upper corolla lip 2-lobed, pointing forward, lower corolla lip 3-lobed, bent downward, forming the extended spur, another ½–¾ in. long, with an orangeish-yellow, rounded projection (the palate) on the lower lip (lower-left photo). The common name "butter and eggs" refers to the yellow and orangeish yellow color combination of the corolla. **Blooms** July to September.

SPOTTED MONKEYFLOWER
Mimulus guttatus

(Seep Monkeyflower, Common Yellow Monkeyflower)
Figwort Family, Scrophulariaceae

Leafy perennial up to 20 in. tall, in shallow water or mud near streams or springs, in more northern mountains, foothill scrub up to mixed conifer forests, 5,000–10,000 ft. **Stems** from rhizomes, erect to reclining, some branching. **Leaves** opposite, ovate to oblong, ¾–2 in. long, ⅜–1½ in. wide, sessile above, clasping stem, on petioles below, irregularly toothed margins. **Flowers** irregular, solitary, on stalks loosely clustered at top of stem, with leaf-like bracts. Calyx bell shaped, 5 angled, pleated, with 5 triangular lobes. Corolla ½–¾ in. long, 5-lobed, yellow with reddish spots, the 2 upper lobes bent backwards, lower 3 lobes bent downward. **Blooms** June into August.

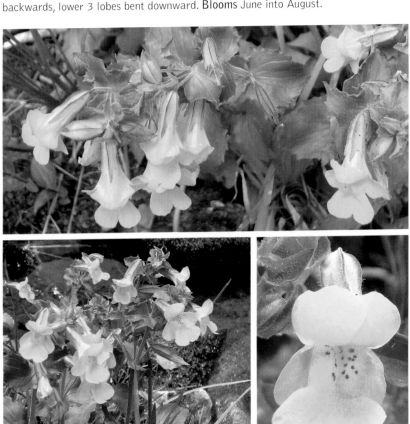

YELLOW OWL-CLOVER
Orthocarpus luteus

Figwort Family, Scrophulariaceae

Hemiparasitic (see *Castilleja integra*) annual up to 12 in. tall, on hills and mountain slopes and in damp meadows and moist clearings in more northern mountains, ponderosa pine and mixed conifer forests, 6,000–9,500 ft. **Stems** erect, unbranched, hairy, dark red. **Leaves** alternate, sessile, linear to lanceolate, up to ½–1½ in. long, upper leaves becoming bract-like and 3-lobed above. **Flowers** bilaterally symmetrical, tilted upward in a loose terminal cluster to 6 in. long; each flower subtended by a pointed, 3- to 5-lobed, leaf-like bract ca. ½–¾ in. long (right photo). Corolla yellow, upper two fused lips longer, forming a short beak extending over the shorter but slightly wider lower lips. **Blooms** July and August. Not related to clover or other members of the pea family. No reported uses by southwestern tribes; red stems pounded into animal skins, horsehair, and feathers as a red dye by the more northern Blackfoot.

WOOLLY MULLEIN   *Verbascum thapsus*

Figwort Family, Scrophulariaceae

Stout, erect, introduced biennial, widespread on roadsides, open slopes, and other disturbed sites, from piñon-juniper woodland up to spruce-fir forest, 6,000–9,000 ft. Two years required to reproduce. First year produces only a rosette of velvety basal leaves; tall, stout, flowering stalk produced the second year. **Stems** solitary, up to 7 ft. tall. **Leaves** 4–6 in. long, covered with woolly, felt-like gray hairs. Stem leaves alternate, sessile, becoming smaller toward top of stem; leaf bases extend to stem. **Flowers** almost sessile, ¾–1 in. wide, yellow, densely aggregated into a cylindrical cluster at top of stem; 5 petals, yellow; 5 stamens, orange; 1 stigma. **Blooms** June into September. The plant stalks have been used since Greek and Roman times as torches after having their tips dipped in tallow. The name "mullein" comes from the Latin "mollis," meaning soft, in reference to the leaves.

GOLDEN SMOKE
(Scrambled Eggs)
Fumatory Family, Fumariaceae

Corydalis aurea

Common annual or perennial with watery juice, 8–16 in. tall; in foothill scrub up to mixed conifer forest, 6,500–10,000 ft.; restricted to somewhat moist, shady areas near springs or readily available underground water. Easily identified by its brilliant yellow flower clusters and soft, leafy **stems** mostly along the ground, but weakly ascending. **Leaves** bluish green, alternate, delicately dissected and deeply pinnately divided, final leaflets elliptical, ⅓ in. long or less, margin smooth; somewhat similar to leaves of celery or parsley; said to have a smoky odor, hence the common name. **Flowers** in clusters; 2 sepals, papery; 4 petals, ½–¾ in. long, bright yellow, in 2 pairs; the 2 outer petals unlike, spreading, one of them with a sack-like spur at the base; 2 inner petals narrowed at base. **Blooms** mid-May into September. Infusion of plant used by Navajo as treatment for stomachache, backache, menstrual difficulties, and sore throat, also to soak watermelon seeds in as a fertilizer before planting.

GOLDEN CURRANT   *Ribes aureum*

Gooseberry Family, Grossulariaceae

Spineless riparian shrub up to 6 ft. tall, in canyons, along margins of streams, or on slopes in piñon-juniper woodland and mixed conifer forest, 6,500–9,000 ft. **Leaves** alternate, petiolate, ca. 2½ in. wide, smooth, 3 distinct lobes, margin with irregular round teeth. **Flowers** perfect, on short stalks in clusters of 3–10. Sepals and petals fused at base, forming a bright-yellow, trumpet-like body ¼–½ in. long, opening into 5 yellow, oblong-ovate petals. Five sepals. Flowers have a pleasant, spicy odor. **Fruit:** smooth, tasty, round berry ca. ¼–⅜ in. diameter, reddish purple or black when mature. **Blooms** late April into early June.

BUFFALO GOURD

Cucurbita foetidissima

Gourd Family, Cucurbitaceae

Perennial herb, common in disturbed soils and open areas of foothill scrub and piñon-juniper woodland, 4,000–7,500 ft. Has a sweetish, somewhat unpleasant odor, hence the specific epithet "foetidissima." **Stems** low, prostrate, trailing on the ground. **Leaves** large, alternate, gray green, rough to the touch, triangular to ovate, pointed, 3–10 in. long with irregularly serrated edges. **Flowers** unisexual; male and female flowers on same plant but physically separated; female flowers more prominent, ridged, hairy. Corolla funnel shaped, bright yellow, 3–6 in. long with tips of the 5 petals pointed, mostly hidden under leaves. Young, **immature fruit** green, easily recognizable below base of corolla (middle-right photo). **Mature fruit** 2–3 in. diameter; green with white, lengthwise stripes and blotches (upper photo); bitter and inedible, even poisonous; eventually maturing into dry structures with a hard-crust shell (lower photo). **Blooms** June to September. Apache used dried, ground leaves for "green paint" in making sand paintings and for dermatological treatment of boils and sores for both humans and horses; pulverized roots used as a laxative by Tewa; cut gourds and leaves used as insect repellent by Sandia and Kewa; fresh gourd chunks used as soap by Cochiti and Sandia.

TWINBERRY HONEYSUCKLE

Lonicera involucrata

Honeysuckle Family, Caprifoliaceae

Woody shrub in open woods near streams, more common in northern mountains, ponderosa pine to spruce-fir forests, 7,500–10,000 ft. **Stems** mostly erect to ascending up to 6 ft. tall, somewhat 4-angled when young, older bark shreddy. **Leaves** opposite, simple, prominently veined, ascending, ovate to elliptical, ca. 2½–5½ in. long, pointed at tip, tapering to rounded at base, upper surface green and smooth, paler with veins hairy below. **Flowers** mostly axillary, in 2s or 3s on stalks ca. 1¼ in. long, corolla yellow, ca. ⅓–½ in. long, funnel form, base enclosed by 2 sets of oval to heart shaped, green to purple, leaf-like bracts (two middle photos). The bracts open later, exposing the **fruits:** globose, shiny, purplish-black berries ca. ⅓ in. diameter, initially green, turning red, maturing to purple black (four lower photos). **Blooms** June and July. The berries are considered poisonous, but many northern tribes had numerous medicinal uses for the plant. Navajo used the plant as a ceremonial emetic.

CRAG LILY

Anthericum torreyi
(*Echeandia flavescens*)

Lily Family, Liliaceae

Erect, delicate perennial from clustered roots on open, gravelly, rocky soil and meadows, in grassland scrub to piñon pine–juniper woodland to ponderosa pine forest, 6,000–8,000 ft. **Flowering stalks** leafless, 8–16 in. tall. **Leaves** grass-like, basal, linear, sometimes longer than the flowering stalks. **Flowers** in loose clusters on curved stalks along upper stalks, 6 petaloid tepals, ca. ⅓–½ in. long, yellow, bent backwards, with midvein darkened; lower 3 narrow, sepal-like, upper 3 broader, petal-like. Six stamens, erect, yellow; 1 style. **Fruit:** an oblong, erect capsule ca. ⅓–½ in. long (upper-right photo). **Blooms** July and August. Cold infusion of roots taken by Navajo to ease delivery of placenta.

FAWN LILY
(Avalanche Lily, Glacier Lily)
Lily Family, Liliaceae

Erythronium grandiflorum

Perennial from a large, deep bulb, high in subalpine elevations near melting or receding snow in the higher mountains of northern New Mexico, ca. 10,000 ft., and into the subalpine and alpine zones above. **Stems** up to 12 in. high, slender, unbranched with a crookneck. **Leaves** basal, elliptic to 6 in. long and sheathed around stem at base, parallel veined, narrowed to a petiole. **Flowers** usually solitary, nodding at base, 6 bright yellow tepals, spreading and recurring upward at base, exposing 6 yellowish to purplish anthers and a style (lower-middle and lower-right photos). Seed pods reddish, club shaped. **Blooms** late May through June, depending on time of snow melt. Bulbs were a staple food for Indian tribes in more northern Rocky Mountains.

GARDEN YELLOWROCKET
(Wintercress)
Mustard Family, Brassicaceae

Barbarea vulgaris

Introduced biennial or perennial, up to 24 in. tall, in wet, disturbed ground; waste areas; along streams; piñon-juniper woodland and ponderosa pine forest, 4,000–7,000 ft.; not common in New Mexico. **Stems** erect, branched, smooth. Upper **stem leaves** shallowly lobed or toothed. **Flowers** in dense terminal clusters at stem and branch apices, each on a short pedicel. Four sepals. Four petals, yellow, to ca. ⅓ in. long. **Fruit**: single, spreading, elongated silique, ca. ¾–1¼ in. long, with a slender beak (lower-right photo) (see also Western Wallflower). **Blooms** April to June. This specimen found only once, in and along the stream in Holy Ghost Canyon, Pecos River valley. Identification kindly provided by Timothy Lowrey, University of New Mexico.

LITTLE-POD FALSE FLAX
Camelina microcarpa

Mustard Family, Brassicaceae

Common annual, introduced weed often in fields or along roadsides in more northern mountains, grassland scrub to ponderosa pine forest, 4,500–8,000 ft. **Stems** erect, 12–36 in. tall, herbage harshly pubescent, branched toward the top, becoming stiff or even woody when mature. Early **basal leaves** large, rounded. **Stem leaves** alternate, reduced toward top, lanceolate, pointed at tip, base clasping the stalk (somewhat similar to Dalmatian toadflax), margins mostly entire except for a few outward-pointing projections. **Flowers** in a loose raceme at stem and branch ends, 4 petals, initially white, becoming soft yellow when open. **Fruit:** a smooth, stalked, teardrop-shaped pod (silique) ca. ¼ in. long, about twice the length of the style remnant extending from the top (lower photos). **Blooms** June into August.

TWISTPOD DRABA
(Heller's Whitlow-Grass)
Mustard Family, Brassicaceae

Draba helleriana

Erect or reclining perennial, common on wooded and open slopes in ponderosa pine and spruce-fir forests, 7,000–11,000 ft. One to several **stems** up to 10 in. tall with coarse, sometimes stiff hairs. **Basal leaves** oblanceolate, ½–2 in. long, smooth margin, clustered at stem base on short petioles; **stem leaves** alternate, lanceolate to oblanceolate, ½–1½ in. long, margin smooth or lightly toothed. **Flowers** on ascending stalks in a cluster at stem apex. Sepals on unopened flowers distinctly hairy. Four bright yellow petals at right angles, bending outward; 6 prominent yellow stamens. **Fruit:** a 1½ in. long pod with pointed tip; with maturity becoming flattened and twisted in a "corkscrew" shape; hence the common name. **Blooms** June through August. Used by Navajo for cough relief, sore kidneys, gonorrhea, and as a ceremonial emetic.

WESTERN WALLFLOWER

Erysimum capitatum

Mustard Family, Brassicaceae

Coarse biennial up to 32 in. tall; common in piñon-juniper woodland up to spruce-fir forest, 7,000–11,000 ft. **Stems** branched or unbranched, erect, stiff, hairy. **Basal leaves** up to 6 in. long, petiolate; **stem leaves** sessile, alternate, narrow, pointed at tip. **Flowers** ca. ¾ in. wide, on stout stalks in dense terminal clusters; 4 petals, much wider at tip than at base. Flowers most commonly yellow, but vary to orange, burnt orange, and orange-maroon, depending on altitude or location; typically yellow at lower elevations and orange at higher elevations. **Fruit:** erect, slender, 4-angled, single pod (silique), 2–4 in. long (lower-right photo). **Blooms** May to September. Used by Navajo as pulverized pods sniffed to cause sneezing for "congested nose"; poultice of warmed root applied for toothache; used by Puebloan tribes to make yellow paint.

FENDLER'S BLADDERPOD
Lesquerella fendleri

Mustard Family, Brassicaceae

Small, low-growing, clumped, early perennial common in foothill scrub and piñon-juniper woodland, 6,000–7,500 ft., especially in springs following wet winters, in more central mountains. Several **stems**, mostly unbranched, up to 10 in. tall. **Basal leaves** elliptic, mostly linear, ½–1½ in. long; **stem leaves** smaller, alternate, somewhat ovate, tapering to the petiole, ¼–1 in. long. Herbage covered with tiny, star-shaped hairs. **Flowers** perfect, on straight, slender stalks 2½–4¾ in. long, in dense clusters at stem ends. Four petals, ½ in. long, bright yellow, fused at their base. **Fruit:** ellipsoidal to almost spherical 2-chambered pod, ca. ⅛ in. diameter, smooth, on pedicels (upper-right photo). **Blooms** late March into June. Plant infusion taken as an emetic and crushed plants mixed with salt as a rub for swellings by Keres; used by Navajo as an infusion to counteract the effect of spider bites.

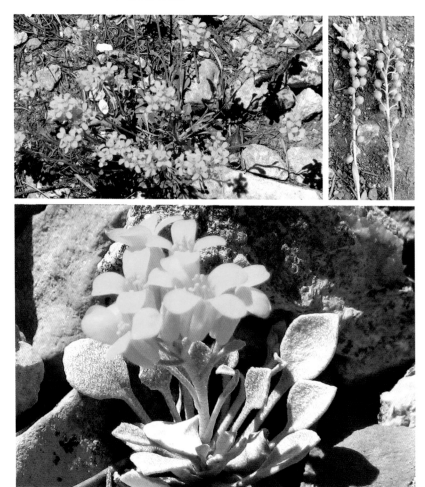

SIERRA BLANCA BLADDERPOD

Lesquerella pinetorum
(*Physaria pinetorum*)

Mustard Family, Brassicaceae

Perennial herb, from foothill scrub to spruce-fir forest, 8,000–10,000 ft.; 4–12 in. high. **Stems** one to several, erect to reclining, usually grayish green with star-shaped hairs. **Basal leaves** rhombic to elliptic, ½–3 in. long, tapering basally to a long, slender petiole. **Stem leaves** petiolate, alternate, spatulate to oblanceolate, up to 4 in. long, ½ in. wide. **Flowers** on pedicels at stem ends, yellow; 4 sepals, ovate to oblong; 4 petals, spatulate, up to ½ in. long; 6 stamens, 4 equal, 2 shorter. **Fruit:** an elliptical to spherical 2-chambered pod up to ⅓ in. long, with the slender style remnant extending from the top (lower-right photo). **Blooms** April into June.

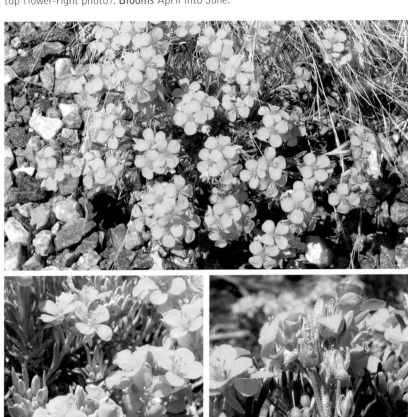

IVEY'S BLADDERPOD

Physaria iveyana

Mustard Family, Brassicaceae

A recently described new species of bladderpod, restricted as yet to exposed, windswept, limestone outcrops along the crest and somewhat south of the crest of the Sandia Mountains, spruce-fir to subalpine forest zone, ca. 11,000 ft. Long-lived, ground-hugging perennial from a taproot. **Stems** erect, closely branched, less than ca. ½ in. long, with branches ascending to erect; forming compact, rock-hugging tufts of herbage 2–4 in. diameter (lower-right photo). Growing typically in fissures of limestone outcrops or in nearly barren limestone rubble (upper photo). **Leaves** pale green to gray green with dense, short, stellate hairs giving a gray cast; spatulate to elliptic, ca. ¼–½ in. long including the petiole, margins entire. **Flowers** on short pedicels barely exceeding the basal leaves; 4 sepals; 4 petals, yellow, less than ½ in. long; 6 stamens. **Fruit:** a somewhat spherical pod longer than wide, less than ¼ in. long, coppery purple at maturity (lower-right photo). **Blooms** mid-May to mid-June (O'Kane, Smith, and Arp 2012).

ROUGH MENODORA
(Frog's Eyes)
Olive Family, Oleaceae

Menodora scabra

Erect perennial, somewhat woody at the base, slightly rough to the touch, up to 12 in. tall; on meadows, dry hills, and mesas; sandy arroyos; often on rocky soil in more central mountains; foothill scrub and piñon-juniper woodland; 5,000–7,000 ft. **Stems** few to many, branched above. **Leaves** grayish green, sessile, opposite near the base, alternate above, oblong to lanceolate, ca. ⅜–1 in. long. **Flowers** scattered in loose groups near ends of stems and branches. Calyx ca. ¼ in. long, with 8–11 linear lobes that later extend up and around the fruits (lower-left photo). Five or six petals with fused tubular base ca. ¼–⅓ in. long, yellow when open. Two stamens, protruding. **Fruit:** membranous, 2-lobed capsule, green, becoming reddish brown; each lobe splits into 2 hemispheres when mature, 2 seeds in each lobe. **Blooms** May into September. Najavo used cold infusion of plant for heartburn and to facilitate labor; root decoction used for backbone pain.

YELLOW LADY'S SLIPPER ORCHID *Cypripedium parviflorum* var. *pubescens*

Orchid Family, Orchidaceae

Perennial; ca. 7–24 in. tall in shaded, moderately moist, mixed conifer and spruce-fir forests; generally above 8,000 ft.; in more northern mountains. This plant has the largest flower of any of the wild orchids in New Mexico. Stems, bracts, and leaves all finely pubescent; stems arising from rhizomes. Leaves on stem, alternate, 4–6 on blooming plants, ovate to lanceolate, up to 5½ in. long, 2 in. wide, somewhat inward folded lengthwise, fine hairs underneath, few hairs above. Typically 1 **flower** per plant, subtended by a leaf-like bract ca. 2¾ in. long at base of ovary. Three sepals. Three petals; 2 lateral, greenish yellow, ca. 2 in. long, twisted; basal petal (lip) bright yellow, pouch or slipper shaped, ca. 1½ in high, 1¼ in wide, opening with an incurving margin. Yellow staminode just inside the pouch. **Blooms** April into July.

MOUNTAIN PARSLEY

Pseudocymopterus montanus

Parsley Family, Apiaceae

Erect perennial, often abundant in aspen groves or coniferous forest openings, ponderosa pine to spruce-fir forest, 8,000–11,000 ft. **Stems** 1–3 ft. tall, slender, smooth except for short stiff hairs just below flower cluster. Each stem terminates in a dense cluster of yellow flowers. **Leaves** highly variable in size and degree of dissection, mostly basal on long petioles; 1–4 stem leaves similar to basal leaves; pinnately divided with further dividing of leaflets, ultimate segments narrow. Many small **flowers**, each ca. ⅛–¼ in. across, borne in a compact, compound umbel containing 5–9 secondary branches, each terminating in a single, small flower; flower clusters up to 2 in. across (lower-right photo), extending above the leaves. Sepals and petals extremely small, partially encased by bracts incurving with an almost closed, spherical appearance (lower-left photo). **Blooms** May through September. Roots peeled, baked, and ground as an occasional substitute for cornmeal by Navajo.

BLADDER SENNA

Colutea arborescens
(*C. vaseyi*)

Pea Family, Fabaceae

Perennial, deciduous, drought-tolerant, woody shrub indigenous to Europe and North Africa, introduced into North America, now grown as an ornamental in several of the United States and in Ontario, Canada. Small population of it in the Sandias, likely an escape from horticultural planting; on sunny, dry road cuts; ponderosa pine zone, ca. 7,500 ft. **Stems** 6–8 ft tall, 4–8 ft. wide, from a common base, woody, leggy, without spines. **Leaves** 3–5 in. long, odd-pinnately divided into 9–13 round to slightly ovoid leaflets ca. 1 in. long and wide. **Flowers** pea-like, bright yellow, single or in clusters of 2 or 3, sometimes more, each ca. 1 in. long, the banner petal broadly recurved upward, revealing delicate red penciling on the inside surface (middle-right and lower-middle photos). **Fruit:** an inflated, bladder-like, papery, slightly reddish-yellow to tan pod, ca. 1–1½ in. long with an indented suture down its length and a small beak at its terminus; contains a "string" of olive, brown, or black seeds. **Blooms** June into August. Kindly identified by Eugene Jercinovic.

WRIGHT'S DEERVETCH
Lotus wrightii

(Wright's Trefoil, Red and Yellow Pea)
Pea Family, Fabaceae

Perennial; up to 20 in. tall; on rocky slopes, dry hills, mesas; piñon-juniper woodland to ponderosa pine forests, 6,000–9,000 ft.; in more central mountains. **Stems** erect to ascending, numerous, branched. **Leaves** essentially sessile or nearly so, in groups of 1–3 on short stalks. Calyx (lower-right photo), tubular at base, ¼–⅓ in. long, with 5 slender teeth extending about the same length. Five petals, initially yellow, becoming red with age; top petal up to ⅝ in. long, curling upward; 2 lateral petals, 2 bottom petals fused into a keel (upper-right photos). **Fruit:** straight pod up to ½ in. long, hairy. **Blooms** June through September. Decoction of leaves used by Navajo for stomachache; considered by Isleta an excellent grazing plant for sheep. A common plant for deer grazing.

BLACK MEDIC

Medicago lupulina

Pea Family, Fabaceae

Introduced annual or short-lived perennial, now widespread in the United States, on roadsides and other disturbed places in foothill scrub up to spruce-fir forests, 4,000–10,500 ft. **Stems** trailing to somewhat ascending, 12–24 in. long, branched at the base, smooth to lightly hairy. **Leaves** alternate, on short petioles, with 3 obovate leaflets ca. ⅓–⅝ in. long, lightly toothed at the apex. **Flowers** small, in dense cylindrical clusters, ca. ¼–½ in. long, at ends of branches from leaf axils. **Fruits** small, veined, black, clustered in pods at ends of flower stalks (upper-right photo). **Blooms** May into October.

YELLOW SWEETCLOVER   *Melilotus officinalis*

Pea Family, Fabaceae

Erect, introduced biennial, well-adapted and widespread throughout the United States. On roadsides and disturbed valley bottoms, often in association with native white clover, from foothill scrub up to spruce-fir forest, 6,500–10,000 ft. **Stems** up to 6 ft. tall, branched above. **Leaves** alternate, on short petioles; divided into three small elliptic leaflets ⅓–1½ in. long, with minute teeth along edge of upper half of blades. **Flowers** yellow, in elongated, loose, many-flowered clusters on upper stem branches and stem apex. Individual flowers pea-like, small, up to ¼ in. long; 2 lower petals fused into a keel. **Blooms** May into October. An excellent honey producer; browsed by deer.

GOLDEN PEA

Pea Family, Fabaceae

Thermopsis montana
(*T. rhombifolia* var. *montana*)

Perennial, common along roadsides and in open areas and aspen glades in mixed conifer and spruce-fir forests, 7,000–11,000 ft. Vigorous rootstocks often produce large stands of striking yellow flowers. One to several **stems**, hollow, 15–24 in. tall, with large clusters of bright yellow flowers at the end. **Leaves** alternate, with ½–1½ in. long petioles; palmately divided into three ¾–4 in. long pointed, elliptic leaflets originating from a common point. Seven to thirty **flowers** in loose clusters on 4–12 in. long stalks arising from stem; similar to sweet pea. Individual flowers ¾–1 in. long, bilaterally symmetrical, 5 petals differentiated into the upper "banner"; two lateral "wings"; and the larger, lower "keel" formed by the coalescence of two petals. Seed produced in upright, finely hairy pods (the legume **fruit**) (lower-right photo), 1½–2 in. long. **Blooms** April through June. Used by Navajo as an inhalant for headache, a decoction for coughs, and a fumigant for sore eyes.

YELLOW SKY PILOT
Polemonium brandegeei

(Brandegee Sky Pilot)
Phlox Family, Polemoniaceae

Perennial herb, mostly on rock outcrops in open areas of spruce-fir forest, 9,000–11,000 ft.; usually in more northern mountains; in the Sandias on open ridges and in rock fissures along crest of summit. **Stems** simple, basally clustered, 4–12 in. tall, stems and leaves glandular pubescent, aromatic, somewhat sticky to the touch. **Leaves** alternate, upright, elongated, 6–10 in. long; basal leaves crowded, pinnately divided; many leaflets ca. ¼ in. long, narrowly oblong to oval, closely spaced along leaf midvein, often appearing whorled. **Flowers** in short clusters at stem tip; corolla basally fused; forming a slender, funnel-shaped tube ¾–1 in. long; longer than wide; 5 petals opening broadly toward apex, cream yellow to golden yellow. **Blooms** May into July.

IVY-LEAFED GROUND CHERRY

Physalis hederifolia

Potato Family, Solanaceae

Perennial, up to 24 in. tall; in sunny foothill scrub and piñon-juniper woodland, 5,500–7,500 ft. Herbage with dense mixture of hairs, long and short, simple and forked. **Stems** erect or spreading, often diffusely branched, leafy. **Leaves** alternate, ¾–2 in. long, distinctly petiolate, blades oval to lanceolate with pinnately incised lobes, margins smooth or wavy toothed. **Flowers** solitary, on drooping stalks from leaf axils. Five petals, dull yellow, funnel shaped, with 5 lobes ca. ½ in. across, often bent backwards. Five sepals, initially with short triangular lobes that grow to form the papery, lantern-shaped enclosure around the fruit. **Fruit:** a fleshy berry ca. ¼ in. diameter, completely enclosed within the expanded calyx (lower photos). **Blooms** July through September. Fruit eaten raw or cooked by Apache. Fruit boiled in small quantities of water, crushed, and used as a condiment by Zuni.

PURSLANE

Portulaca oleacea

Purslane Family, Portulacaceae

Fleshy, prostrate annual introduced from Europe as an edible potherb plant, now widespread throughout much of North America as a common weed, especially persistent in soil that remains moist much of the time, 4,000–8,000 ft. (upper-left, lower-right: in more moist soil; upper-right and lower-left: in drier soil). **Stems** smooth, reddish brown, radiating from a central rooting point up to 16 in. long, forming dense vegetative mats. **Leaves** shiny, succulent, flat, teardrop shaped (obovate or spatulate), ca. 1¼ in. long, margin often with reddish tinge, entire. **Flowers** perfect, up to ⅜ in. wide, sessile, single or in small clusters. Two sepals, most often 5 petals, yellow, notched at ends. **Blooms** July into September. Up to 50,000 seeds per plant and can remain dormant in the soil for years. Cooked with meat and eaten like spinach by Western Keres, Apache, Navajo, Hopi, and San Felipe. Plants oven dried, stored, and used as greens during winter by Isleta. Used as a medicine for stomachache and diarrhea by Western Keres and Navajo.

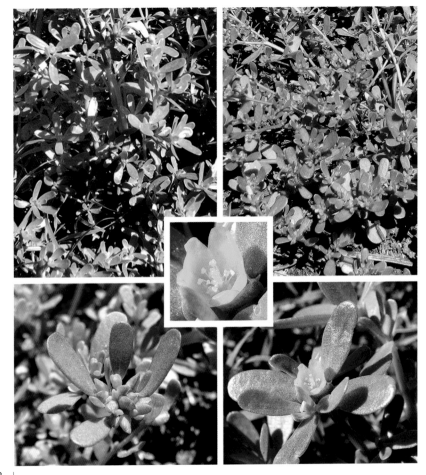

AGRIMONY

Agrimonia striata

Rose Family, Rosaceae

Erect perennial 20–40 in. tall; often in moist woods, open meadows, and piñon-juniper and ponderosa pine forests, 7,000–9,000 ft.; typically in more northern mountains. Stems with long and spreading hairs below, shorter and sometimes glandular hairs above. Leaves alternate; pinnately divided into 5–13 opposite, coarsely toothed leaflets 1½–3 in. long. Those larger leaflets interspersed with much smaller leaflets (lower-middle photo) in the leaf axis, ca. ½–¾ in. long. Flowers on short stalks in slender, linear cluster (raceme) along stem end. Floral cups 5-lobed with a ring of hooked bristles at their summit, hardening with maturity. Five petals less than ¼ in. long, yellow, rounded ends; 5 to numerous stamens. Fruit: berry, the hardened floral cup, containing 1 or 2 seeds. Blooms June through August. No reported use of this plant by southwestern tribes; other species of *Agrimonia* used by several eastern tribes, primarily for gastrointestinal problems.

SHRUBBY CINQUEFOIL

Dasiphora fruticosa
(*Potentilla fruticosa*)

Rose Family, Rosaceae

Small shrub up to 40 in. tall, widespread in moist meadows and open slopes and along stream banks, ponderosa pine to spruce-fir forests, 8,000–11,500 ft. in more northern mountains. **Stems** much branched, older stems with brown shreddy bark. **Leaves** alternate, pinnately compound, 3–7 crowded leaflets, each ½–¾ in. long, hairy and grayish, especially on underside (the name *Dasiphora* comes from the Greek *dasy*, hairy or thick). **Flowers** ca. 1 in. wide; 5 sepals, 5 petals, yellow, up to ca. ⅝ in. long and almost as wide; 25–30 stamens. **Blooms** June and July. Excellent browse for sheep, goats, and deer.

YELLOW AVENS

Geum aleppicum

Rose Family, Rosaceae

Erect perennial often found in damp woods and forest openings along streams, more common in northern mountains, ponderosa pine to spruce-fir forest, 6,500–10,000 ft. **Stems** branched, 16–36 in. tall with coarse hairs. **Basal leaves** ovate in outline, up to 6 in. long, palmately divided into 5–9 irregularly toothed leaflets, veins prominent. **Stem leaves** smaller, subtended by leaflet-like stipules, alternate with 3–5 leaflets. **Flowers** perfect, in loose clusters on long stalks at stem and branch ends; 5 sepals, ovate, alternating with 5 narrow bractlets; petals yellow, obovate to round; stamens and pistils numerous, the latter forming a fruiting sphere with long, bristly styles (middle-right photo). **Blooms** May into August.

215

SILVERWEED CINQUEFOIL

Potentilla anserina
(Argentina anserina)

Rose Family, Rosaceae

Perennial, to 8 in. high, forming a creeping mat from spreading stolons, widespread, commonly on moist ground and damp meadows, piñon-juniper woodland to spruce-fir forest, 7,500–9,500 ft. **Stems** prostrate, leafy to 3 ft. long, rooting at the nodes. Main **stem leaves** ca. 3–5 in. long, in a rosette, pinnately divided into leaflets ca. ½–1 in. long, elliptical; green above, lighter colored and densely hairy beneath; margins distinctly serrate. **Flowers** solitary at ends of silky pedicels, with small green bracts subtending the sepals (middle-inset photo), petals bright yellow, ca. ¼–½ in. long, 20–25 stamens. **Blooms** May into August. No reports found for uses by southwestern tribes, but stem runners (stolons) used to tie leggings and to hold them in place by the more northern Blackfoot.

GRACEFUL CINQUEFOIL
(Beautiful Cinquefoil, Pretty Cinquefoil)
Rose Family, Rosaceae

Potentilla gracilis var. *pulcherrima*

Widespread perennial in meadows and exposed areas of ponderosa pine up to spruce-fir forests, 7,000–11,000 ft. **Stems** erect to ascending, 10–20 in. tall, silky haired. **Leaves** mostly basal, on petioles up to 7 in. long; deeply palmately divided with 5–9 blue-green leaflets originating from a common point, each 1–2 in. long; margin coarsely toothed, undersurface white and hairy. **Stem leaves** few, alternate, reduced upward. **Flowers** borne in loose, open clusters at stem tip. Floral cup shallow, 5 petals, showy, bright yellow with diffuse brownish-orange streaks near the base, ca. ¼ in. long, wider at tip than at base; 20 stamens, yellow; many styles, yellow (upper-left photo). **Blooms** June into September.

WOOLLY CINQUEFOIL
Potentilla hippiana

Rose Family, Rosaceae

Ascending to erect perennial 4–20 in. tall, in clumps, widespread in meadows and aspen glades, ponderosa pine to spruce-fir forest, 7,000–10,000 ft. **Stems** slender, woolly, branching at top. **Basal leaves** crowded, on long petioles, pinnately divided with up to 13 oblanceolate leaflets, ¼–1½ in. long, with deeply toothed margins. **Stem leaves** alternate, few, similar to basal leaves. Both types hairy on top with short, wooly hairs giving a distinctly whitish-gray cast to lower leaf surface. **Flowers** perfect, on stalks in loose clusters at stem and branch ends (lower-right photo). Calyx with 5 green, lanceolate sepals. Five petals, yellow, ca. ½ in. wide, narrowing toward the base and extending in an almost flat plane. About 20 stamens; numerous pistils. **Blooms** June into August. Used by Navajo to expedite childbirth and as a poultice or lotion applied to burns and injuries; also as a powder applied to wounds made by a bear. The name *Potentilla* was given to the genus by Linneaus in 1753; it is derived from "potent," as some members of the genus were considered to have potent curative powers.

THREE-LEAF SUMAC

Rhus trilobata

(Skunkbush, Lemonadeberry)

(Rhus aromatica var. trilobata)

Sumac Family, Anacardiaceae

Widely scattered shrub up to 5 ft. tall, in foothill scrub to ponderosa pine forest, 5,000–7,500 ft. **Leaves** alternate, compound, palmately divided into 3 sessile leaflets, each ca. ½–1½ in. long, narrowing toward the base, margin coarsely toothed. Leaves do not appear in spring until after flowering; summer leaves green, turning red orange in autumn; somewhat foul smelling when crushed, hence the common name skunkbush. **Flowers** small; whitish yellow to tannish yellow; in small, dense clusters; 5 petals (upper-right photos). **Blooms** April through June. **Fruit** spherical, in dense clusters, red to orange at maturity, extremely hairy, sticky to the touch. Fruit eaten fresh and dried, as a jam, and as a refreshing drink variously by Acoma, Apache, and Hopi; stems used by Navajo, Apache, Keres, and Tewa for making rough baskets and by Navajo as a source of black dye for baskets and leather.

RUSSIAN KNAPWEED

Acroptilon repens
(Centaurea repens)

Aster Family, Asteraceae

Introduced, noxious, invasive, deep-rooted perennial forming large colonies by adventitious shoots from widely spreading roots. On waste ground, margins of cultivated fields and on roadsides throughout much of the state, 4,500–7,000 ft. Stems erect, openly branched, 18–36 in. tall, covered with fine white hairs. Lower leaves deeply lobed, 2–4 in. long, stem leaves alternate, smaller, sessile with entire to serrate margins. Flower heads mostly solitary at ends of leafy branches, disk flowers only, ca. 1¼–1½ in. across, pink to lavender; involucre rounded cone to urn shaped, ca. ½–¾ in. high with several series of hairy, overlapping, dark green to gray phyllaries (lower photos). Blooms late June through September.

CANADA THISTLE
(Creeping Thistle)
Aster Family, Asteraceae

Cirsium arvense

Introduced perennial noxious weed, from creeping rootstocks, restricted to disturbed habitats and open areas in northern counties, usually in low-lying areas, 5,000–8,000 ft. Stems 12–36 in. tall, ridged, branching above. Leaves alternate, sessile, pinnately lobed, lanceolate in outline, up to 6 in. long with spine-tipped wavy margins. Pistillate and staminate flower heads on separate plants. Flower heads solitary or in loose clusters, heads ¾–1 in. long, ½–¾ in. diameter. Pistillate flower heads with disk flowers only, pink to light purple; mature achenes brownish, radiating in a spherical array. Involucre vase shaped, narrowing toward the top; phyllaries dark tipped, lacking spines, in many series (lower-left photo). Blooms June to September.

WAVYLEAF THISTLE   *Cirsium undulatum*

Aster Family, Asteraceae

Stout, erect biennial up to 3½ ft. tall, on dry slopes in piñon-juniper woodland up to spruce-fir forest, 7,000–9,500 ft. Herbage with persistently white, woolly hairs. **Basal leaves** in a rosette, 3–10 in. long, margin spiny, toothed. **Stem leaves** alternate, sessile, lanceolate, margins wavy toothed or lobed, spiny, usually woolly on both sides; smaller than basal leaves. **Flower heads** borne singly or in groups of 2 or 3 at stem or branch ends, ¾–1¼ in. wide; **ray flowers** absent. **Disk flowers** rose purple. Involucre prominent, urn shaped, ca. ¾–1 in. high; phyllaries with short-tipped spines (middle-right photo). Mature seed head dusty brown. **Blooms** June through September. Comanche used raw roots for food and root decoction for treatment of gonorrhea; cold infusion of roots used by Navajo as a wash for eye diseases of humans and livestock.

WILD COSMOS
(Southwestern Cosmos)
Aster Family, Asteraceae

Cosmos parviflorus

Annual, widespread in open meadows, hillsides, canyons; along roadsides; in grassland scrub to ponderosa pine forest zone, 5,500–9,000 ft. **Stems** smooth, very slender, up to 32 in. tall. **Leaves** light green, opposite, two to three times pinnatifid into delicate, thread-like divisions (lower-left photo). The combination of tall, slender stems and finely divided, thread-like leaves gives the plant a very open, "airy" character, even in dense populations (upper-left photo). **Flower heads** small, ca. 1 in. or less in. diameter, borne singly on elongated pedicels; usually 8 rays, pale pink, up to ½ in. long, somewhat creased, notched at the ends; disk yellow, fertile, less than ¼ in. diameter. Involucre with 2 series of phyllaries, outer ones 6–8, ca. ½ in. long, slender with long-pointed tips; inner series shorter, wider, not spreading (lower-middle and lower-right photos). **Blooms** late July into October. Cold infusion of leaves used as a ceremonial lotion by Navajo.

SHOWY FLEABANE
(Showy Daisy, Oregon Fleabane)
Aster Family, Asteraceae

Erigeron speciosus

Perennial, along roadsides, in mountain meadows, ponderosa pine forest to mixed conifer forest zones, 7,000–10,000 ft. One of many throughout the western mountain areas; wild fleabanes are often difficult to differentiate from one another. Very common in the more northern mountains in late summer into autumn. **Stems** smooth to sparsely hairy, sometimes woody at base, up to ca. 2½ ft. tall, branched. **Leaves** alternate, 2–4 in. long with finely haired margins, often somewhat wavy in appearance. Lower leaves oblanceolate, tapering to a thin petiole with flattened edges. Upper leaves lanceolate, sessile. **Flower heads** several, at ends of stems and branched. Disk ca. ½–¾ in. across, yellow. Many ray flowers, narrow, pink to light purple, length about equal to diameter of disk. Involucre bowl shaped, ca. ¼–⅓ in. high, phyllaries linear with fine, pink hairs at ends (lower-left photo). **Blooms** July through September. Decoction of the plant used by Navajo as a contraceptive and for menstrual pain.

SKELETON WEED   *Stephanomeria pauciflora*
(Wire Lettuce)
Aster Family, Asteraceae

Perennial, in arid, open, disturbed areas and foothill scrub; piñon-juniper woodland, 5,000–7,500 ft. **Stems** up to 20 in. tall; scantily to copiously branched; branches stiff, ascending or spreading, smooth or with short, stiff hairs. Stem sap milky. **Lower leaves** on plant sparse, alternate, irregularly pinnatifid, linear to narrowly lanceolate, up to 2 in. long, smooth and waxy. **Upper leaves** reduced to scales, giving branches an almost leafless appearance. The paucity of leaves and reduction of upper leaves to scales make the plant well-adapted to arid environments. **Flower heads** at ends of branches; 3–6 fertile **ray flowers** per head, pink with purple linear stripes, notched at ends; **disk flowers** absent; involucre cylindrical, up to ½ in. long; pappus: white, plumose. **Blooms** June through September. Root infusion used by Hopi to increase mother's milk supply and by Navajo to hasten delivery of placenta in childbirth; root used as chewing gum.

ROCKY MOUNTAIN CLEMATIS
(Alpine Clematis)
Buttercup Family, Ranunculaceae

Clematis columbiana
(*C. pseudoalpina*)

Perennial, in shaded, moist areas of more central mountains, in ponderosa pine to spruce-fir forest, 7,000–10,000 ft. **Vines** herbaceous to somewhat woody, trailing, often branched, twining along the ground or clinging on and growing over other low plants, sometimes into shrubs. **Leaves** opposite, pinnately compound, divided into groups of three; each of those further divided into 3 leaflets, usually with lobed or coarsely toothed margins. **Flowers** solitary or in small clusters, long stalked, delicate, 1–2 in. across; 4 prominent, pointed, petal-like sepals (left photos), initially pale pink to light purple, rapidly fading. Many tightly packed, yellow stamens in center of flower. Sepals and flower stalks finely hairy. At maturity, many seeds present, each with a long, finely feathered tail (upper-right photo). **Blooms** late May into June.

STRAWBERRY HEDGEHOG CACTUS
(Fendler's Hedgehog Cactus)
Cactus Family, Cactaceae

Echinocereus fendleri

Often single stemmed, sometimes several to many clumped together; easily recognized by their striking flower color; on gravelly slopes or rocky hills, in foothill scrub and piñon-juniper woodlands, 6,000–7,500 ft. **Stems** 3–12 in. tall, dark green, somewhat egg shaped to cylindrical, 3–4 in. diameter, with 8–16 longitudinal ribs; up to 10 spines per cluster borne along crest of the ribs; radial spines 5–9, straight, ⅜–¾ in. long; 0–1 central spines, shorter. **Flowers** on upper ¼ of stem but below apex, funnel shaped, 2–2¾ in. long and wide. Overlapping rows of numerous, broadly pointed, deep pink to magenta petals surround numerous stigmas with green lobes and yellow anthers. Outermost petals, greenish centers with violet edges. **Fruits** below the flowers, round, fleshy, turning red when mature, with small clusters of white spines. **Blooms** late April into June. Raw fruit used for food by Apache; stems roasted and eaten by Cochiti; fruits dried and used as a source of sweetening by Hopi.

INDIAN HEMP

Apocynum cannabinum

(Spreading Dogbane)
Dogbane Family, Apocynaceae

Perennial, 20–36 in. tall, in open areas and on waste ground in piñon-juniper woodland and ponderosa pine forest, 4,500–8,000 ft. **Stems** erect or ascending, smooth, with milky juice and tough, fibrous bark. **Leaves** opposite, ovate to lanceolate, ¾–4 in. long, short stalked, smooth margin, ascending or spreading, soft hairs underneath. **Flowers** small, ca. ¾ in. long, in large clusters at branch ends. Corolla somewhat bell shaped, ¼ in. long, the 5 lobes erect, slightly spreading or recurved at the tip, white to pinkish white. **Fruit:** slender, pendulous, brown pod ca. 3 in. long (lower-right photo). **Blooms** June through August. Gummy stem latex mixed with clean clay for chewing gum by Isleta; used by many tribes throughout North America to make thread and even rope.

FIREWEED

Evening Primrose Family, Onagraceae

Chamerion angustifolium
(*Epilobium angustifolium*)

Stout, erect perennial common in mixed conifer forest up to subalpine forest, 7,500–11,000 ft., especially in recently burned areas, hence its common name, or in other cool areas with full sunlight. **Stems** simple or branched, up to 6 ft. tall, commonly shorter. **Leaves** alternate, lanceolate, essentially sessile, 2–6 in. long, ¼–1¼ in. wide, smooth margin. **Flowers** on short stalks in loose clusters toward stem end. Four sepals, purple to magenta, spreading, elongated, prominent between the petals. Four petals, spreading, pink to magenta, ½–¾ in. long, tapering to a narrow base. Eight stamens with purplish anthers. Stigma 4 lobed, curled downward (middle photo). **Blooms** late July into September. Within a few years following a fire, fireweed will be replaced by more shade-tolerant species as trees occupy more of the area.

WILLOW HERB

Epilobium saximontanum

Evening Primrose Family, Onagraceae

A seldom-found perennial in saturated ground, even in small streams in more northern mountains, ponderosa pine to mixed conifer forest, 8,000–10,000 ft. **Stems** to 16 in. tall, reddish, finely haired, branched toward top. **Leaves** opposite, upper ones alternate, sessile or short petioled, ¾–1½ in. long, ovate lanceolate to elliptic, tips pointed, margins entire to finely serrated. **Flowers** very small; ca. ¼–½ in. long or shorter; borne at tips of slender, elongated pedicels. Five sepals, green; 5 petals, pink to white, bilobed, less than ⅛ in. long with delicate, purple guidelines (upper-right photo). **Fruit:** an elongated, slender capsule up to 2 in. long, finely haired (lower-middle and lower-right photos). **Blooms** July to September. Identification kindly proved by Timothy Lowrey, University of New Mexico.

PURPLE-WHITE OWL-CLOVER

Orthocarpus purpureoalbus

Figwort Family, Scrophulariaceae

Erect, hemiparasitic (see Foothills Paintbrush) up to 16 in. tall on open slopes and meadows, foothill scrub to ponderosa pine forest, 6,000–9,000 ft. Despite its common name, the plant is not related to any clover. **Stems** unbranched except near base, glandular, hairy. **Leaves** dark green, to 1½ in. long, narrowly linear, entire or 3-cleft division, thread-like. **Flowers** loosely spaced in a spike-like inflorescence on upper part of stem; 3 lobed; linear bracts ¾ in. with pointed tips subtending the flowers; corolla ca. ¾ in. long, white (right photos), becoming pink to light purple; tip of the initially white, hooded upper lip (galea) purple. **Blooms** July to September. Decoction used by Navajo as a cathartic; cold infusion taken for heartburn.

ELEPHANT HEAD   *Pedicularis groenlandica*

Figwort Family, Scrophulariaceae

Perennial, typically associated with bogs and wet meadows in more northern mountains, mixed conifer to spruce-fir forest, 8,500–12,000 ft. **Stems** unbranched to ca. 24 in. tall. Most easily recognized by its flowers. **Leaves** mostly basal, 2–4½ in. long, deeply incised almost to the midvein, finely toothed, resembling fern fronds; lower leaves petiolate, upper leaves sessile. **Flowers** in dense, 4–10 in. long terminal clusters; pink to reddish pink, sometimes white. Individual flowers ca. ⅜–½ in. long, conspicuously lobed; the united, hooded, 4–10 in. long upper corolla lobes arching and curling downward, with a blunt tip curving upward (together forming the "trunk"); that plus the 2 side lobes (the "ears") and a smaller lobe fitting under the trunk make the flower resemble a miniature elephant's head. **Blooms** June to August. No reports of use by southwestern tribes, but used by Cheyenne as an infusion to stop or loosen long-lasting cough.

SAND PENSTEMON *Penstemon ambiguus*
(Bush Penstemon, Plains Pink Penstemon)
Figwort Family, Scrophulariaceae

Shrubby perennial up to 18 in. across, with highly branched stems up to 24 in. tall; on sandy soil in full sun in foothill scrub, 5,500–6,000 ft. Leaves opposite, narrow, ca. 1 in. long, in-rolled, sharply tipped. Few to numerous flowers, 1 per flower stalk, many flowering stalks arising from main stem. Sepals short, pointed, surrounding base of tubular corolla, which is pale pink on the outside, deep pink inside (lower-middle and left photos). Corolla opens into 5 rounded, flat-faced lobes, white above with short, pink guidelines, pinkish below; upper 2 lobes bending upward, 3 lower lobes projecting forward. Blooms May into August. Appearance of the flowers was an indicator for Tewa and Hopi that watermelon planting season was over. Navajo used it as a poultice for scorpion and eagle bites.

233

PALMER'S PENSTEMON   *Penstemon palmeri*
(Balloon Penstemon)
Figwort Family, Scrophulariaceae

Perennial; up to 3 ft. tall or more; on gravelly soil, dry meadows, and arroyos; in piñon-juniper woodland, 6,000–7,000 ft. **Stems** one to several, stout, smooth, somewhat brittle. **Leaves** opposite, gray green, waxy; **median stem leaves** (left photo) sessile, at their base often clasping and encircling stem (upper-middle photo); **upper leaves** smaller, not joined around the stem. **Flowers** irregular, stalked, 1–1¼ in. long, white or pale pink with red guidelines. Prior to opening, corolla has an inflated-balloon appearance (lower-right photo); upon opening, 3 lower lobes are about twice as long as upper pair. Lower lip bearded, staminode extended, strongly bearded with long yellow hairs (middle-right and upper-right photos). **Blooms** June into September.

ONE-SIDED PENSTEMON
(Side-Bells Penstemon)
Figwort Family, Scrophulariaceae

Penstemon secundiflorus

Early blooming, erect perennial up to 20 in. tall, on dry hills and in sandy soil in foothill scrub and piñon-juniper woodland, 5,500–6,500 ft. **Stems** and leaves smooth. **Leaves** opposite, sessile, slender, lanceolate, ca. 3 in. long, shorter toward stem base; often folded upward along midrib. **Flowers** on short branches along one side of stem, subtended by erect, leaf-like floral bracts. Sepals ca. ¼ in. long with 5 lanceolate lobes, often pinkish to purplish. Petal color variable, pinkish purple, purple, red violet, sometimes medium blue, rarely white; fused basally, opening wide into 5 lobes up to 1 in. across; inside of lower lip hairy. Anthers smooth; staminode heavily bearded with yellow hairs. **Blooms** late May into July.

WANDBLOOM PENSTEMON   *Penstemon virgatus*

Figwort Family, Scrophulariaceae

Slender, erect perennial, up to 32 in. tall, often solitary, in piñon-juniper woodland and ponderosa pine forest, 7,000–8,500 ft. **Stems** straight, typically single; stems and leaves smooth to finely hairy. **Leaves** opposite, narrow, linear, ca. ¾–4½ in. long. **Flowers** on stalks along one side of stem in clusters of 2–4; pallid white, light pink, or pale lavender. Five sepals with blunt or pointed tips, papery and somewhat ragged edges. Corolla inflated; tubular; ca. ¾–1¼ in. long; 2 upper lobes projecting forward and upward; 3 lower lobes projecting forward, downward, and slightly backward; with reddish-purple guidelines; slightly hairy. Four stamens (lower-right photo), projecting; staminode lacking hairs. **Blooms** June through August.

NARROWLEAF FOUR O'CLOCK

Mirabilis linearis
(*Oxybaphus linearis*)

Four o'clock Family, Nyctaginaceae

Erect perennial on plains, hills, and wooded slopes; grassland scrub to mixed conifer forest; 5,000–9,000 ft. **Stems** mostly erect, to 24 in. tall, densely and finely haired. **Leaves** sessile, opposite, linear to linear lanceolate, to ca. 4 in. long, ¼ in. wide, often curling downward, margins entire to sometimes bearing a few teeth. **Flowers** at stem and branch ends in groups of mostly 2 or 3, the groups subtended by hairy bracts forming an involucre turning translucent tan at maturity, up to ¼ in. long (middle photos). Sepals only, 5 lobes fused at base, funnel to bell shaped, to ca. ¼ in. long, pinkish white to rose purple. Three to five stamens on long pink filaments extending beyond sepals, anthers yellowish tan (lower-left photo). One stigma on long filamentous style extending beyond sepals. **Fruit:** two erect, slightly hairy, spindle-shaped capsules (middle photos). **Blooms** July to September. Navajo used root infusion for stomach disorders and for postpartum treatment and crushed whole plant for a poultice applied to burns. Zuni used roots to induce urination and as an emetic.

RED-STEMMED FILAREE

Erodium circutarium

(Heronbill, Stork's Bill)
Geranium Family, Geraniaceae

Introduced annual; common along roadsides and other open, disturbed areas in foothill scrub and piñon-juniper woodland, 5,000–7,000 ft. Commonly tightly tufted, 1–1½ in. tall. **Stems** either absent or prostrate with branches sprawling, usually less than a few inches long. Stems, leaves, and sepals finely hairy. **Leaves** 1¼–4 in. long, pinnately divided, each segment further divided, irregularly toothed, often unequal in size; petiole less than ¼ the length of the blade. **Flowers** ca. ½ in. across, in small clusters on a stalk; 5 sepals with alternating, longitudinal, soft green and white stripes (upper-middle photo); 5 petals, rose pink to light purple, up to ¼ in. long. One 5-lobed **seed pod** per flower, with styles united into a rigid, straight to curved column 1½–2 in. long, resembling somewhat a heron or stork's bill (lower-left and lower-right photos). **Blooms** March into September.

BOG WINTERGREEN
Pyrola asarifolia
(Pink Wintergreen, Liverleaf Wintergreen)
Heath Family, Ericaceae

Perennial along stream banks and marshy areas in shaded subalpine forests in more northern mountains, mixed conifer to spruce-fir forest, 9,000–11,000 ft. Flowering stems (scapes), commonly 4–8 in. tall, green to reddish, slender, smooth, unbranched, bearing 5–25 reddish flowers toward the top. Leaves basal, to 3 in. long, glossy, thick, broadly elliptic to heart shaped, long stalked, margins entire or faintly round toothed. Flowers whitish pink to pinkish red, in a terminal raceme, not one sided, hanging down on short stalks. Blooms July and August.

NODDING ONION

Allium cernuun

Lily Family, Liliaceae

Stemless perennial herb up to 20 in. tall, produced from clustered bulbs in ponderosa pine up to spruce-fir forest, 6,500–11,000 ft. All plant parts, when crushed, produce a distinctive onion odor. Bulb scales purplish pink, papery to slightly fibrous. Four to six leaves arising from bulb at base of flowering stalk, flat, linear, up to 10 in. long, ¼ in. wide. Flowering stalks, 4–20 in. tall, extend above length of leaves, bearing an umbel of pink to white flowers. Stalks bend downward near tip, making the umbel flower cluster upside down. Flowers reddish pink, bell shaped, ca. ¼ in. long; one head-like stigma (lower-right photo) and up to 6 stamens extend beyond petals and sepals. Blooms mid-July through September. Used by several Pueblo Indian tribes and Navajo for food, raw or cooked; applied as a poultice for external infections and for sore throats.

GEYER'S ONION

Allium geyeri

Lily Family, Liliaceae

Strongly scented perennial, 6–20 in. tall, from a fibrous-coated bulb, outer scales of which extend above and around base of stem. On rock outcrops and meadows, from piñon-juniper woodland up to spruce-fir forest, 6,500–11,000 ft. **Flower stalks** erect, exceeding length of leaves. **Leaves** originate from the bulb, usually 3 per flowering stem, ca. ⅛ in. wide, up to 10 in. long. **Flowers** borne in an erect umbel cluster on individual, short stalks originating from a single point at the apex of the flowering stalk, subtended by 2 or 3 single-veined, membranous bracts (upper-right photo). Flowers perfect, bell shaped, pink to white, ¼–⅜ in. long. Stamens shorter than petals. **Blooms** mid-June through September. Used by Keres and other Pueblo Indian tribes, mostly for seasoning.

SHOWY MILKWEED　　　　　　　　　　　*Asclepias speciosa*

Milkweed Family, Asclepiadaceae

Stout, erect perennial; up to 4 ft. tall or taller; widespread on damp, open ground; often near streams and roadside ditches; in scrub grassland to ponderosa pine forest, 5,500–8,500 ft. **Stems** unbranched. **Leaves** gray green; on short petioles; opposite; up to 7 in. long; lanceolate; prominently veined; thick but soft; underside with short, woolly hairs. As in all milkweeds, leaves and stems contain a white, sticky latex sap that oozes out when the plant is injured. **Flowers** perfect; purplish pink; in stalked, 3 in. wide umbel clusters at stem apex and in axils of upper leaves. Five corolla lobes, pinkish red, ⅜ in. long. Upon opening, 5 outwardly radiating, pinkish white, concave, elongated, pointed tip, triangular "hoods" and their 5 inwardly curved "horns" (upper-inset photo) become more prominent than the corolla lobes. See Broadleaf Milkweed for more complete description of milkweed flower anatomy. **Fruit:** greenish-tan, vertically oriented, woolly pod up to 4 in. long, with soft spines, splitting lengthwise when mature to reveal flat, brown seeds with numerous attached, long, silky hairs that facilitate wind dissemination (lower photos). **Blooms** June to August. Used by Navajo as a ceremonial emetic; the hardened milky latex was used as a chewing gum by Acoma, Laguna, and Apache.

FIELD MINT

Mentha arvensis

Mint Family, Lamiaceae

Widespread, aromatic perennial from creeping rootstock; clusters common in moist meadows and canyon bottoms from scrub grassland to mixed conifer forests, 5,000–9,000 ft. **Stems** erect, 6–10 in. tall, often branched, 4-angled. **Leaves** opposite, ovate to elliptic, ¾–2 in. long with short petioles, toothed margins, smooth above, somewhat hairy veins below. **Flowers** perfect, in dense clusters surrounding the stem in upper leaf axils; corolla tubular, pink to purplish, 5 petals to ¼ in. long, 2-lipped, the upper one often notched at the tip, the lower lip 3-lobed. Four stamens, distinctly dark pink to purple, extending well beyond corolla. Style with stigma extending, dichotomously forked at tip (lower-right photo). **Fruit** consists of 4 fused nutlets. **Blooms** June to September. Used by Navajo as dermatological lotion for swellings, cold infusion for fever, dried leaves as a flavoring for meat or cornmeal mush.

BERGAMOT
(Beebalm)
Mint Family, Lamiaceae

Monarda fistulosa var. *menthifolia*

Coarse, erect, aromatic perennial 12–32 in. tall, on open or wooded slopes, ponderosa pine forests, 6,000–8,500 ft. **Stems** 4-angled, unbranched, with short, soft hairs near the top, sometimes woolly. **Leaves** velvety, opposite, with short petioles, ovate to lanceolate, 1½–2 in. long, ½–1¼ in. wide, prominently veined, finely serrated margin. **Flowers** solitary, in a dense cluster at stem apex, ½–1 in. diameter excluding corolla, subtended by leaf-like bracts bent backward. Calyx: pink-lavender tubular extensions (upper-left photo) ca. ¼–½ in. long, opening at tips to expose pink, 2-lipped corolla, the lower lip 3-lobed, bending downward (upper-right photo). Two stamens, protruding. Entire floral head with its many individual flowers 2–3 in. diameter. The specific epithet (*fistulosa*) comes from Latin and means "resembling a pipe"; it describes the narrow, elongated floral tube. The common name *bergamot* comes from the plant's aroma, which is similar to that of the Bergamot orange. **Blooms** July through September. Cold infusion used by Navajo as a lotion for gunshot or arrow wounds and as an eye medicine; plant used as a poultice for sore throat by Tewa; ground leaves used as a seasoning for sausage, other meats, and stews by Acoma, Laguna, Isleta, and San Ildefonso.

WRIGHT'S THELYPODIUM

Thelypodium wrightii

Mustard Family, Brassicaceae

Erect biennial with smooth herbage, widespread, on mountain slopes, often in open woods or brushy areas, piñon pine woodland to ponderosa pine forest, 7,000–8,500 ft. **Stems** erect, to 3 ft. tall, often less, with many short branches. **Basal leaves** 4–6 in. long, pinnatifid; **stem leaves** becoming smaller upward, linear lanceolate, ca. 1¼–3½ in. long, up to ¾ in. wide, simple to pinnatifid, margins smooth to wavy edged. **Flowers** perfect, on slender pedicels at branch and stem ends in dense clusters 1–2 in. across. Four sepals; 4 petals, tapering, white to pale purple, longer than sepals; 6 stamens (lower-left photo). **Fruit** (silique): a slender, smooth, flattened, somewhat lumpy pod ca. 1¼–3 in. long, widely spaced on upper stem; fruit and fruit stalks horizontal or bent somewhat downward (upper-right photo). **Blooms** June through September. Used by several Pueblo Indian tribes for food; young plant boiled and eaten as greens; boiled, pressed, dried, and stored for winter use; or made into a stew with wild onions, wild celery, and tallow or bits of meat.

PERENNIAL PEAVINE
(Everlasting Pea)
Pea Family, Fabaceae

Lathyrus latifolius

Introduced garden ornamental, now naturalized to most areas of North America; can be invasive. Dense herbaceous perennial from rhizomes, generally in disturbed habitats with somewhat wet and sunny to partially shaded areas in more northern mountains, 6,000–9,000 ft. **Stems** ascending to erect, smooth, broadly winged, twining with many tendrils, forming large growths up to 3 ft. high covering many square yards. **Leaves** alternate, up to 6 in. long but with only 2 pinnate leaflets ca. ¾ in. long, on broadly winged stalks (middle-right photo), margins entire. **Flowers** pea-like, in dense raceme clusters on long pedicels from the leaf axils; 5–15 per cluster; pink to reddish pink, purplish red, to white; ca. ½ in. long; calyx green, ca. ¼ in. long, lobe tips pointed (upper-right photo); corolla 5-lobed, the large upper petal (the banner) almost as long, as wide, ca. ½ in., curled somewhat downward over the 2 smaller lateral petals and the yet smaller lower petal (the keel). **Fruit:** a straight, narrow pod to 4 in. long with 10–15 seeds. **Blooms** June through August.

NEW MEXICO LOCUST
Robinia neomexicana

Pea Family, Fabaceae

Tree or shrub up to 24 ft. tall, widespread along stream banks, in canyons, in open woods, along roadsides in scrub grassland to mixed conifer forests, 4,500–9,000 ft.; older stems with 2 sharp, stout, paired, red to brown spines at the base of each leaf. Can form dense thickets by vigorous sprouting from extensive roots. **Leaves** alternate, 7–10 in. long, odd-pinnately divided into 9–19 ovate leaflets ½–1½ in. long, each on a short petiole, rounded at both ends, margins entire. **Flowers** in dense clusters 2–4 in. long; 5 petals, pink to light red, sometimes white, 1 in. long; top petal broadly heart shaped; 2 shorter lateral petals; 2 bottom petals united into a keel between the lateral petals. **Fruits:** reddish-brown pods, papery with dense, rigid hairs, 1½–3¼ in. long, hanging downward (upper-left photo). **Blooms** May into July. The tough, elastic wood was used to make high quality bows by Apache, Walatowa (Jemez), and Tewa; branches used to make arrow shafts by Western Keres; fruits and pods eaten raw or boiled, dried, and stored for winter food use by Apache.

ALSIKE CLOVER   *Trifolium hybridum*

Pea Family, Fabaceae

Common, cultivated, sometimes short-lived perennial species introduced from Europe, now established in moist meadows and along trails in more northern mountains, ponderosa pine to mixed conifer forest, 7,000–9,000 ft. **Stems** erect or ascending, typically in small, low clusters. **Leaves** palmately compound with 3 smooth, ovate to oval leaflets 2 in. long, margins smooth to minutely serrate; rounded at apex. **Flowers** in heads at ends of pedicels, 1–3 in. long; not subtended by leaves; corolla pink to tinged with white, lower ones becoming reflexed after anthesis. **Blooms** June into September. Named by Linneaus after the hamlet of Alsike near his summer cottage in Uppland, Sweden.

HOLY GHOST IPOMOPSIS   *Ipomopsis sancti-spiritus*

Phlox Family, Polemoniaceae

Biennial to short-lived perennial, identified as a new species in 1988, on the list of
New Mexico Rare Plants. Restricted to one location, the Holy Ghost Canyon in the
upper Pecos River drainage north of Pecos, New Mexico; on relatively steep, west-
to southwest-facing slopes in open ponderosa pine forest, ca. 7,700–8,200 ft. **Stems**
erect, 12–32 in. tall, mostly solitary, sometimes branched near the base. **Basal leaves**
in a rosette (lower-left photo), senescent at flowering; **stem leaves** and **basal leaves**
deeply pinnatifid into 9–15 linear segments ca. ⅛–½ in. long; leaf size gradually reduced toward top of stem (lower-middle and lower-right photos). **Flowers** in clusters of
6–11 lateral inflorescences restricted to upper half of stem (middle-right photo). Calyx
5-lobed, cylindrical, ca. ¼ in. long. Corolla of 5 pink petals fused from the base upward
in a trumpet-shaped structure up to ca. ¾ in. long, opening to 5 spreading lobes, slightly
reflexed at their ends. **Fruit:** a capsule. **Blooms** July to September.

WOOD'S ROSE
Rosa woodsii

(Wood's Wild Rose)
Rose Family, Rosaceae

Much branched woody shrub up to 5 ft. tall. Common in riparian areas and on moist to open mountain slopes, piñon-juniper woodland up to mixed conifer forest, 6,000–9,000 ft. **Stems** brown or gray with slender prickles between the nodes and 1 or 2 larger thorns below base of each petiole. **Leaves** alternate, deeply pinnately divided into 5–9 oval leaflets ¾–1½ in. long with toothed margin. **Flowers** stalked, 2 in. across, solitary or in loose clusters at ends of new branches. Floral cup urn shaped; 5 prominent petals, each somewhat heart shaped, ½–1 in. long, varying shades of pink to pinkish white. Stamens numerous, with yellow anthers. **Fruit** (the mature floral cup) red to orange, spherical to elliptical. **Blooms** May into August. Rose hips used as food by Navajo and Apache; thorns used by Navajo to make needles for leather work.

SANDIA ALUMROOT
Heuchera pulchella

(Coralbells, Sandia Mountain Alumroot)
Saxifrage Family, Saxifragaceae

Rare perennial species endemic to the mountains of central New Mexico; in the Sandia Mountains, restricted mostly to cliffs and rocky crevices along and near the crest, spruce-fir forest, ca. 10,600 ft. Very shallow rooted, growing in thin layers of soil and plant litter on rock ledges. Stems are horizontal rhizomes that bear leaves on 1–2½ in. long petioles, broadly oval to heart shaped, deeply 5-palmately lobed, ca. ¼–¾ in. wide, forming a basal "understory" around the base of the floral stalks. Leafless floral stalks 4–8 in. tall, with 15 or more small pink to burgundy flowers scattered along upper portions of stalk; sepals somewhat spreading, darker red on tips. Floral cup densely and finely hairy. Blooms July into September. Although not reported for this species of *Heuchera*, the healing properties of the tannin-containing roots of several other species were used by Native Americans across North America as a decoction for many intestinal, skin, and eye disorders.

DEVIL'S CLAW
(Unicorn Plant)
Sesame Family, Pedaliaceae

Proboscidea parviflora

Coarse, viscid-pubescent annual on dry, sandy soil; on plains and mesas, along roadsides, and in disturbed soils up to 7,000 ft. **Stems** initially single, later spreading to 3 ft. **Leaves** dark green, petiolate, lower leaves mostly opposite, triangular to heart shaped, entire to shallowly lobed, to 7 in. long, very hairy and sticky. Few **flowers**, terminal, large and showy, to 1½ in. long, ¾ in. wide; 5 pink to reddish-purple corolla lobes, 2 pointing upward, 2 laterally, and 1 lower lobe with yellowish throat (upper-right photo). **Fruit:** sticky, hairy, fleshy pods up to 8 in. long or longer, dark green with curved tip. Fleshy, outer skin (lower-right photo) shed at maturity, revealing a woody shell ending in 2 diverging, inward-curving prongs (lower-left photo). **Blooms** April into October. Dry seed pods used by Pima in southwestern Arizona in basket weaving; regarded as a pest on sheep ranges, as the pronged pods become entangled in the fleece.

TEASEL   *Dipsacus fullonum*
(Common Teasel)   (*D. sylvestris*)
Teasel Family, Dipsacaceae

Erect, introduced biennial, in moist habitats near springs and acequias in piñon-juniper woodland to ponderosa pine forest, 5,000–8,500 ft.; declared a noxious, invasive weed in many states. **Stems** up to 4 ft. tall, stout, single or branched above; corrugated with sharp, downward-pointed prickles along the ribs. First year's **leaves** a rosette of wrinkled, broadly lanceolate leaves. Second year's **stem leaves** up to 10 in. long, lanceolate, toothed margin, opposite, with bases of each pair fused, conspicuously veined with stiff prickles on lower midrib. **Flower heads** egg shaped, ca. 2–3 in. long, with tiny, sharp bracts extending from each flower and a subtendings whorl of 6–10 long, narrow, prickly bracts curving upward, around and beyond the head (upper-middle photo). **Flowers** small, numerous, with pinkish-white corolla, opening first in a belt around the middle of the head (upper-right photo), sequentially toward the top and bottom (lower-middle photo). **Blooms** June to September. The rigid, dry heads were used by Navajo to card wool.

ARIZONA VALERIAN   *Valeriana arizonica*

Valerian Family, Valerianaceae

Early perennial, mostly 6–18 in. tall; usually in damp woods, in piñon-juniper woodland up to mixed conifer forest, 6,000–9,000 ft. **Stems** usually smooth. **Basal leaves** on petioles arising from a common base on underground rhizomes, ovate to elliptic, somewhat shiny, up to 2 in. long, margins smooth; **stem leaves** opposite, reduced, pinnately divided in 1–3 opposite pairs, tip pointed. **Flowers** in several small, stalked, hemispherical clusters (cymes) at stem apex, varying from light pink to white (lower-right photo). Corolla trumpet-like, ca. ⅜ in. long with 5 petal lobes fused at base (upper-left photo). Usually 3 stamens, protruding beyond surface of flower cluster as does the single, 3-lobed style. **Blooms** early May through June. Other species of *Valeriana* are well known for their medicinal properties, with root decoctions used as sedative (a safe remedy for stress-induced anxiety), poison antidotes, healing of wounds, and more by many Native American tribes; no specific uses of *V. arizonica* have been reported.

VIOLET WOODSORREL   *Oxalis violaceae*

Woodsorrel Family, Oxalidaceae

Delicate perennial growing from a bulb; can form a ground cover in damp forest openings; characterized by its clover-like leaves, rose violet to pink flowers, and bitter taste. In open to shaded slopes, wooded and grassy areas of ponderosa pine up to mixed conifer forest, 7,000–9,000 ft. **Stems** absent. **Leaves** single, borne on slender petioles 2½–5 in. long arising from a common point at base of plant. Each leaf divided into 3 heart-shaped leaflets at the petiole tip, often folded along midrib; leaflets ½–1 in. wide. Two to ten **flowers** borne on short stalks at top of flower stalks 4–10 in. long. Five petals, various shades of pink or violet, united at base, initially trumpet-like, then flaring open, revealing their white base and deep pink guidelines. Ten yellow stamens and 5 green styles with stigmas radiate from the ovary at the base of the flower (middle photo). **Blooms** June into August, sometimes again in September. Leaves eaten raw or cooked with other leaves and bulbs by Apache.

MUSK THISTLE
Carduus nutans

(Nodding Thistle)

Aster Family, Asteraceae

Robust biennial, native to southern Europe and western Asia, introduced in the nineteenth century, now a widespread noxious weed across much of North America. Very aggressive invader of pastures and of range and forest lands, along roadsides, stream banks, and other areas, grassland scrub to ponderosa pine forest, 5,000–8,000 ft. **Stems** to 4 ft. tall with rigid spines and numerous branches. **Leaves** in first year's growth from seed are restricted to a many-leaved rosette, 5 in. long with wavy, lobed margins and marginal yellow spines; overwinters in this stage. Second year's stem has leaves to 6 in. long with base extending to stems, giving a winged appearance; rigidly wavy with sharp marginal spines; upper leaves reduced. **Flower heads** solitary at stem and branch ends, 1½–3 in. wide, nodding somewhat. **Disk flowers** only, purple to deep rose. Involucre prominent with many rows of green lanceolate, overlapping, spine-tipped phyllaries, becoming purple with maturity, pointing downward. **Blooms** June to August.

BULL THISTLE

Cirsium vulgare

Aster Family, Asteraceae

Introduced biennial from Eurasia, with a short, fleshy taproot, common on waste ground, grassland scrub to ponderosa pine forest, 4,500–7,500 ft., more common in the northern mountains. **Stems** stiff, coarse, to 3 ft. tall, much branched, strongly ribbed, with stiff, sharp spines. **Leaves** alternate, sessile, 4–6 in. long with leaf bases extending down the stem, upper surface with coarse hairs, rough to the touch, lower surface with sharp spines along midrib; lanceolate in outline, deeply toothed or lobed, spined leaves with sharply pointed tips. **Flower heads** solitary at stem and branch ends, 1½–2 in. wide; **disk flowers** only, rose purple. Involucre (upper-right photo) vase shaped, narrowing to the top; phyllaries flattened and overlapping at bases, sharply spined toward their tips and pointing outward, with cobwebby hairs along their margins. Pappus: soft, woolly white bristles (lower-right photo). **Blooms** July and August.

257

DOTTED GAYFEATHER

Liatris punctata

Aster Family, Asteraceae

Erect perennial, often found on sandy soil in open areas of foothill scrub up to ponderosa pine forest, 5,000–8,000 ft. **Stems** unbranched, mostly single or few, up to 32 in. tall, typically shorter. **Leaves** alternate, numerous, stiff, linear, up to 5 in. long, ⅓ in. wide, minutely dotted; hairs along edge. **Flower heads** crowded into several oblong spikes on short branches arising from upper portion of main stem; 4–6 heads per spike; rose-purple **disk flowers** up to ⅝ in. long with numerous elongated, curved, abruptly long-pointed bracts of the same color (lower-middle photo); fading to white. **Ray flowers** absent. **Blooms** August into October.

PURPLE ASTER
(Bigelow's Tansy, Sticky Aster)
Aster Family, Asteraceae

Machaeranthera bigelovii
(*Dieteria bigelovii*)

Annual or biennial, 20–40 in. tall, widespread in open meadows and along roadsides, in ponderosa pine up to mixed conifer forest, 7,000–9,000 ft. One of the most common, colorful wildflowers of the Sandias and Manzanos in late summer well into autumn. Stems usually branched, glandular, often rough with stiff hairs on the upper parts. Leaves alternate, oblong to lanceolate, 2–4 in. long, often glandular, somewhat rough to the touch. Flower heads showy, on short stalks at ends of stems or branches. Ray flowers purple or violet, ca. ¼–⅝ in. long. Disk flowers yellow, perfect. Involucres ca. ⅜–⅝ in. high. Phyllaries numerous, in several overlapping series, with slender green tips bending backward. Blooms late May into October. This and other closely related *Machaeranthera* spp. used by Hopi, Navajo, Zuni, and Pueblo Indian tribes as an emetic decoction for upset stomach; whole plants used as a dry powder to stimulate sneezing to clear nasal congestion. Used by Hopi as a strong stimulant, especially for women in labor. Ground petals mixed with white clay used by Acoma as a dye for wool.

259

ROCKY MOUNTAIN TOWNSEND DAISY
(Tall Easter Daisy)
Aster Family, Asteraceae

Townsendia eximia

Erect biennial in ponderosa pine forest up to rock outcrops in spruce-fir forest, 7,000–10,000 ft. **Stems** hairy, simple or occasionally branched, 8–20 in. tall. **Leaves** alternate, spatulate below, lanceolate toward stem tip, up to 2¾ in. long, tip sharply pointed, smooth or sometimes with hairs lying flat, margin entire. **Flower heads** showy, at stem and branch tips, ca. 1½ in. wide; **ray flowers** ½–¾ in. long, purple as head begins to open, becoming purplish white with age. **Disk flowers** yellow. Involucre ca. ½ in. high, wider than high; numerous overlapping, lanceolate phyllaries with green centers and lighter, papery margins (upper-right photo); sometimes hairy on margins. **Blooms** late June through September.

PARRY'S BELLFLOWER
(Purple Bellflower)
Bellflower Family, Campanulaceae

Campanula parryi

Erect perennial, common in higher, more northern mountain meadows, subalpine slopes to near timberline, 7,000–11,000 ft., often in wet ground. Similar to harebell (*C. rotundifolia*) except flowers typically erect rather than nodding. **Stems** up to 12 in. tall, unbranched or sometimes with one or more lateral branches. **Leaves** sessile; basal leaves spatulate, up to 2 in. long; stem leaves upright, linear, to 10 in. long, margins entire. **Flowers** solitary at stem tips, erect, bell shaped at anthesis, up to 1 in. long. Five sepals, erect, linear, extending almost to the reflexed petal tips (upper-right photo). Five petals, blue to purple, to ca. ¾ in. long. Five stamens, 1 style with trilobed stigma. **Blooms** July to September. Dry plants used by Navajo as a dust applied to sores. Zuni chewed blossoms and applied saliva and poultice to skin to remove hair.

261

LEATHERFLOWER

Clematis bigelovii

Buttercup Family, Ranunculaceae

Erect, perennial, 12–20 in. high, not vining, on mountain slopes in ponderosa pine to spruce-fir forest, 7,500–9,000 ft. **Stem** elongated, unbranched, flexible, with short hairs; base often woody. **Leaves** opposite, pinnately lobed, with leaflets again pinnately divided into trilobed leaflets ca. ½–1½ in. long, up to ca. ½ in. wide, rounded at the tips, smooth. **Flowers** most commonly one per stem, nodding, usually upside down, urn or bell shaped, up to 1 in. long, brownish purple or purple, darker on the inside than on the hairy outside. Petals absent; 4 thick, leathery sepals pressed firmly together at their base, flaring outward and curling backward at their ends. Compact mass of green, feathery styles extend from ovaries (upper-right photo). **Blooms** mid-May through July. Flowers used by Keres for bouquets.

SAPELLO CANYON LARKSPUR
(Ugly Delphinium)
Buttercup Family, Ranunculaceae

Delphinium sapellonis

Erect perennial restricted to New Mexico, near streams or in moist, mixed conifer and spruce-fir forests (often under aspen), 8,000–10,000 ft. **Stem** slender, hollow, 3–6 ft. tall (shorter in drier habitats), sparingly branched, lower portion smooth, hairy to glandular in the inflorescence. **Leaves** alternate, on petioles 2–4¾ in. long, blades 3–6 in. long, 1½–4 in. wide, deeply palmately divided with lobes incised or coarsely toothed; lower leaves early deciduous. **Flowers** perfect, on stalks in loose clusters at stem end; 5 sepals, dull brown or greenish, purplish veined, the upper sepal forming a basal spur with the 2 laterals pointing forward and the 2 lower ones bending downward. Four petals, upper pair spurred, smooth; lower pair cleft with yellow hairs. **Blooms** July and August.

PLAINS LARKSPUR

Delphinium wootonii
(*D. virescens*)

Buttercup Family, Ranunculaceae

Stout perennial, 5–15 in. high, on plains and foothill scrub, 5,000–7,000 ft. **Stems** erect, with short, curling hairs. **Basal leaves** grayish, alternate, on short petioles; rarely extend beyond basal quarter of plant, palmately dissected into overall kidney- or fan-shaped lobes, ½–1¼ in. long, 1–1½ in. wide. Lobes further dissected into very narrow, fork-like segments. **Flowers** bluish purple to white, on strongly ascending stalks, in a loose cluster on upper stem. Five sepals, showy, petaloid, the upper with an ascending, trumpet-like spur up to 1 in. long. Four petals, upper 2 spurred into the upper sepal, lower 2 inside the lateral sepals. **Blooms** May through June.

ROCKY MOUNTAIN BEEPLANT

Cleome serrulata

Caper Family, Capparidaceae

Robust annual on disturbed soils and open areas, grassland scrub to piñon-juniper woodland and ponderosa pine forest, 5,000–8,000 ft. **Stems** erect, up to 3½ ft. tall. **Leaves** alternate, petiolate; 3 lanceolate leaflets per leaf, each up to 2¾ in. long, smooth margin. Uppermost portion of stem below head with many tiny, pointed, nonpetiolate leaves less than ¼ in. long. **Flowers** crowded in terminal, hemispherical clusters. Four sepals, bright purple, most apparent when enclosing unopened flowers in center of flower cluster (top photo). Four petals with constricted, stalk-like base, ¼–½ in. long, light purple to white; elongated purple stamens each tipped with a small anther projecting well beyond the petals. **Fruits:** cylindrical pods 1–2 in. long, hanging downward on a conspicuous stalk. **Blooms** July and August. Young plants and seeds utilized in a wide range of foods by Navajo and Pueblo Indian tribes; Zuni, Tewa, and Keres boiled paste to make black mineral paint for decorating pottery.

RED-WHISKER CLAMMYWEED   *Polanisia dodecandra*

Caper Family, Capparidaceae

Coarse, sticky, hairy perennial on dry plains and hills, in gravelly or sandy soil, dry stream beds or arroyos, in foothill scrub and piñon-juniper woodland, 4,500–7,000 ft. **Stems** erect, branched, 20–40 in. tall. **Leaves** alternate with three petiolate, palmately divided, oblong to lanceolate leaflets ½–1 in. long, margins entire. Petioles and leaf blade midveins hairy. Small, closely spaced, pointed leaves on upper portions of stem. **Flowers** in crowded terminal clusters. Four petals, white, up to ½ in. long. Conspicuous, long, purplish, whisker-like stamens extend well beyond the petals. **Fruit:** thin, bean-like pod 1¼–2 in. long, upright at end of elongated pedicels (upper-right photo). **Blooms** May to October. Used by several Pueblo Indian tribes for food, either as a stew with wild onions, meat, or tallow or boiled, pressed into balls, dried, and stored for winter. Used for smoking and in ceremonies by Zuni and Isleta.

DWARF LOUSEWORT   *Pedicularis centranthera*

Figwort Family, Scrophulariaceae

Short, erect perennial. Its short stature and crinkly, purplish, fern-like leaves and purple flowers are the plant's distinguishing characteristics; found in open to partly shaded areas of piñon-juniper woodland and ponderosa pine forests, 6,000–9,000 ft. One of the earliest plants to bloom in spring. **Stems** unbranched, up to 6 in. tall; mostly smooth, sometimes woolly below flower cluster. **Leaves** 2–6 in. long, deeply pinnately divided, with clefts between lobes not extending more than ⅔ the distance to the midrib; lobe bases often overlapping, crinkly, edges doubly toothed. After flowering, leaves become less prostrate and more arched, 6–8 in. high. **Flowers** in dense clusters borne on stalks that extend beyond the often horizontally oriented leaves. Flowers purple, tubular with curved, hooded lobes that enclose the stamens. **Blooms** late March through early June. Dwarf lousewort, a hemiparasite, produces only some of its energy by photosynthesis and parasitizes roots of other plants for a significant amount of its nutrition.

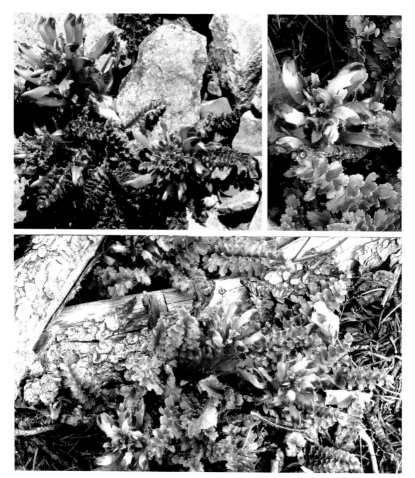

RYDBERG'S PENSTEMON   *Penstemon rydbergii*

Figwort Family, Scrophulariaceae

Perennial, often in large clusters, in open, moist meadows in more northern mountains, ponderosa pine to mixed conifer forest, 7,000–9,000 ft. **Stems** numerous, 12–16 in. tall, smooth below, often pubescent above; short, sterile shoots often present. **Leaves** opposite, those at base and on sterile shoots oblanceolate to elliptic, to 4 in. long, smooth, margins entire; relatively few leaves on flowering stems, of similar shape, smaller, sometimes clasping the stem. **Flowers** in fascicles of two or more, closely spaced or interrupted on the spike-like inflorescence, not restricted to one side. Corolla lobes bluish purple to dark blue, broad, not highly separated, paper-like, margins irregular, whitish hairs at the base of lower lobes; throat narrow to slightly expanded, anthers black on curved filaments. **Blooms** July and August.

ROCKY MOUNTAIN PENSTEMON

Penstemon strictus

Figwort Family, Scrophulariaceae

Erect perennial, often forming large colonies in open woods or along roadsides in ponderosa pine up to spruce-fir forest, 8,000–11,000 ft. **Stems** many, ascending to erect, smooth, strong, 12–28 in. tall, arising from a woody rootstock. **Leaves** sessile, opposite, dark green, smooth; **basal** and **lower leaves** lanceolate to linear, up to 6 in. long, with smooth edges; **upper leaves** lanceolate, up to 4 in. long, often folded upward along the midrib. **Flowers** along one side of upper stem on erect stalks in groups of 1–3. Five sepals, fused, greenish toward base, bluish purple toward tip. Five petals, bluish purple, lobed, basally fused, forming a tubular corolla ¾–1¼ in. long, broadly inflated; 2 upper petals projecting; 3 lower petals fused, deeply 3-lobed, bent downward. Five stamens; 4 fertile with anthers protruding, with fuzzy whitish hairs visible in throat of the flower; 1 sterile stamen, the staminode. **Fruit:** a conical capsule. **Blooms** June into August.

WHIPPLE'S PENSTEMON
(Dusky Penstemon)
Figwort Family, Scrophulariaceae

Penstemon whippleanus

Erect perennial, common in mixed conifer and spruce-fir forests, 8,500–11,000 ft. Easily recognized by its large leaves and plump, dark purple, widely opening flower petals. **Stems** smooth, 1–2½ ft. tall. **Basal leaves** petiolate, lanceolate to ovate, 1½–3 in. long, ½–1½ in. wide, hairs absent. **Stem leaves** opposite, sessile, lanceolate, 1–2½ in. long, ½–1½ in. wide, base clasping stems, margins smooth. **Flowers** irregular, deep purple, 2–4 borne on short pedicels in whorled clusters at the base of opposite stem leaves along upper half of stem. Flowers broadly inflated, tubular, up to 2¼ in. long. Petals with sparse, long hairs inside the 3-lobed lower lip petals; upper lip petals 2-lobed. Five sepals, greenish white, deeply cleft with long, pointed tips. Many extremely short hairs on outer surface of both sepals and petals. **Blooms** July through mid-September.

COLORADO FOUR O'CLOCK
Mirabilis multiflora
(Wild Four o'clock, Desert Four o'clock)
Four o'clock Family, Nyctaginaceae

Low, spreading perennial up to ca. 12 in. high, 24 in. across; widespread on plains, hills, and low mountains, foothill scrub and piñon-juniper woodland, 4,000–7,500 ft. Stems ascending to trailing, widely and loosely branched, smooth to hairy, up to 2 ft. long. Leaves opposite, ovate, rounded to indented at base, margin smooth, petioles fleshy, ca. ¾ in. long, blade ca. 1½ in. long. Flowers mostly in terminal clusters of 5–8 or solitary in leaf axils, subtended by 5 bracts. Petals absent. Sepals purplish red to rose pink, fused into a funnel- or bell-shaped tube ca. 1¼–2 in. long. Five stamens, unequal, protruding. Flowers open in the late afternoon, remaining so throughout the night, facilitating their pollination by moths. Blooms June through September. Used by Zuni as an infusion of powdered root for overeating; roots chewed by Hopi doctors to induce visions while making diagnoses.

VELVET UMBRELLAWORT
(Mountain Four o'clock)
Four o'clock Family, Nyctaginaceae

Mirabilis oblongifolia
(*M. alibida, M. comatus*)

Erect perennial in open areas of foothill scrub up to rocky outcrops in spruce-fir forest, 5,000–11,000 ft. **Stems** 20–40 in. tall; dichotomously branched (upper photo). **Leaves** opposite, sessile, restricted to the base of leaf branches, deltoid ovate to lanceolate deltoid; edges somewhat wavy, smooth margin. One leaf usually larger than the other, up to 4 in. long. **Flowers** borne singly or in clusters, subtended by a glandular, hairy involucre (right photo, second from bottom). Petals absent; sepals pink, lavender, or magenta; fused into a 5-lobed tube ca. ½ in. long, ½ in wide. Rarely do flowers on the same plant, or even the same branch, open simultaneously. Typical of many four o'clocks, this flower opens in the late afternoon and is closed by the middle of the following day. **Fruit:** small, 5-ribbed achene, usually not constricted at base, subtended by the light tan, papery, 5-lobed involucre (upper-right photo). **Blooms** June through September. Used by Navajo as a soaked, split-root poultice for treatment of burns and dermatological aid for spider bites; also made into scalp lotion for dandruff; flowers boiled to make dyes.

PURPLE GERANIUM
(Fremont Geranium)
Geranium Family, Geraniaceae

Geranium caespitosum

Perennial occurring in open or partially shaded ponderosa pine to spruce-fir forest, 6,500–11,000 ft. Often intermixed with Richardson's geranium at higher elevations; can better tolerate heat and drier environments at lower elevations than Richardson's geranium. **Stems** reddish brown, clustered and much branched, 8–28 in. long, ascending or spreading, covered with short, soft, downward pointing hairs. **Leaves** opposite, with long petioles, palmately 5-lobed, up to 4 in. wide with coarsely toothed or lobed margins. **Flowers** prominent, ca. 1½ in. diameter, solitary or loosely arranged on flower stalks. Five petals, rose purple to deep purple, reflexed, oblong to oval, up to ¾ in. long; finely hairy toward base. Five sepals radiating outward below and between the petals, greenish white, tips pointed. Ten stamens, anthers tan to tannish gold. Styles united with stamens forming a central column. **Fruit:** a slender pod containing seed, elongated, ca. 1½ in. long (lower-right photo). **Blooms** May into September.

273

ANTELOPE HORN MILKWEED
Asclepias asperula
(Plains Milkweed; called "Inmortal" by Hispanic herbalists)
Milkweed Family, Asclepiadaceae

Perennial, widespread on dry plains and slopes, foothill scrub to ponderosa pine forest, 4,000–8,000 ft. **Stems** clustered, unbranched, mostly erect, ascending from base up to 16 in. tall with short, stiff hairs. **Leaves** alternate, often nearly opposite, mostly 2–6 in. long, narrow, linear to lanceolate, tapering to an often upward-bending tip (middle-left photo). **Flowers** perfect, in a globular to spherical cluster at the stem apex. Five sepals, reddish yellow (lower-right photo), enclose the buds, opening to expose 5 petals; the central, barrel-shaped corona; and 5 purple, radiating hoods and horns (middle-inset photo). (See Broadleaf Milkweed for more complete description of milkweed flower anatomy). **Fruit:** smooth or slightly spiny pods, single or in pairs. **Blooms** June through August. Infusion of the plant used by Navajo as a ceremonial emetic and as a lotion for mad dog or mad coyote bites on humans and animals. **Note:** In the field, one readily sees both yellowish green and purple as characteristic colors of this plant's flowers, but as the purple color of the hoods predominates over the green color of the opened petals, we have chosen to place it in the purple rather than in the green flower color group.

GIANT HYSSOP   *Agastache pallidiflora*

Mint Family, Lamiaceae

Erect perennial on rocky slopes and outcrops, in ponderosa pine to spruce-fir forest, 7,500–9,500 ft. **Stems** 8 in.–4 ft. tall, single or clustered, square with stiff, downward-pointing hairs. **Leaves** opposite, with short petioles, generally triangular shaped, ¾–2 in. long, ½–1½ in. wide, margin serrated to round toothed, finely hairy. Successive pairs of leaves perpendicular to those immediately above and below. **Flowers** small, densely clustered in 1¼–3½ in. long cylindrical heads at stem ends. Petals deep pink to light purple, fused to form tubular corolla ca. ½ in. long, opening at the end to form one upper and one enlarged lower lip, the latter facilitating insect feeding. **Blooms** July through September. Seed used by Apache and Comanche as a staple food; by Acoma and Laguna as a spice; and by Navajo as a cough medicine, dermatological aid, disinfectant, and to reduce fever.

HEAL-ALL
(Self-Heal)
Mint Family, Lamiaceae

Prunella vulgaris

Introduced perennial, often dwarf and prostrate, 6–12 in. tall; on moist soils of more or less shaded meadows and along stream banks and roadsides of upper foothills to mixed conifer forest, 5,500–9,500 ft., common in more northern mountains. **Stems** up to 20 in. long, prostrate to ascending or erect, smooth or hairy. **Middle stem leaves** often yellowish green, petiolate, opposite, up to 2¾ in. long, ca. ½ as wide as long, base broadly rounded, veins prominent underneath, margins entire (upper-right photo). **Flowers** in short, blunt, terminal spikes ½–2 in. long, interspersed with broad kidney-shaped to broadly ovate bracts. Calyx reddish purple at base, brown toward tips; corolla small, to ¼ in. long with 5 lobes fused at base, pinkish to purple, opening into 2 lips, the upper three fused and the lower two fused almost to their tips. **Blooms** June through August. Reports of many medicinal and other uses in different regions of the county, such as the Pacific Northwest and eastern states, where adequate moisture provides for more robust growth than in the semiarid Southwest.

SLIMLEAF PURPLE MUSTARD

Schoenocrambe linearifolia
(*Sisymbrium linearifolium*)

Mustard Family, Brassicaceae

Erect perennial on dry ground in meadows and open areas of piñon-juniper woodland to ponderosa pine forest, 6,000–8,000 ft. **Stems** 16–24 in. tall, branched above, smooth. **Basal leaves** 2–4 in. long, lanceolate, toothed margin; **stem leaves** alternate, 2–4 in. long, often folded upward along midrib, margin smooth. **Flowers** in loose clusters at top of stem, 4 sepals ca. ¼ in. long and 4 spatulate, light-purple petals ca. ½–¾ in. long, tapering to a long, narrow base, often with deep purple veins. Six stamens, 4 equal, 2 shorter. **Fruit:** a slender, nearly erect pod 1½–2½ in. long, with 2 longitudinal compartments, each with one row of seeds. **Blooms** June into September. Cold infusion used by Navajo as a mouthwash for sore gums.

CALYPSO ORCHID
(Fairy Slipper Orchid)
Orchid Family, Orchidaceae

Calypso bulbosa

Small, delicate, difficult-to-find orchid; occurs in well-rotted understory of shady mixed conifer and spruce-fir forests above 8,000 ft. Above ground, the plant consists of only one basal, ovate **leaf** up to 2¼ in. long, the base of which wraps around the single, 4–8 in. tall, purplish-brown flowering stalk; the latter bears a single irregular **flower** at its apex. The pendulose, drooping flower has 3 sepals and 2 petals, generally of similar size and color, all rose to purple color, that extend outward above the large, lighter colored, spotted, slipper-like third petal, the lip, which extends downward. The reproductive part of orchid flowers, the pistils and stamens, structurally separated in most other flowers, are fused into one organ, the column, located within the lip. (Note: a somewhat analogous fusion of pistils and stamens to form an encased column may also be found in milkweeds). **Blooms** late April into June. Although chlorophyllous, all orchids depend largely for their nutrition on a specific soil-borne fungus within their roots that extends into the soil, where it absorbs and transports soil nutrients into the orchid roots.

BEAKPOD MILKVETCH
(Specklepod Milkvetch)
Pea Family, Fabaceae

Astragalus lentiginosus

Perennial, usually found in open, gravelly canyons and washes or rocky slopes, foothill scrub to piñon pine–juniper woodland, 5,000–7,500 ft. Stems often arise from reclining bases, curving upward, 6–16 in. long and with appressed hairs. Leaves alternate, pinnately compound; leaflets mostly 15–21, lightly hairy beneath, elliptic to ovate. Flowers pea-like, in loose clusters at stem apices, pinkish purple or white; upper petal (banner) ⅝–¾ in. long. Fruit: a rounded, somewhat longer than wide pod with a distinct furrow lengthwise; color changes from green to speckled purple with age; ¾–1¼ in. long with a recurved tip when mature. Considered poisonous to livestock. Blooms March into June. Used as a charm in some prayers by Navajo.

SMALL-FLOWERED MILKVETCH
Astragalus nuttallianus
(Nuttall's Milkvetch)
Pea Family, Fabaceae

Low-growing, spreading annual on sandy soils and slopes in foothill scrub and piñon-juniper woodland, 5,000–8,000 ft. **Stems** slender, to 10 in. long, reclining to ascending. Stems and leaves with fine, unbranched, flat-lying hairs or almost hairless. **Leaves** alternate, to ca. 4 in. long, pinnately divided with 7–9 leaflets up to ½ in. long. One to seven flowers on flowering stalks ca. 1–3 in. long; petals purplish blue to purple, top petal ca. ¼ in. long with a distinct white eye, 2 lateral petals, 2 bottom petals fused into a keel. **Fruit:** a smooth, oblong, curved pod, yellowish red to red, ½–1 in. long (lower-right photo). **Blooms** March through May.

PURPLE PRAIRIE CLOVER

Dalea purpurea

Pea Family, Fabaceae

Perennial, often in dense, somewhat isolated clusters on open hills and plains and along roadsides, grassland scrub to ponderosa pine forest, 5,000–7,000 ft. **Stems** erect, smooth to sparsely hairy, 12–20 in. high, often forming a compact base. **Leaves** palmately compound, 3–5 leaflets to ca. ½ in. long, mostly folded lengthwise. **Flowers** borne in dense, cylindric to ovoid-globose spikes ¼–2 in. long at stem ends, progressing from base of spike to top (lower-right photo). **Blooms** July to September. Note: this plant varies widely in the state; some varieties variously smooth to pubescent, others typically smooth. Leaves used by Navajo to make tea and also to treat pneumonia. Comanche chewed roots for their sweet flavor.

PURPLE LOCOWEED
(Lambert's Locoweed)
Pea Family, Fabaceae

Oxytropis lambertii

Stemless, tufted perennial, up to 12 in. tall. Common between 5,000 and 10,000 ft. in foothill scrub to rocky outcrops in spruce-fir forest. Similar to silvery locoweed growing at lower elevations but often with more uniformly dark purple flowers than the light purple to white flowers of silvery locoweed. Flower stalks, leaves, and leaflets covered with fine, silvery hairs. **Leaves** 3–12 in. long with 7–5 pinnately divided leaflets arising from basal crowns. Among the differences from Showy Locoweed is the absence of small, leaf-like stipules at base of leaflets. **Flowers** pea-like, bright reddish lavender to purple, borne on 4–12 in. leafless stalks; each flower ca. ½–1 in. long with beaked keel composed of the two fused bottom petals. **Blooms** June into September. As with other locoweed species, this can be lethally toxic to many kinds of livestock.

SHOWY LOCOWEED
Oxytropis splendens

Pea Family, Fabaceae

Clustered perennial lacking true stems, in more northern mountain meadows, ponderosa pine to mixed conifer forest, 8,000–10,000 ft. **Leaves** arise from basal crown; long, pinnately divided into many leaflets, each up to 1 in. long, various shapes (linear lanceolate to oblong lanceolate or oblong elliptic), silky hairs on both surfaces with small, leaf-like stipules at their base, attached to leaf midrib (lower-left photo). Many **flowers**, in racemes 2–4 in. long, at top of flower stalks. Calyx densely hairy; corolla dark blue to dark purple, ca. ⅓–⅔ in. long. **Fruit:** mature seed pods hairy, erect or spreading. **Blooms** June and July. All locoweed species, to varying degrees, are toxic to livestock.

SCURF PEA

Psoralidium tenuiflorum

Pea Family, Fabaceae

Erect perennial to 24 in. tall, widespread in dry plains and low hills, 4,500–7,000 ft., typically in the central mountains. One to several **stems**, much branched. Herbage dotted glandular with short, stiff hairs, thus the common name "scurf" pea. **Leaves** alternate, widely spaced, palmately compound, a few 5-foliate near base, generally 3-foliate above; leaflets oblanceolate, up to ½ in. long; leaf petioles shorter than leaflets. **Flowers** 2–10 in. long, slender, in loose clusters up to 2 in. long on stem and branch ends. Individual flowers on a short stalk; calyx 5-lobed, about equal and as long as the tube; corolla with 5 petals, one upper and 2 lateral petals, pale; bottom 2 petals fused into a keel between the laterals, deep purple. **Fruit:** ellipsoidal, dotted glandular, ca. ⅓ in. long. **Blooms** May into September. Navajo applied a poultice of moistened leaves to any body part for purification and as a disinfectant; an infusion was taken for influenza; also used several ways for sheep with coughs.

ALPINE CLOVER

Trifolium dasyphyllum

Pea Family, Fabaceae

Low perennial, in spruce-fir forest zone, ca. 10,000–11,500 and higher; in the Sandias, restricted to the crest area, ca. 10,700 ft., in open areas between limestone outcrops. True **stems** lacking; flowering stalks angled upward or spreading, up to 6 in. long; herbage smooth or nearly so. **Leaves** basal, on elongated petioles from plant base, 3 palmately divided leaflets ca. ½–1¼ in. long, elliptic, ends pointed. Flower stalks finely hairy, longer than the petiolate leaves. **Flower heads** pinkish purple, globose, somewhat loose, ca. ½–1 in. wide with 10–30 radiating, pea-like flowers per head. Corolla ca. ⅜–⅝ in. long, pinkish purple. **Blooms** June through August.

AMERICAN VETCH

Vicia americana

Pea Family, Fabaceae

Slender, climbing perennial clinging to other plants or structures by coiling tendrils that arise at end of each leaf. Often in dense, extensive groups, especially on open or wooded slopes in ponderosa pine up to subalpine forest, 7,000–11,000 ft. **Stems** smooth, up to 4 ft. long. **Leaves** alternate, even-pinnately divided, 6–16 leaflets, each ½–1½ in. long, generally ovate, smooth margins. Two to five **flowers** per cluster, ½–1¼ in. long, pea-like on 1¼–3 in. long stalks arising from leaf axils; petals pinkish-white, bluish-purple to pink to reddish-lavender. **Fruit:** a slender, flattened elliptical pod ca. ¼ in. long. **Blooms** May through September. Seeds were used as food by Acoma, Keres and Laguna and as an infusion for eyewash by Navajo.

SANTA FE PHLOX
Phlox nana

Phlox Family, Polemoniaceae

Low perennial, often in dense populations on grassy areas of plains, hills, and mountain slopes, in piñon-juniper woodland and ponderosa pine forest, 5,000–7,500 ft. **Stems** erect or ascending, much branched; mostly 4–10 in. tall with many glandular hairs on upper portions and in the flower cluster. **Leaves** opposite, ascending or erect, narrowly lanceolate, ca. ½–1¾ in. long, margins smooth. **Flowers** scattered at stem and branch ends, usually up to 1–1½ in. across, tubular shaped at base; 5 petals, mostly ½–¾ in. long, opening abruptly, various shades of light purple to whitish pink; irregularly toothed margins. **Blooms** May to September.

287

SILVERLEAF NIGHTSHADE
Solanum elaeagnifolium

(Purple Nightshade)
Potato Family, Solanaceae

Erect perennial from creeping rhizomes, somewhat woody at base; typically on coarse-textured, sandy soils and disturbed sites in foothill scrub and piñon-juniper woodland, 5,000–7,000 ft. **Stems** up to 2 ft. tall with sharp, slender spines up to ¼ in. long. **Leaves** alternate, narrowly lanceolate to oblong, up to 4 in. long, 1 in. wide, covered with silvery-white hairs that give the plant a dusky, silvery-gray color; sharp spines along lower midrib; margin wavy, sometimes with a white edge. **Flowers** on stalks, solitary or in small clusters at ends of stems or branches. Petals lavender to light purple, sometimes white, fused toward their base. Five prominent yellow anthers, ¼–⅓ in. long, protruding upward. **Fruit:** a small greenish-yellow to brown, globose berry ca. ¼–⅜ in. diameter, turning brownish yellow to reddish brown with age. **Blooms** June to October. Reportedly toxic to humans and most livestock species. Reported medicinal uses of silverleaf nightshade by Navajo and other tribes based perhaps on similar but nontoxic members of the genus.

CLIFF PRIMROSE
(Rusby Primrose)
Primrose Family, Primulaceae

Primula rusbyi

Perennial often found on damp rocky ledges and in fissures on rock cliffs and in rocky meadows, in mixed conifer and spruce-fir forest, 8,000–11,000 ft. Scape (leafless flowering **stem**) 6–10 in. tall, arising from cluster of **basal leaves. Leaves** up to 4 in. long, mostly broader above, tapering to the base, finely hairy underneath, finely toothed edges. Few to many **flowers**, in terminal clusters; various shades of purple to violet, funnel shaped, ⅜–¾ in. wide; 5 petals, with notched lobes at ends; sepals and individual flower stalks with a mealy covering. **Blooms** May to September.

DAKOTA VERVAIN

(Pink Vervain, Verbena)
Verbena Family, Verbenaceae

Glandularia bipinnatifida
(*Verbena bipinnatifida*)

Reclining to ascending perennial; widespread on open slopes and in foothill scrub, piñon-juniper woodland, and open areas of ponderosa pine forest, 5,000–8,000 ft. **Stems** 4-angled, up to 12 in. tall, often with diffusely branched hairs near base. **Leaves** petiolate, opposite, ¾–2½ in. long, deeply divided into 3–5 pinnatifid segments, stiff hairs above and beneath. **Flowers** in somewhat flattened clusters at stem ends; each flower tubular with 5 pink to purple petals, ⅜–½ in. long, fused toward their base, each having a distinct notch at its apex. Continued, or repeated, flowering occurs at the apex of the elongated inflorescence, producing a terminal cluster of new flowers subtended by more mature flowers below. **Blooms** often for months (late March to October), sometimes with repeated blooming cycles if there is sufficient moisture. A very drought-tolerant plant. Crushed leaves rubbed on snakebites by Keres; leaf infusion used as a gargle for sore throat.

WEED VERBENA
(Prostrate Verbena)
Verbena Family, Verbenaceae

Verbena bracteata

Prostrate to upright annual, a weed typically on waste ground, foothill scrub to ponderosa pine forest, 6,500–8,500 ft. Photos show somewhat more vertical growth typical in more moist, shady, northern mountains (lower-left and lower-right photos) and more prostrate growth in dry, exposed areas of more central mountains (other four photos). Many **stems**, prostrate, reclining to ascending, 6–12 in. tall when there is sufficient moisture, diffusely branched, curving upward at ends and forming spike-like flower clusters; herbage hairy. **Leaves** opposite, petioles broad with flat edges; blades up to ca. 1½ in. long, divided pinnately into 3 segments, the center one larger, 2 lateral segments smaller, finely hairy, margins entire to irregularly toothed (lower-middle photo). **Flowers** sessile, small, at stem ends in cylindrical clusters with distinct bracts (lower-right photo) subtending the flowers; corolla blue to lavender to light purple. **Blooms** May to September. Used by Navajo as a poultice applied to centipede bites.

SPIKE VERBENA
Verbena macdougalii
(New Mexico Vervain)
Verbena Family, Verbenaceae

Hairy perennial, 2–4 ft. tall, common on roadsides and openings in ponderosa pine and mixed conifer forest, 6,500–8,000 ft. Stems stout, 2 to several, sparingly branched, 4-sided with a dense, terminal, flower-bearing spike up to 2¾ in. long, ¾ in. diameter; resembles members of the mint family but lacks the aromatic mint aroma. Leaves opposite, generally sessile, oblong to elliptical, 1½–2½ in. long, ½–1½ in. wide, densely hairy with saw-toothed margins. Tubular, purple flowers, ½ in. long, begin blooming as a ring around the spike base. As the spike elongates, successive rings of purple flowers form progressively up the length of the spike. Blooms June through August. An infusion of the herbage was taken internally and applied as a lotion by Navajo for fever, also used as a lotion and a fumigant in various ceremonies.

INDIAN BLANKET
(Firewheel, Gaillardia)
Aster Family, Asteraceae

Gaillardia pulchella

Colorful annual 5–20 in. tall; in piñon-juniper woodland and ponderosa pine forest, 5,000–7,000 ft. **Leaves** alternate, sessile, linear to oblong, up to 4 in. long, surface marked by resinous dots. Conspicuous **flower heads**, single, on long leafless stems; **ray flowers** sterile, red to maroon, ¼–¾ in. long with yellow tips having three teeth; red color fades toward base of each ray flower upon maturity, leaving it mostly yellow. **Disk flowers** purplish. Ray flowers eventually drop, leaving stalked, spherical heads with small, radiating, reddish to white disk flowers, each containing a seed (lower-middle photo). **Blooms** late June through August. Keres rubbed plant on mothers' breasts to wean infants. A similar but distinctly yellow-flowered relative, the Yellow Blanket Flower, *G. pinnatifida,* with pinnately divided leaves and fewer ray flowers, occurs occasionally in the Sandias and Manzanos between 4,000 and 7,000 ft.

293

SORREL WILD BUCKWHEAT   *Eriogonum polycladon*

Buckwheat Family, Polygonaceae

Perennial, 12–20 in. tall; in scattered locales on dry rocky hills, canyons, sandy arroyos; foothill scrub and piñon-juniper woodland, 3,500–7,000 ft. **Stems** erect, leafy, finely hairy, with only a few ascending branches; panicle inflorescences laterally and at the top branches. **Leaves** alternate, oblong ovate to broadly oblanceolate, ca. 3–7 in. long, margins entire, tips pointed, arising from stems or from basal crown, with finely haired underside. **Flowers** very small, with pinkish-red, petal-like sepals, petals lacking. **Fruit:** red, 3-sided, with a single 3-seeded, angular carpel. **Blooms** June to October.

RED COLUMBINE
Aquilegia desertorum

Buttercup Family, Ranunculaceae

Delicate, erect perennial with distinct drooping red to yellow flowers; on rocky slopes and valley bottoms in ponderosa pine forest up to spruce-fir forest, 7,000–10,000 ft. Stems slender, lightly hairy, bending downward near top, 12–24 in. tall. Stem leaves alternate, petiolate below, becoming sessile above, mostly hairless, compound, divided into 3 leaflets, each of which is palmately divided into 3 lobes; the ultimate leaflets ½–1¼ in. long with round-toothed margins. Basal leaves similar, on long petioles. Flowers perfect, 1¼–1½ in. long, nodding, on long stalks; five red sepals project forward, each with ¾–1¼ in. spur projecting backward; petals yellow, less prominent, extend backward into the sepal spurs. Many yellow stamens and five styles extend forward beyond sepals and petals (lower-right photo). Blooms June into August. Used by Navajo as a ceremonial fumigant for headache or severe pain.

CANE CHOLLA CACTUS
(Tree Cholla Cactus)
Cactus Family, Cactaceae

Cylindropuntia imbricata

Upright, brushy to tree-like cactus 2–8 ft. tall, common in foothill scrub and piñon-juniper woodland, 4,000–7,500 ft. **Stems** cylindrical, jointed, fleshy; latticed; the diamond shaped pattern of the underlying woody skeleton commonly visible on dead portions of plants. Spines sharp, ½–1¼ in. long, radiating in small groups of 2–5 over entire body. **Flowers** at tips of branches, red to magenta, up to 3 in. diameter, 1½–2 in. long. **Fruits:** fleshy, bright yellow when mature, spherical to hemispherical, ca. 1 in. across, deeply pitted and grooved; no spines, not juicy. Remain on branch apices at least one year. **Blooms** late May through July. Considered as "starvation food"; many Pueblo Indian tribes utilized stored, roasted young stem joints in times of famine. Dried fruit was ground, mixed with cornmeal, and made into a mush. Stem needles used for sewing and tattooing.

SCARLET HEDGEHOG CACTUS   *Echinocereus* sp.

Cactus Family, Cactaceae

One of several species of *Echinocereus*, often identified as *E. coccineus* in central New Mexico, with some species and subspecies appearing quite similar. Precise identification often requires laboratory verification, including ploidy number (the number of chromosome sets). Common in dry foothill scrub, often in partially shaded areas under scrub bushes (as this specimen) up to exposed rock outcrops in mixed conifer forest, 4,000–9,000 ft. **Stems** several to numerous, 3–6 in. tall with 9–12 ribs bearing small areoles from which spines arise; stems usually branching near the base to form dense mounds often covering several square feet. Rigid **spines** in groups; 0–4 central spines and 5–20 radial spines. **Flowers** on stem ribs, broadly funnel shaped, 1¼–4 in. long, 1½–3 in. across; many bright red overlapping tepals, 1–2 in. long with a central column of styles, commonly with green stigmas surrounded by numerous stamens, commonly pink. Some species and varieties have bisexual flowers, as here; others have only pistillate or staminate populations. **Fruit** somewhat spherical, juicy, with spines; reddish with age; spines deciduous. **Blooms** mid-May into June. Used by Cochiti, Isleta, and Keres for a variety of foods, including roasted stem pith and fruit, pulp baked with sugar to make candy and sweet pickles, fruits made into a conserve after spines removed by burning.

CLARET CUP CACTUS   *Echinocereus triglochidiatus*

Cactus Family, Cactaceae

Succulent perennial, often among piñon pine and junipers on rocky, gravely, or sandy slopes; canyon walls; or grassy areas, 5,500–7,500 ft. Numerous varieties of this cactus exist; various common names often applied to different varieties and species. **Stems** solitary to several, loosely clustered, up to 8 or more in. tall, 3 in. diameter, 6 or more broad parallel ribs with slight swellings (areoles) from which spines arise. Spines stout, gray or tan, up to 2½ in. long, 2 or more (commonly 3) per cluster, radially spreading. **Flowers** borne below **stem** tips, tubular, funnel shaped, 1½–3¼ in. long, 1–2½ in. diameter, remain open for several days; petals scarlet red, stiff, waxy, rounded to pointed at tips; stamens numerous. **Fruit** (lower-right photo): varies with species, round to oval, ¾–1½ in., green with pinkish cast or bright red; some spines, usually dropping off with maturity. **Blooms** May and June. Baked stems eaten like squash by Isleta, Keres, and Cochiti; fresh stems used for making relishes and sauces; dried pulp used as candles.

FENDLER'S SPURGE

Euphorbia Family, Euphorbiaceae

Euphorbia fendleri var. *fendleri*
(*Chamaesyce fendleri*)

Low, spreading, mat- or clump-forming perennial from woody rootstock on open, dry slopes of foothill scrub and piñon-juniper woodland, up to 7,000 ft. Many **stems**, smooth, reddish brown, up to 5–6 in. long with many short branches growing in a zig-zag pattern caused by the lack of growth of the terminal stem bud and the growth of the lateral buds to form a sprawling web of stems. **Leaves** opposite, small, up to ⅓ in. long, lacking hairs, broadly elliptic, generally coming to a point. The tiny red inflorescence (cyathium), a cup-like structure borne at branch tips, bears a ring of 25–35 tiny, **staminate flowers** around one central **pistillate flower**. Four short, whitish, petal-like glands occur around the apex of the cyathium (middle-left photo). **Fruit:** a small, ovoid, 3-compartmented capsule on a short stalk, extending from top of cyathium following fertilization (see *Euphorbia davidii*). **Blooms** May to October. Many uses by Navajo: infusion or decoction for stomachache and for diarrhea, topical treatment of warts and poison ivy, hot poultice for toothache, as a hemostatic agent for cuts. Identification kindly provided by Eugene Jercinovic and Robert Sivinski.

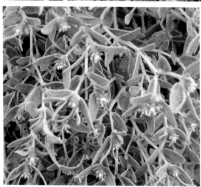

SCARLET GAURA   *Gaura coccinea*

Evening Primrose Family, Onagraceae

Perennial, common on open areas, disturbed sites, and foothill scrub up to ponderosa pine forest, 5,000–7,000 ft. **Stems** smooth or hairy, sparsely branched, 8–16 in. high. **Leaves** alternate, mostly sessile, smooth to hairy; lower leaves lanceolate to oblong, ca. 2¼ in. long, upper leaves usually linear. Margins wavy or smooth. **Flowers** in spike-like clusters along upper portion of stem with older flowers below; individual flowers subtended by bracts; 4 sepals, bent backwards after flower opens. Four petals, spoon shaped, tapering to a narrow base, ca. ¼ in. long, white when they open in the afternoon to evening, turning pink the next morning following fertilization, then drying and turning scarlet. Eight stamens, located just below the 4 petals; elongated with maroon to reddish-brown anthers extending beyond the 4 petals (upper-right photo). Stigma 4-lobed, light green, on long style. **Blooms** mid- to late May through August. Used by Navajo as an infusion to settle a child's stomach after vomiting.

SMALL-FLOWERED GAURA

Gaura mollis
(*G. parviflora*)

Evening Primrose Family, Onagraceae

Large annual or biennial with somewhat small flowers; on plains, roadsides, disturbed ground; foothill scrub to ponderosa pine forest, 4,000–8,000 ft. **Stems** coarse, reddish, hairy, erect, up to 6 ft. tall. **Leaves** alternate, hairy, 1¼–6 in. long; **basal leaves** large, broadest above the middle, tapering to base; **upper leaves** smaller, sessile, lanceolate. **Flowers** in slender, spike-like clusters on upper portions of stem, with older flowers at base of cluster. Four sepals, bending backward after opening. Four petals, spoon shaped with narrow base, white when opening in the afternoon, turning pink the next morning, red later that day. Eight stamens, elongated with maroon to reddish-brown anthers extending beyond the petals. Stigma 4-lobed, light green, at end of style. **Blooms** May through July. Root decoction taken by Hopi for snakebite; fresh fruit eaten or root chewed by Zuni medicine man before sucking snakebite; poultice applied to wound. Navajo stewed the plant with meat or ate by itself. Fresh, soft leaves worn by Isleta as a headband for its cooling effect in hot weather.

FOOTHILLS PAINTBRUSH

Castilleja integra

Figwort Family, Scrophulariaceae

Perennial, 4–12 in. tall, widely distributed, usually on dry, open slopes between 5,000 and 10,000 ft. This paintbrush is only one of several similar, related, often hybridizing native species, many often referred to as Indian paintbrush or simply paintbrush. Some of these species extend throughout the Great Plains region of the United States. **Stems** stout; **leaves** alternate, sessile, linear, up to 2½ in. long, upper surface smooth, lower finely hairy, sometimes matted. Inflorescence, a dense spike; the bright scarlet color restricted to petal-like **bracts** beneath the green **floral structures**. Bracts must be examined closely to identify paintbrush species. **Blooms** June through August. Seed borne in flask-shaped **fruits** (capsules) in the axils of bracts, adjacent to stem. Paintbrushes are all hemiparasites; that is, they obtain part of their nutrition by photosynthesis but also obtain significant nutrition from parasitizing roots of other plants, especially grasses and oaks. Used by Navajo as a wound dressing and by Apache and Zuni as a pigment to color deerskins. Jemez mixed dried flower bracts with chile seed as a food preservative, to prevent foods from spoiling during storage.

WYOMING NARROWLEAF PAINTBRUSH
Castilleja lineariifolia
(Wyoming Indian Paintbrush)
Figwort Family, Scrophulariaceae

State flower of Wyoming. Perennial, usually in open woods or brushy slopes in more northern mountains, ponderosa pine to spruce-fir forest, 7,000–12,000 ft. **Stems** often clustered, often with a few branches, purplish, up to ca. 30 in. tall. **Leaves** alternate, up to ca. 3¼ in. long, very narrow, lower leaves deeply divided (lower-left photos); upper leaves pinnately 3–5 lobed with in-rolled edges (upper-left photo). **Flowers** on short pedicels in leaf axils in a dense, softly hairy, spike-like raceme (right photos). Petals largely red with green bases, up to 1 in. long, more noticeable than the subtending bracts, in contrast to many other paintbrush species. Bracts bright red, often shorter than petals, divided into 3 narrow lobes at the tip (middle photo). **Fruit:** a pointed, cylindrical capsule. **Blooms** June to September. A semiparasitic plant, as are all paintbrushes, depending on root parasitism of other plants, especially grasses, for much of their nutrition. Decoction of plant used as a contraceptive by Hopi and Tewa, also to ease menstrual difficulties; chewed root and juniper bark mixed with clay used as a ceremonial paint; used by Navajo as a treatment for stomachache.

SCARLET PAINTBRUSH
Castilleja miniata

Figwort Family, Scrophulariaceae

Erect perennial common at higher elevations in mixed conifer and spruce-fir forest, 7,500–11,000 ft. Elevation range overlaps that of foothills paintbrush. **Stems** few to several, often branched. **Leaves** alternate, sessile, lanceolate, 1¼–3 in. long, margins smooth; wider than foothills paintbrush leaves. **Flowers** sessile, numerous on upper stem. Petals green, 2-lipped, up to 1¾ in. long; each flower subtended by a lanceolate, brilliant red, hairy bract but green toward its base; the aggregate of those bracts provides the plant's ragged, crimson paintbrush appearance. **Fruit:** a slender, pointed capsule extending well beyond tips of petals and bracts. **Blooms** June into September. Scarlet paintbrush is, as are all other paintbrushes, a semiparasite, obtaining a portion of its nutrition by photosynthesis but the majority by parasitism of other plant roots, most commonly grasses. Root bark of other paintbrush species used by Apache and Zuni for dyeing deerskin black; other tribes applied snail slime to paintbrush flowers to trap hummingbirds.

BIRD BEAK

(Clubflower)

Figwort Family, Scrophulariaceae

Cordylanthus wrightii

Perennial characterized by its erect, highly branched growth habit; its many almost thread-like leaves; and its compact, terminal spikes of flowers partially enclosed by pointed bracts; found in open areas of piñon-juniper woodland and ponderosa pine forest, 5,000–7,500 ft. **Stems** erect, up to 14 in. tall, solitary, highly branched, almost smooth to glandular-hairy. **Leaves** alternate, ¼–1¼ in. long, deeply divided into 3–5 thread-like segments. Two to eight **flowers**; sessile; asymmetric; in tight, spike-like clusters at branch ends; each flower subtended by 1 or more narrow, sharply pointed green bracts (upper-right photo). Corolla various shades of rose purple, tubular, with 2 lips, the upper somewhat arched, up to 1 in. long. **Blooms** mid-July into September. Decoction used by Navajo for syphilis, leg and body aches, and menstrual pain.

FERNLEAF LOUSEWORT
(Giant Lousewort)
Figwort Family, Scrophulariaceae

Pedicularis procera

Erect, perennial herb in damp woods and along streams in mixed conifer and spruce-fir forest, 7,000–11,000 ft. **Stems** stout, up to ca. 4 ft. tall. **Stem leaves** alternate, 6–14 in. long, deeply pinnatifid almost to midrib, with toothed margins, somewhat similar to fern fronds; upper leaves on short petioles; **basal leaves** on longer petioles. Many **flowers** in a dense, hairy, cylindrical to pointed conical cluster 4–14 in. long, interspersed with linear, finely haired, pointed, smooth-edged bracts longer than the flowers (upper-middle photos). Corolla tubular, strongly 2-lipped, upper lip curved downward, grayish to yellowish green with prominent pinkish-red streaks and coloration, enclosing the 4 stamens (lower photo). Younger, smaller flowers toward the tip. Mature **fruits** brown, dry, splitting open lengthwise. **Blooms** July and August.

SCARLET PENSTEMON

Penstemon barbatus ssp. *torreyi*

Figwort Family, Scrophulariaceae

Erect perennial on open, dry slopes in piñon-juniper woodland up to mixed conifer forest, 6,000–9,000 ft. One to a few **stems**, smooth, up to 3 ft. tall, arising from a basal mat of leaves. **Basal** and **lower stem leaves** 1½–3 in. long, oblanceolate; **upper stem leaves** sessile, opposite, linear, widely spaced, up to 2¾ in. long. **Flowers** broadening toward tips, 1–4 on slender, ascending stalks from each leaf axil on upper half of stem. Corolla tubular, 1–1¼ in. long, consisting of 5 fused, bright red petals, the 2 upper petals straight, the 3 lower petals bent backward; a few yellow-white hairs sometimes at base of lower lip; 4 stamens, (upper-right photo). **Blooms** June into August. Infusions and decoctions used by Navajo for menstrual pain, stomachache, burns, coughs, and as a diuretic; by Keres for bouquets and decorations in dances.

MOUNTAIN FIGWORT

Scrophularia montana

Figwort Family, Scrophulariaceae

Erect perennial, 2–6 ft. tall; this species is reported only in New Mexico. Common along roadsides and other open areas in mixed conifer and spruce-fir forest, 7,000–11,000 ft. The single, 4-ribbed **stem** bears numerous, short-stalked flowers along its upper half. **Leaves** opposite, on short petioles, lanceolate, 3–6 in. long, each leaf pair perpendicular to ones immediately above and below; may also occur in whorls of 3–5 leaves around the stem. **Flowers** small, ca. ¾ in. long, in loosely branched clusters; sepals green; petals, pale maroon, fused to form an urn-shaped tube flaring open toward the apex (lower-right photo). **Blooms** June to September; often utilized by hummingbirds as a nectar source. Other more widespread species of figwort have been reported primarily for medicinal uses, including eyewashes, skin infections and injuries, aids in childbirth and for cramps following delivery.

RUSSIAN THISTLE

Salsoa tragus
(*S. iberica, S. kalivar*)

Goosefoot Family, Chenopodiaceae

Highly branched annual forming dense clumps up to 3 ft. in diameter. Introduced from Russia in the late 1800s, it has become naturalized and is a troublesome, noxious weed throughout the western United States. Well-adapted to dryland agriculture, also on dry mesas, disturbed soils, and overgrazed rangelands, 3,000–9,000 ft. **Stems** erect, branched, usually red or purple striped; breaking off at ground level when mature and becoming tumbleweeds. **Leaves** alternate, up to 2½ in. long, extremely narrow, margins entire, spine tipped, often rigid (upper-left photo). **Flowers** sessile, saucer shaped, in leaf axils, subtended by a pair of sharp-pointed, rigid bracts; petals absent; sepals initially colorless, translucent, petal-like bodies, later turning pink, then red (upper-right photo). **Blooms** July to September. Each plant can produce up to 250,000 seeds, which are scattered by wind blowing the tumbleweeds. Rapid seed germination and seedling establishment occur after brief and limited amounts of precipitation. Ironically, the drought-resistant tumbleweed provided feed for cattle when no other feed was available during much of the Dust Bowl era of the 1930s (Utah State University, Cooperative Extension Service; Washington State University).

PINESAP
Monotropa hypopitys

Heath Family, Ericaceae

Delicate, bright red, somewhat waxy-appearing perennial, up to 12 in. tall, most commonly in shaded understory of coniferous forests, 7,500–9,500 ft. **Young stems** have a "shepherd's crook" appearance. **Leaves** alternate, inconspicuous, scale-like, ca. ½ in. long, partially wrapped around stem. **Flowers** bell shaped, perfect, drooping or perpendicular to stem, single or in loose clusters, often primarily on one side of stem. Four to five sepals and petals up to ½ in. long. Plant brown when mature. Being devoid of chlorophyll, the plant obtains its nutrition through the intermediate parasitic activity of mycorrhizal fungi attached to and connecting pinesap roots and conifer tree roots, there absorbing nutrients that are transferred back to the pinesap's roots. **Blooms** late June through August.

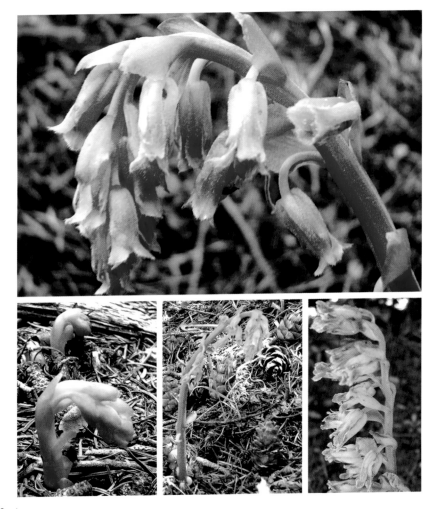

PINEDROPS

Pterospora andromedea

Heath Family, Ericaceae

Common, nonchlorophyllous herb in partial shade in ponderosa pine forest between 7,000 and 9,000 ft. **Stems** erect, fleshy, unbranched, 12–20 in. tall. **Leaves** scale-like, only on lower portions of stem. Numerous **flowers** on upper ⅔–¾ of stem, each on a short, down-curving stalk; petals white to reddish pink, fused, tubular, urn shaped with five short lobes. **Fruit:** a somewhat flattened, round capsule ⅓–½ in. across. **Blooms** late June into August. Plant turns dark purplish brown upon maturity. Stems become fibrous and dry in autumn and persist into following year. Lacking chlorophyll, these plants are parasitic, depending primarily on ponderosa pine roots for their nutrition through the intermediate activity of a specific mycorrhizal fungus.

SCARLET MORNING GLORY
Ipomoea cristulata

Morning Glory Family, Convolvulaceae

Twining annual vine in moist open fields and along roadsides, grassland scrub to piñon pine–juniper zone, 4,000–7,000 ft. **Stems** simple or branched, 3–6 ft. long, twining on other plants, fence wires, and other supports. **Leaves** alternate, on slender stalks up to 5 in. long, ovate in outline to ca. 4 in. long, 3 in. wide, smooth edged or deeply lobed, especially above; typically with 3 lobes pointing toward leaf tip and 2 lobes pointing toward the base (lower-right photo). One to few **flowers** on stalks from leaf axils. Five sepals, unequal; corolla bright red, trumpet shaped, up to 1½ in. long, the 5 petals never separating at their expanded ends. **Blooms** July through September.

STRIPED CORALROOT ORCHID

Corallorhiza striata

Orchid Family, Orchidaceae

Erect, leafless perennial, lacking chlorophyll, reddish purple, tan or yellow, in piñon-juniper woodland up to spruce-fir forest, 6,500–9,500 ft. **Stems** 6–16 in. tall, wrapped by several tubular papery bracts, **leaves** absent. Seven to twenty-five **flowers** on short pedicels up to ¼ in. long, clustered mostly on upper half of stem. Sepals and petals closely spaced, both tannish yellow with lengthwise, darker red to purple stripes. Two of the three petals shorter than the sepals; one is larger, more elliptical with a thick margin, and more strongly striped. One fertile stamen fused with 3 stigmas to form a yellow column up to ¼ in. long, curving outward from the base of the large petal. **Fruit:** when mature, an ellipsoidal, faintly striped seed capsule ca. ½ in. long, hanging from the flower. **Blooms** late May into August. Being unable to provide its own nutrition by photosynthesis, coral-root orchid depends on a specific, mycorrhizal soil fungus that obtains nutrients saprophytically from decaying litter in the forest soil and transfers some of those nutrients into the coral-like root mass of the orchid. Right photo courtesy of Judy Dain.

STREAM ORCHID

Epipactis gigantea

Orchid Family, Orchidaceae

Erect perennial up to 3 or more ft. tall, from underground rhizomes; in damp woods and spring seeps in calcareous soils in piñon-juniper woodland, 7,000–8,000 ft. **Leaves** alternate, sessile, clasping to stem, finely hairy above, conspicuously veined, narrowly lanceolate, up to 6 in. long, tip pointed. Four to eighteen **flowers** on short nodding pedicels, loosely scattered on top ⅓ of plant, ca. 1½ in. wide; 3 sepals, pointed, slightly concave, greenish to faintly rose tinted; 3 petals, rose to intense pink, fading to green at tip, ovate, up to ca. ¾ in. long, shorter than the sepals. Central column ⅓–½ in. tall, bearing greenish-yellow anthers. **Blooms** May to July. Used by Navajo as a ceremonial medicine in girls' puberty rites and to purify newborn infants.

SKYROCKET
(Scarlet Gilia)
Phlox Family, Polemoniaceae

Ipomopsis aggregata

Erect biennial, with clusters of bright red, trumpet-shaped flowers on slender, often solitary stems up to 2–2½ ft. tall. Common in a wide range of environments, from foothill scrub to mixed conifer forest, 5,000–9,000 ft. Basal leaves in a rosette; stem leaves alternate, ¾–3 in. long, pinnately divided into narrow segments; leaves smaller toward top of stem. Stout stems up to ca. 4 ft. tall. Flowers on short pedicels along much of the plant's height. Five petals, up to ca. 1½ in. long, bright red, fused at base to form a tubular trumpet shape; pointed tips of petals flared widely at the apex of the fused base, often with numerous, various-sized yellow blotches on inner surface of flared petals. Five prominent, yellow stamens extend beyond opening of fused petals. The bright red, narrowly tubular flower is typical of many plants pollinated by hummingbirds. Blooms June into September. Used by Navajo for spider bites and as a laxative and an emetic for stomach disorders; boiled for a dye by Hopi.

PRAIRIE SMOKE   *Geum triflorum*
(Purple Avens)
Rose Family, Rosaceae

Perennial from short, thick rhizomes on wet meadows and moist stream banks on mountain slopes, ponderosa pine to mixed conifer forest, 7,000–9,000 ft.; more common in northern mountains. **Stems** erect to ascending, ca. 8–20 in. high, unbranched, softly hairy to scaly, typically pubescent, often forming clumps 8–16 in. wide or more. **Leaves** mostly basal, 1–8 in. long, pinnately divided with 7–19 larger and smaller leaflets, those obovate in outline, divided into 2–5 segments toothed or cleft into linear lobes, softly haired along the margins. **Flowers** typically in loose clusters of 3, sometimes more, at stem ends, erect to drooping. Calyx lobes ca. ¼ in. long, tinged with reddish purple; petals oval, yellow to tinged with purple, about equally long as or slightly longer than calyx lobes. Styles plumose, remaining attached to individual one-seed **fruits** (achenes); mature, plumose heads up to 1¼ in. long. **Blooms** May and June.

KING'S CROWN
(Rosewort)
Stonecrop Family, Crassulaceae

Sedum integrifolium

Erect perennial from thick, fleshy, scaly rootstock. Found in the Sandias near the crest; more common in more northern mountains on moist, rocky outcrops in spruce-fir and subalpine forest, to 12,000 ft. **Stems** up to 12 in. tall. **Leaves** alternate, succulent, smooth, crowded along and encircling stem; oblong to ovate, pointed at tips, up to ca. 1 in. long, margin smooth; appear to radiate from stem. **Flowers** borne in a single, dense cluster at stem end; flowers unisexual or bisexual; petals deep reddish purple, up to ¼ in. long with spreading ends. **Fruits:** reddish clusters of pointed, spreading capsules. **Blooms** May into September.

SMOOTH SUMAC
Rhus glabra
(Scarlet Sumac)
Sumac Family, Anacardiaceae

Small tree or shrub, usually 3–10 ft. tall, occurring along streams or rocky canyon bottoms in piñon-juniper woodland up to mixed conifer forest, 5,500–8,000 ft. **Stems** and branches gray brown and smooth. **Leaves** deeply pinnately divided into 13–17 smooth leaflets ca. 3–3½ in. long with longest leaves near the middle; lanceolate to ovate, thin, not leathery, upper surface dark green, whitish beneath. Dioecious plant with male and female flowers on separate plants; female plants shown here. **Female flowers** in dense, pyramidal, terminal clusters 4–6 in. long; of short duration, depending on available moisture; yellowish white to green (upper-left photo). **Fruits** ca. ⅛ in. diameter, bearing one seed, borne in dense clusters, finely hairy; turning red with maturity and remaining so over winter (lower photo). **Blooms** commonly mid-May to July, also at different times throughout summer depending on habitat and available moisture. Bark eaten by Apache children as a delicacy. Roots chewed by Navajo for sore mouth and tongue; decoction of shredded bark taken for ulcers and venereal diseases. **Note:** Smooth Sumac is included in both the green and red color groups in this book in order to show the small, rather inconspicuous green flowers, which do not bloom long, compared with the much more prominent, easily visible red fruits, which can be seen for several months.

CHICORY

Cichorium intybus

Aster Family, Asteraceae

Erect perennial, native of the Mediterranean region, widely established across North America; common along roadsides, on disturbed sites, or in plains bordering mountains; up to 32 in. tall; in scrub grassland to lower ponderosa pine forest, 4,000 to 7,000 ft. **Stems** much branched with a few stiff hairs. Both **basal** and **stem leaves** alternate to about 6 in. long; basal leaves usually broader above the middle, tapering toward base, often clasping the stem. Upper leaves smaller, margins smooth or with some teeth or lobes, almost inconspicuous toward stem and branch ends. **Flower heads** large, 1–1½ in. wide, sessile, in small clusters at stem tips or singly along branches. **Ray flowers** blue to deep purple blue to lavender, occasionally white, 5-toothed at the squared-off tips. Involucre oblong, in 2 series, inner phyllaries linear, longer and more numerous than the ovate, outer ones. **Blooms** June into August. Ground roots long used as a coffee substitute or amendment; a few reported uses by eastern Native American tribes as a tonic for nerves and a wash and poultice applied to chancres and fever blisters.

SPREADING FLEABANE

Erigeron sp.

Aster Family, Asteraceae

Biennial or short-lived perennial, 4–20 in. tall. One of several related, difficult to differentiate species of fleabanes, daisies, and asters common along roadsides, in meadows, on dry foothills, and in open scrub in piñon-juniper and ponderosa pine forest, 5,500–9,000 ft. **Stems** curving upward or lying on the ground with ends pointing upward; stems and leaves covered with many short grayish hairs. **Lower leaves** petiolate in a tuft, oblong to lanceolate, early deciduous, slightly longer than the alternate, linear, **stem leaves**, ca. ½–¾ in. long, smaller toward stem tip. **Flower heads** ca. 1–1½ in. diameter, solitary or in small groups, on slender stems, often nodding, prior to opening; involucre with linear phyllaries. **Ray flowers** numerous, narrow, tightly spaced; white, bluish lavender, or pink, up to ca. ⅜ in. long, pink to light red when first emerging from involucre; **disk flowers** yellow, in a flat disk. **Blooms** May to September. Used extensively by Navajo for stomachache, headache, menstrual cramps, snakebite, sore throat, animal bites, and other skin wounds; also as an eyewash and an aid in childbirth.

SMOOTH BLUE ASTER
(Smooth Aster)
Aster Family, Asteraceae

Symphotrichum laeve
(*Aster laevis* var. *laevis*)

Herbaceous perennial common in late summer and early autumn, often scattered on roadsides, in open areas, in canyon bottoms, and on dry mountain slopes in piñon-juniper woodland and ponderosa pine forest, 6,500–8,500 ft. **Stems** slender, erect, smooth, sometimes reddish green; reportedly up to 4 ft. tall; in the Sandias commonly 18–24 in. tall. **Leaves** alternate, smooth and almost waxy, elliptic to lanceolate, up to 4 in. long, ¾ in. wide; tips pointed; lower leaves clasping the stem; margins entire to lightly serrated. **Flower heads** solitary or in loose clusters at stem and branch ends. About 10–15 **ray flowers** blue to violet, up to ca. ½ in. long. **Disk flowers** yellow, turning reddish brown. Involucre cylindrical, ca. ⅓ in. high with overlapping series of phyllaries, whitish at base, green at tips (middle-right photo). **Blooms** August into October. Identification and synonymy kindly provided by Timothy Lowrey, University of New Mexico.

HAREBELL
(Bluebell)
Bellflower Family, Campanulaceae

Campanula rotundifolia

Erect perennial common on mountain sides, in meadows, and along streams and road-sides in ponderosa pine to spruce-fir forest, 7,500–11,000 ft. One or several slender stems, 6–24 in. tall with bell-shaped flowers dangling from tops of stems or stem branches. Upper stem **leaves** narrow, grass-like in appearance, ½–3 in. long, less than ¼ in. wide. **Flowers** on stalks, solitary, often drooping. Calyx lobes long, slender, pointed. Corolla bell shaped, consisting of 5 fused, delicate, blue to blue-violet petals, ½–1 in. long, each with a terminal lobe, often curling outward. One prominent, elongated pistil inside the corolla (lower-right photo). **Blooms** June into September. Used by Navajo as a ceremonial fumigant and a medication for heart ailments.

FRANCISCAN BLUEBELLS *Mertensia franciscana*

Borage Family, Boraginaceae

Robust erect perennial, widespread along moist stream banks, in meadows, and on open slopes in ponderosa pine to spruce-fir forest in more northern mountains, 7,000–11,500 ft., often growing in clusters. **Stems** erect or spreading, 12–20 in. tall or taller. **Basal leaves** alternate, 2–4 in. long, lanceolate to elliptic, petiole sometimes longer than the blade. **Stem leaves** alternate, elliptic to ovate, with evident lateral veins; petioles progressively shorter up the stalk. Leaves densely covered with fine, short hairs difficult to see with the unaided eye. **Flowers** blue or pink, funnel shaped, on short stalks, in loose, pendulous clusters at stem end. Five sepals, short with pointed tips, fringed with hairs on the margins. Five petals, fused for most of their length, opening to rounded lobes toward the tips and forming the characteristic, inflated funnel-to-bell shape, ca. ¼–⅝ in. long. **Blooms** June to August.

LANCELEAF BLUEBELLS
(Rocky Mountain Bluebells)
Borage Family, Boraginaceae

Mertensia lanceolata

Erect to ascending perennial, 8–16 in. high, in well-shaded ponderosa pine to spruce-fir forest, 7,000–11,000 ft. **Stems** simple to unbranched, smooth or finely hairy. **Basal leaves** petiolate; **stem leaves** alternate, sessile, mostly lanceolate or nearly so, up to ca. 3 in. long, 1½ in. wide with prominent midvein. **Flowers** perfect, borne at stem and branch ends, often nodding on stalks in loose clusters. Calyx ca. ⅓ in. long, tubular with 5 incised, lanceolate lobes. Corolla light blue to white, funnel shaped, up to ca. ⅓ in. long, fused at base with 5 flared lobes, hairy inside. Five stamens. **Blooms** late April into July. The closely related Franciscan bluebell (*M. franciscana*), common in the more northern New Mexico mountains, is more robust with larger, more deeply veined leaves and slightly longer corollas. Despite the common name "bluebell," the most apparent color of this plant's flowers is often white to bluish white.

MONK'S HOOD   *Aconitum columbianum*

Buttercup Family, Ranunculaceae

Tall, single-stemmed perennial in scattered groups at higher elevations in shaded to partly open areas of mixed conifer to spruce-fir forest, 8,000–11,000 ft. **Stems** mostly unbranched, 2–6 ft. tall; lower stem smooth, hairy above. **Leaves** alternate, petiolate, progressively reduced above, 2–4 in. wide, deeply palmately divided into 3–5 lobes, coarsely toothed or incised. **Flowers** irregular, showy, on pedicels, dark blue violet to creamy white in loose, elongated, narrow clusters at stem end or from upper leaf axils. Five sepals, more prominent than the 2–5 petals; uppermost sepal finely hairy, helmet shaped, forming a beaked hood pointing forward; 2 oval, lateral sepals flaring outward; 2 lower ones narrow, dangling underneath. The two upper petals hooded but hidden under the upper sepal (lower-left photo). Numerous stamens, 3–5 pistils. **Blooms** mid-July to mid-August. The plant is quite poisonous, affecting the heart and the central nervous system. Assassins in ancient Greece and Rome used other species with highly concentrated toxins in the roots to prepare death potions.

BLUE COLUMBINE
(Rocky Mountain Columbine)
Buttercup Family, Ranunculaceae

Aquilegia caerulea

Native perennial on rocky slopes, moist ground, woods, and meadows in northern mountains, mixed conifer to subalpine forest, 7,000–12,000 ft. **Stems** up to 24 in. high, mostly erect, often clustered. **Leaves** deeply palmately divided into 3 leaflets, those divided further into 3, scallop-shaped leaflets somewhat similar to those of Meadowrue. **Flowers** nodding prior to opening, erect when open (right photo), ca. 2½–3½ in. long and across. Five sepals, medium to dark blue, ca. ¼–1½ in. long with pointed tips. Base of fused sepals projects backwards as a slender, tubular spur (lower-left photo). Five petals, white or light blue, smaller than sepals, tips rounded (right photo). Stamens numerous, forming the golden center of the flower, ca. ½–1 in. long. **Blooms** June and July. No report found of uses by New Mexico tribes, but seeds were chewed or a root infusion was used to treat abdominal pain, and seeds were used as a treatment for head lice by several western Native American tribes (Extension Utah State University). The Blue Columbine, also known as the Colorado Columbine, is the Colorado state flower.

BARBEY'S LARKSPUR
(Subalpine Larkspur)
Buttercup Family, Ranunculaceae

Delphinium barbeyi

Perennial in moist, shady, northern mountains, mixed conifer to spruce-fir forest, 8,000–11,000 ft. **Stems** single, smooth, hollow, 2–7 ft. tall. **Leaves** alternate, widely spaced on stem, large, generally round in outline, broader than long, 4–7 in. wide, palmately lobed into 3–7 pointed lobes, each with 5–9 pointed, coarsely toothed smaller segments. Ten to fifty **flowers** per inflorescence, on pedicels 1–2 in. long; before opening (upper-right photo), inflated tubular sepal with a rear-pointing spur, showy, dark blue, tapering toward the tip. Open flowers (lower-right photo) large, showy; sepals dark bluish purple, ½–1 in. long, recurving toward their tips; dense white hairs near their base; petals small, somewhat hidden, partially surrounding the numerous stamens. **Blooms** July and August. Highly toxic, especially in early stages of growth to cattle, although less so for horses and sheep.

INFLATED PENSTEMON

Penstemon inflatus

Figwort Family, Scrophulariaceae

Slender, erect perennial common in ponderosa pine forest up to rocky meadows in spruce-fir forest, 7,500–11,000 ft. **Stems** one to several, up to 2 ft. high. **Leaves** smooth, slightly waxy; basal and lower stem leaves lanceolate, 1¼–3¼ in. long; stem leaves opposite, sessile, similar to lower leaves, becoming narrower toward the upper stem. **Flowers** in clusters of 2–4; each cluster stalk subtended by 2 linear, pointed bracts (upper-left photos). Five sepals, green, pointed. Corolla tubular, distinctly blue to blue lavender, ca. ¾–1 in. long; 2 upper lobes bent upward, 3 lower lobes bent downward, distinctly white throat, hairy, with straight bluish guidelines on lower throat; 5 distinct stamens, one sterile (the stamenode) that is orange bearded for ca. ½ its length and does not project out of the throat (lower photos). **Blooms** early June to July.

JAMES' PENSTEMON

Penstemon jamesii

Figwort Family, Scrophulariaceae

Erect perennial on plains and along roadsides, often in large colonies in open areas of piñon-juniper woodland, 5,000–7,000 ft.; more common in central mountains. One to several stems up to 20 in. tall, smooth to downy surface. Leaves often shiny, dark green to gray green, smooth or hairy, margins smooth or toothed. Lower leaves petiolate, linear to lanceolate, 1–3 in. long; stem leaves opposite, linear to lanceolate, somewhat larger but progressively shorter toward stem apex. Flowers commonly in groups of two on short stalks in crowded clusters on one side of upper stem; pink, lavender, lavender blue to lavender white with visible purple guidelines inside the white, broadly inflated throat; 2 upper lobes bent upward; 3 lower-lobed petals bent downward with white area extending from the base of the lobes into the throat. Surface of sepals, petals, and bracts very finely hairy. Four yellow stamens and 1 sterile, hairy stamenode visible in the open throat. Blooms May to June. Used by Navajo as an infusion for sore throat, as an emetic, and as a lotion to purify a newborn infant before nursing.

WILD BLUE FLAX
Linum lewisii

(Prairie Flax)
Flax Family, Linaceae

Erect perennial in open meadows in piñon-juniper woodland up to mixed conifer forest, 5,000–10,000 ft. **Stems** 8–20 in. tall, slender, often clustered, branched or unbranched. **Leaves** alternate, sessile, crowded along the stem, linear, ca. ⅜–1¼ in. long, sometimes in-rolled lengthwise. **Flowers** in loose, often 1-sided clusters on short stalks near tops of stems; 5 petals, separate, narrowing toward their base, blue with dark veins, sometimes white, ⅜–⅝ in. long; 5 styles, alternating with 5 stamens. Individual flowers open only for one day, opening in the morning with petals falling by late afternoon. **Fruit:** a small, rounded, berry-like capsule ca. ¼ in. diameter, drooping at the end of the slender flower/fruit stalk (lower-right photo). **Blooms** June into August. Closely related and similar in appearance to cultivated flax, which is used for linseed oil and the stem fibers for linen. Oil from the seed used by Navajo for washing hair and the faces of children and adolescents and as an eyewash; seed used for food; in some tribes, stems used as cordage for making strings, mats, and bedding.

PLEATED GENTIAN *Gentiana affinis*

Gentian Family, Gentianaceae

Erect perennial on moist, open mountain meadows, ponderosa pine to spruce-fir forest, 7,000–10,000 ft., in more northern mountains. **Stems** 8–12 in. tall, often clustered in groups of 10 or more, upper third of stem distinctly maroon (an easy key to identification before flowers form). **Leaves** opposite, numerous, closely spaced on stem, sessile, lanceolate to ovate, up to 1⅜ in. long but not more than five times as long as they are wide; margins entire. **Flowers** perfect; in short, often dense clusters at stem end or in upper leaf axils. Short, leaf-like bracts with rounded ends subtend the bell-shaped calyx, which is composed of 5 unequal lobes. Corolla tubular, blue to purple blue; 5 petals, joined for most of their length, lobed toward tips. Fused basal portions reveal distinct, externally beaded ridges where fused. Four or five stamens, 2 stigmas. Flowers close in overcast weather. **Blooms** August to September. Used by Navajo as a snuff for headaches, to revive those who have fainted, and as an antidote for witchcraft.

FRINGED GENTIAN

Gentianopsis thermalis

Gentian Family, Gentianaceae

Erect annual in moist mountain meadows, bogs, and slopes, ponderosa pine to mixed conifer forest, 8,000–9,500 ft. in more northern mountains. **Stems** smooth, up to 16 in. tall. **Stem leaves** sessile, opposite, lanceolate, 2 in. long. **Flowers** solitary, terminal, vase shaped, blue to deep purple, not subtended by bracts. Four sepals with angled, pointed extensions. Four petals, fused, having a vase-like appearance above the fused portions of the calyx (upper-middle photo), 1–2 in. long; lobed toward apex, broadly flattening outward, fringed, toothed at apex. The official flower of Yellowstone National Park, with the specific epithet *thermalis* coming from the plant's original collection there in a region of numerous hot springs. **Blooms** July to October.

ROCKY MOUNTAIN IRIS

Iris missouriensis

Iris Family, Iridaceae

Common perennial from rhizomes, in meadows and along roadsides in mixed conifer to spruce-fir forest, 8,000–9,500 ft. **Flower stalks** slender, erect, up to 2 ft. tall. Resembles cultivated iris but usually has smaller flowers. **Leaves** basal, bluish green, smooth, 8–20 in. long, ¼–½ in. wide, shorter than stalk, V shaped in cross section at their base. Also one short leaf present on flower stalk. **Flowers** single or in limited clusters at apex of flower stalk, each up to 3 in. wide. Most conspicuous are 3 drooping sepals, ca. 2½ in. long, blue to purple with white central areas, often with blue to purple veins. Three petals, blue, erect, smaller and less conspicuous than the sepals. **Blooms** May through July. Generally considered toxic. Most traditional medicinal applications were decoctions, salves, or poultices for treatment of wounds, sores, burns, earaches, or rheumatic pains; taken internally as an emetic. Used by Jemez for ceremonial decorations.

COMMON MORNING GLORY

Ipomoea purpurea

Morning Glory Family, Convolvulaceae

Annual, probably naturalized from Mexico, escaped from ornamental cultivation; found on disturbed sites, in meadows, and on fences; in valley bottoms to piñon-juniper woodland, 4,000–7,000 ft. **Stems** prostrate or trailing, 3–6 ft. long or longer, strongly climbing (upper-left photo), here on a Siberian elm sapling. **Leaves** alternate, ca. 3–5 in. long, variable shape, either heart shaped or 3- or 5-lobed, all leaves with pointed tips; if lobed, each usually broadest at the middle, margins entire (upper-right photo). **Flowers** perfect, on long pedicels from leaf axils bearing up to 5 flowers. Five sepals, finely hairy, ca. ⅜ in. long with pointed tips (middle-left and lower-left photos). Corolla showy, funnel shaped, 2–2¾ in. long; 5 petals, fused their entire length, opening widely toward the tip; white toward their base; blue, red, or purple toward the top; sometimes variegated. Five stamens, not protruding; 1 style with 3 stigmas. **Blooms** July through September.

SILVERY LUPINE

Lupinus argenteus

Pea Family, Fabaceae

Colorful perennial commonly in open areas of ponderosa pine and mixed conifer forest, 7,000–9,000 ft. **Stems** erect, 12–20 in. tall with short, silvery, appressed hairs. Many **leaves**, palmately compound with 5–9 lanceolate leaflets 1⅛–2 in. long radiating from the tip of the petiole and covered with silky hairs on both surfaces. **Flowers** in loose terminal clusters, pea-like, each up to ½ in. long, dark blue to purple with central white area. **Fruit:** a small, elongated pod, ¾–1½ in. long, containing 4–6 seeds. **Blooms** April through September. Roots of lupines contain, as do all members of the pea family, symbiotic nitrogen-fixing bacteria that contribute essential nitrogen to the plant and eventually to the soil. Poisonous to humans and livestock, especially cattle and sheep, lupines have not been used as food or medicines taken internally; however, Navajo made extracts and pastes for topical treatment of poison ivy and other skin disorders.

KING'S LUPINE

Lupinus kingii

Pea Family, Fabaceae

Annual or biennial herb on dry slopes in foothill scrub and piñon-juniper woodland, 6,000–8,000 ft. Lupines can easily interbreed, producing hybrids difficult to identify to species. **Stems** up to 10 in. tall; branched near the base or widely spreading; with silky, often silvery hairs. **Leaves** alternate, petiolate; palmately divided into 4–7 leaflets originating from the same point; oblanceolate, up to ca. ¾ in. long, ¼ in. wide; often folded upward along midvein; silky hairs on both sides. **Flowers** pea-like, seldom over ½ in. long, blue or purple, in dense raceme clusters. Top petals almost round, with a white eyespot (lower-right photo). Two lateral petals longer than top petals, convex, united at top; 2 bottom petals fused to form a curved keel. **Fruit:** hairy pods ca. ¼ in. long, bluish purple; each pod contains 2 seeds (upper-right photo). **Blooms** June to September. Used as an eye medicine by Hopi and by Navajo as a poultice of crushed leaves for poison ivy blisters and other skin irritations.

TRUMPET GILIA

Ipomopsis longiflora ssp. *neomexicana*

Phlox Family, Polemoniaceae

Erect, drought-tolerant annual or biennial, found along roadsides, on disturbed sites, and in sandy soils in foothill scrub to lower ponderosa pine forest, 3,500–7,000 ft. **Stems** ascending to erect, up to 24 in. long, much branched, smooth, with a few cobwebby hairs. **Leaves** smooth, alternate, ¾–2 in. long, pinnately divided with 1–3 separated, linear segments. **Flowers** pale blue to lavender, stalked, in loose clusters near branch ends. Calyx ca. ¼ in. long, far shorter than the long, trumpet-shaped corolla with its narrow tube and 5 spreading lobes, up to 2 in. long. Five stamens, 1 pistil. **Fruit:** elliptical capsules ca. ½ in. long (lower-left photo). **Blooms** June into September. Numerous uses by Hopi, Navajo, Tewa, and Western Keres (Laguna and Acoma), including treatment for stomachache and other gastric disorders, as an emetic to induce vomiting, for postpartum septicemia, to facilitate delivery of placenta, as treatment for headache and sores, and as a veterinary treatment applied daily to heal incision of castrated colts.

JACOB'S LADDER   *Polemonium foliosissimum*

Phlox Family, Polemoniaceae

Erect perennial common in open areas of ponderosa pine up to spruce-fir forest, 7,000–11,000 ft. **Stems** 12–36 in. tall, hairy, often branched, glandular above. **Leaves** alternate, pinnately compound, with 11–25 mostly lanceolate leaflets ⅜–1 in. long, together resembling a ladder somewhat, hence the common name. Foul smelling when crushed. **Flowers** various shades of blue, often with white centers; in somewhat open, round-topped clusters at branch ends; sometimes entirely white. Corolla tubular with petals basally fused, opening into a bell shape with 5 lobed petals ⅜–¾ in. long. Five elongated, white stamens; 1 style, stigma 3-lobed. **Blooms** late June into September.

MANY-FLOWERED GILIA

Ipomopsis multiflora

Phlox Family, Polemoniaceae

Perennial on dry slopes, often in sandy soil in piñon-juniper woodland and ponderosa pine forest, 5,000–6,500 ft. **Stems** up to 10 in. tall, erect or arching with glandular, whitish hairs, somewhat woody at base. **Leaves** alternate, some pinnately divided into narrow, prong-like segments, some linear and undivided. **Flowers** borne on short branches in a rounded, compact cluster. Sepals finely, densely hairy, short, green, with small spine at tip (lower-left photo); surround base of the ¼–½ in. long, trumpet-shaped, blue to lavender corolla that opens into 5 darker lobes, usually with irregular purple markings in the throat. Five stamens, cobalt blue, protruding. One style, stigma 3-lobed. **Blooms** August into September. Powdered whole plant applied by Navajo to face for headache and to wounds.

BIRDBILL DAYFLOWER

Commelina dianthifolia

Spiderwort Family, Commelinaceae

Erect perennial 6–16 in. high, usually on open, rocky areas of piñon-juniper wood-land up to mixed conifer forest, 6,500–9,000 ft. **Stems** smooth, jointed, unbranched to sparsely branched. **Leaves** alternate, grass-like, parallel veined, linear to linear lanceo-late, 4–15 in. long, up to ¼ in. wide, reduced at the base to a petiole wrapping the stem. **Flowers** single, borne on a long stalk up to 8 in. long. Buds initially enclosed within a large, folded, green, crescent-shaped bract (spathe), ca. 1¼–2½ in. long, with a long, ta-pered point (upper photos). Three small sepals; 3 petals, dark blue, opening wide, up to ca. 1 in. across, lower petal slightly smaller; styles and stigmas blue, extending. Flowers last for only one day. **Blooms** August and September. Used as an infusion by Western Keres to give strength to weakened tuberculosis patients.

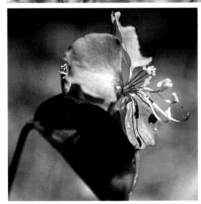

GYPSUM SCORPIONWEED *Phacelia integrifolia*

Waterleaf Family, Hydrophyllaceae

Annual or biennial on exposed, sunny areas of plains, deserts, and foothills in the central mountains and southern portions of northern mountains, 5,000–7,000 ft. Herbage with dense gland-typed hairs, sticky and with foul odor. **Stems** reddish brown, 4–20 in. high, not heavily branched but very leafy. **Leaves** ca. ¾–2½ in. long, lanceolate to oblanceolate with very crinkled appearance, margins curling down and inward with broad, rounded lobes (upper-right photo). Midvein and lateral veins prominent underneath; lateral veins widely spaced (lower-left photo). **Flowers** ca. ⅛–¼ in. across, sessile, borne on one side of elongated, narrow inflorescence, the later uncurling from a "fiddle head" shape as more flowers are formed (lower-middle photo). Corolla bluish white to lavender, ca. ⅛ in. long, tubular to funnel shaped, opening broadly; purple anthers, 1-branched style, and stigmas extend well beyond the corolla (lower-right photo). **Fruit:** small ovoid pods. **Blooms** May through August. Powdered roots or leaves of several species of *Phacelia* were mixed with water and rubbed on sprains, swellings, and rashes by Zuni, Laguna, Acoma, Santa Clara, and San Ildefonso (Dunmire and Tierney 1995).

BURNT-ORANGE DANDELION

Agoseris aurantiaca

(Orange-Flowered Mountain Dandelion)
Aster Family, Asteraceae

Stemless perennial 4–20 in. tall, in meadows and open coniferous forests up to mixed conifer zone, 6,000–10,000 ft.; flower heads borne on flowering stalk (scape) arising from base of plant. **Leaves** in a basal rosette, oblong lanceolate, 2–10 in. long, essentially smooth margin, somewhat grass-like in appearance. One **flower head** per stalk, borne at tip. **Ray flowers** only, burnt orange, radiating outward from the center; wider toward tip than at base; tip rounded. Involucre mostly ¾–1 in. high, with 2 overlapping rows of green, pointed phyllaries, covered with fine white hairs (lower-left photo). Mature flower heads essentially spherical, with white pappus bristles. **Blooms** June to September. Used by Navajo as a lotion for arrow and bullet wounds; wet leaves rubbed on swollen arms, wrists, or ankles; and as a ceremonial emetic.

WOOD LILY *Lilium philadelphicum*
(Rocky Mountain Lily)
Lily Family, Liliaceae

Perennial in moist meadows, grasslands, and open forest, ca. 7,000–9,000 ft. in more northern mountains. **Stems** from chunky bulbs, erect, 1–2 ft. tall, unbranched, smooth, usually with a solitary flower, sometimes more, at stem tip. **Leaves** alternate, near the base, linear to lanceolate, up to 4 in. long, 1 in. wide; upper stem leaves in whorls, smooth, horizontal or drooping at tips, margins entire. **Flowers** erect, not fragrant, widely bell shaped up to 4 in. across; 6 tepals, bright orange to brick red with purple to black spots near the base of each, not united at base (lower photo). Six stamens, extending beyond tepals and of the same color, surrounding the single pistil, also orange. **Blooms** June and July but for only short periods during this time. An endangered species in New Mexico.

NARROWLEAF GLOBEMALLOW   *Sphaeralcea angustifolia*

Mallow Family, Malvaceae

Erect, drought-tolerant perennial up to 4½ ft. tall in open fields and arroyos and along roadsides in foothill scrub and piñon-juniper woodland, 3,500–7,500 ft. **Leaves** alternate, about twice as long as wide, with petioles half the length of the lanceolate blade, often with 2 prominent, lateral lobes near the base; leaf edges often wavy with coarse, irregular teeth. **Flowers** on short pedicels arising from leaf axils, in loose clusters along much of stem. Five distinct, orange petals ¼–½ in. long, notched at apex. Stamens numerous, united, forming a collar around the base of the united styles and numerous stigmas. Mature **fruit**: a disk-like cluster of 10–15 triangular-shaped carpels united at the center, each with 1–3 seeds (lower-right photo). **Blooms** late June into October. Several species of *Sphaeralcea* used by Navajo, Hopi, Tewa, and Keres for treatment of colds, sores, snakebite, stomachache, and diarrhea; as a source of pigment for face paint; as a glue-like substance mixed with mud to make floors hard; and as a glue to hold feathers and cotton on skin during dances.

SCARLET GLOBEMALLOW

Sphaeralcea coccinea

Mallow Family, Malvaceae

Low perennial spread by rhizomes; found on open hills and waste ground, along roadsides, and in piñon-juniper woodland, 5,000–7,000 ft. **Stems** 4–20 in. tall, solitary or clustered, often prostrate at base, whitish or yellowish, hairy. **Leaves** alternate, petiolate, up to 2 in. long, grayish green, hairy; 3–5 lobes deeply incised nearly to midrib, often again lobed or toothed. **Flowers** in clusters, on short stalks at ends of branches. Sepals 5-lobed, less than ½ in. long, densely hairy. Five petals, ⅜–¾ in. long, orange red. Stamens numerous, thread-like, united in a column around base of styles. As do other globemallow species, scarlet globemallow has numerous varieties and subspecies. The genus is most difficult taxonomically. **Blooms** June through September. Used by Navajo as an infusion to stop bleeding, a tonic to cure coughs and cold, and a traditional hair rinse after shampooing to give body and to condition the scalp.

PIGWEED
(Green Amaranth)
Amaranth Family, Amaranthaceae

Amaranthus hybridis

Coarse, erect or ascending monoecious annual up to 4 ft. tall or higher; along roadsides and in arroyos and disturbed sites in foothill scrub and piñon-juniper woodland, 5,000–7,500 ft. **Stems** branched, smooth or with short hairs, often reddish at base. **Leaves** alternate, up to 3½ in. long including the long petiole, lanceolate to ovate lanceolate, without teeth or lobes, rounded to pointed at tip, margin entire. **Flowers** in dense panicles within dense, terminal, or axillary spikes; small, green, with pistillate and staminate flowers on separate parts of the same plant. Stiff, spine-tipped bracts subtend and extend beyond each flower (lower-left photo). **Blooms** August into September. Young plants boiled and eaten as greens or boiled and dried for winter use by Acoma and Laguna.

BIG SAGEBRUSH
(Wormwood)
Aster Family, Asteraceae

Artemisia tridentata

Much-branched perennial, woody shrub (lower-left photo) with an extensive root system, up to 12 ft. tall at maturity, on dry plains, mesas, or rocky slopes in northern and northwestern New Mexico, 5,000–8,500 ft. **Leaves** ¼–2 in. long with small, dense, appressed hairs, which produce the silvery-gray color; apex blunt, mostly 3-lobed (left-inset photo), sometimes 5-lobed; some upper leaves entire. **Flower heads** (lower-middle and lower-right photos) yellowish green, many, in a definite, somewhat broad panicle; 5–12 flowers per head, **rays** and **disks** similar, perfect, fertile. **Blooms** July to October. Used by Apache to make tea; by Navajo for poles of sweat lodges; leafy stems tied together and used as brooms; fibrous bark used for weaving bags, clothing, and mats. Numerous medicinal applications, for example, a decoction of the plant tissue was used as a bath for muscular ailments and a poultice or plugs were placed in the nose for colds. Used by Zuni for many of the same purposes; they also put leaves in shoes for athlete's foot and for a foot deodorant.

PRAIRIE CONE FLOWER
(Mexican Hat)
Aster Family, Asteraceae

Ratabiba columnifera

Erect perennial, widespread on open slopes in piñon-juniper woodland and ponderosa pine forest, 5,000–7,500 ft. **Stems** branched, up to 32 in. tall with stiff bristly hairs. **Leaves** alternate, deeply pinnately divided into 5 or more linear to oblong segments. **Flower heads** on stalks 2–5 in. long at ends of stems or branches; an elongated columnar shaft of tightly compacted, yellowish brown **disk flowers** that bloom from the bottom up, eventually covering the white columnar surface The column of disk flowers is surrounded at its base by nonfunctional, drooping **ray flowers**, ¾–1½ in. long, brownish purple to maroon brown and yellow at the ends, eventually falling from the head (lower-right photo). **Blooms** mid-June into September. Used as a cold infusion by Navajo for fever and as an emetic by Zuni; crushed leaves rubbed on mother's breasts by Keres to wean child.

COCKLEBUR

Xanthium strumarium

Aster Family, Asteraceae

Coarse annual 2–4 ft. tall, common throughout New Mexico along roadsides and in irrigation ditches, vacant lots, moist drainages, dry lake beds, and similar moist, disturbed sites, 3,000–6,000 ft. **Stems** erect, branched, thick, rough, purplish green with distinctive purple to black spots. **Leaves** alternate, triangular to heart shaped, on long petioles, rough on both surfaces, toothed or lobed, ca. 3 in. long. **Pistillate and staminate flowers** small, separate on the same plant, in axils of upper leaves. **Staminate flowers** in clusters; small, spherical, with stamens radiating outward (lower-left photos); **pistillate flowers** yellowish green, in dense clusters situated below the staminate flowers, initially bristly at terminal end only, eventually becoming bristled throughout (middle-right photo) as fruit continues development. **Fruits:** burs, including the stiff, hooked prickles, ca. ¾–1¼ in. long, cylindrical, tapering toward the tip, green maturing to brown (lower-right photo). **Blooms** June to August. When entangled in wool, the burs reduce its value. Both seedlings and seeds contain a substance toxic to livestock.

CURLY DOCK
(Curly-Leaf Dock)
Buckwheat Family, Polygonaceae

Rumex crispus

Introduced, erect perennial common in most moist areas, road ditches, and seeps in piñon-juniper woodland up to mixed conifer forest, 5,000–9,000 ft., also in dry open grassland but smaller in size. **Stems** smooth, up to 4 ft. tall, unbranched below flowers. **Leaves** alternate, surfaces wavy or crispy. **Basal leaves** petiolate, oblong to lanceolate, up to 8 in. long, ½–2 in. wide, pointed. **Stem leaves** similar, smaller. **Flowers** in dense clusters on slender, sometimes drooping stalks at stem end; yellowish green, with 6 sepaloid segments, together forming a paper-like, 3-sided **fruit** with each segment bearing a grain-like seed (middle-right photo). **Blooms** April to September. Many reported uses of seeds and leaves for food by numerous eastern, southern, and northern tribes.

FENDLER'S MEADOWRUE   *Thalictrum fendleri*

Buttercup Family, Ranunculaceae

Erect perennial 12–28 in. high, in meadows and woods, piñon-juniper woodland to mixed conifer forest, 6,500–9,500 ft. **Stems** smooth, branched above. **Leaves** alternate, on short petioles, in groups of 3, those further divided into groups of 3; the ultimate leaflets ca. ⅓–¾ in. long, ovate to obovate to round, 3-lobed at the apex with wavy-toothed margin; similar to leaves of columbine but smaller. **Flowers** on stalks, in open leafy clusters at branch ends or from leaf axils. Plant dioecious, with male (staminate) and female (pistillate) flowers on different plants. **Staminate flowers** (upper-right photo) with 4 or 5 green to whitish sepals ca. ¼–⅛ in. long; petals absent; 7–30 stamens, green, thread-like, hanging downward. **Pistillate flowers** (lower photos) green, in clusters, producing seed-bearing fruits, each a somewhat rounded triangular pod with pointed tips. **Blooms** mid-June through July. Used by Western Keres as an infusion for colds, by Navajo for ceremonial purposes.

GREEN-FLOWERED HEDGEHOG CACTUS *Echinocereus viridiflorus*

Cactus Family, Cactaceae

Small-sized cactus on rocky slopes, mesas, and draws, in open areas or partial shade, 3,500–7,000 ft. **Stems** solitary or in small clusters, up to ca. 2½ in. diameter with 8–16 ribs composed of conical mounds. All clusters of **spines** have 8–12 white radial spines arranged in a flat plane against the surface; many clusters have 4 or 5 red, brown, or cream-colored spines up to 1 in. long extending upward from the surface. **Flowers** arising on sides of stems, often along the lower half, funnel shaped, up to 1½ in. long and wide. Outer petaloid parts linear, greenish yellow to greenish at edges with a darker midline. Petals and sepals indistinguishable from one another. Many stamens, 6–10 stigma lobes, green, fat. **Blooms** April into June. Lower photo courtesy of Kelly Dix.

NARROWLEAF CATTAIL

Typha angustifolia

Cattail Family, Typhaceae

Tall, slender perennial from starchy rhizomes, restricted to open water or saturated soils along lake shores and river banks and in roadside ditches. Apparently statewide at all elevations. **Stems** slender, smooth, rigid, up to 7 or 8 ft. tall. **Leaves** medium green, ca. ¼–½ in. wide, rarely wider, arising from the plant base in a fan-like manner, typically convex along the back side, margins entire. Extremely tiny **pistillate** and **staminate flowers** borne in spikes up to 6 in. long on the same stem, separated by a naked interval (upper-right photo) with staminate flowers above. Following fertilization, the tiny staminate flowers (lower-right photo) fall away, leaving the exposed stem tip; mature pistillate flowers take on the fluffy, tan, "cat tail" appearance (lower-middle photo). **Blooms** May into July. Hopi chewed mature heads with tallow as gum and associated the plant ceremoniously with water.

BROADLEAF CATTAIL
Typha latifolia

Cattail Family, Typhaceae

Tall perennial from starchy, creeping rhizomes in marshy, aquatic habitats scattered throughout the state, 4,000–8,000 ft. **Stems** stout, circular in cross section, up to 9 ft. tall. **Leaves** pale green, 3–5 ft. long, to 1 in. wide, from a common, spongy sheathing base. Numerous **staminate** and **pistillate flowers** borne in separate inflorescences at top of stem, the former above and the latter below; the smaller diameter, tan staminate inflorescence, and dark brown pistillate inflorescence contiguous (lower-right photo). **Fruit:** small, fluffy, wind-disseminated achenes (upper-right photo). **Blooms** May to August. Stem bases, roots, and rhizomes used as food, raw or cooked, by Apache, San Felipe, Keres, and Navajo.

SCOURING RUSH
(Equisetum)
Equisetum (or Horsetail) Family, Equisetaceae

Equisetum hyemale

Although not a flowering plant, this ancient perennial vascular plant from extensive roots is included, as it commonly occurs in New Mexico, often along with cattails in moist terrestrial habitats along streams and lake shores statewide, at 5,000–8,000 ft. **Stems** 3–5 ft. tall, strongly ridged and grooved, hollow between the nodes, usually unbranched. **Leaves** highly reduced, scale-like, fused into an appressed sheath at their bases (upper-right photo), withering and brown when mature and marked by apical and basal dark bands (lower-right photo). Reproductive, unicellular spores, rather than seeds, are produced in brown, cone-like **strobili** 1 in. long at stem apex (lower photos) that eventually break away, leaving the naked stem apex (lower-right photo). Concentrated silicon deposits in stems made them useful in earlier times as sandpaper for smoothing reeds for clarinets and saxophones and to early pioneers for scouring pots and pans.

NOSEBURN   *Tragia ramosa*

Euphorbia Family, Euphorbiaceae

Reclining to erect perennial up to 16 in. tall, on rocky plains and hillsides, mostly in the more central mountains, in scrub grassland to piñon-juniper woodland, 5,000–7,500 ft. All parts of the plant covered with stiff, stinging hairs, certainly a plant fairly named. **Leaves** alternate, on short petioles, lanceolate, ca. ¼–1 in. long, margins toothed with fine, spiny hairs. A monoecious plant with **male** (staminate) and **female** (pistillate) **flowers** separated on the same plant. Overall flowers greenish yellow; anthers yellow (upper-right photo). **Fruit:** a 3-lobed capsule, ca. ¼ in. diameter, with many stinging hairs (lower-right photo). Infusion used by Western Keres as a treatment for ant bites; also, as a "pediatric strengthener," male babies were struck with parts of the plant to increase their pain threshold in battle.

LAMB'S QUARTERS

Chenopodium album

Goosefoot Family, Chenopodiaceae

Erect, introduced, weedy, pale-green annual, 3–5 ft. tall, on waste ground and in disturbed soil. Common throughout New Mexico, 4,000–8,500 ft. **Stems** branched, often reddish veined with powdery coating (upper-middle photo). **Leaves** alternate, rhombic ovate to lanceolate, ½–2 in. long, margins dentate, upper leaf surface smooth (lower-left photo), undersurface mealy, powdery. **Flowers** inconspicuous, in dense green clusters toward upper ends of stem and branches; petals absent; calyx lobes ridged, with white, powdery coating (lower-right photo). **Blooms** July to October. Apache and Zuni cooked the plants as greens; also numerous reports of other Native American tribes' uses of native species of *Chenopodium* (e.g., *C. quinoa*), which contain 15% protein and more than 50% carbohydrate; long used by Andean tribes in South America and now popular in the United States.

FETID GOOSEFOOT

Dysphania graveolens
(*Chenopodium graveolens, Teloxys graveolens*)
Goosefoot Family, Chenopodiaceae

Erect annual up to 18 in. tall; strongly aromatic (skunk-like in some reports, but a rather pleasant, somewhat astringent, witch hazel–like aroma when mature); in open, shady areas; ponderosa pine and mixed conifer forest, 7,000–9,000 ft. Entire plant green, turning red in late summer to autumn. **Stems** erect, often branched, mostly smooth. **Leaves** alternate, ¾–2½ in. long, deltoid ovate to oblong, petiole shorter than blade, margins deeply lobed, resembling small oak leaves. **Flowers** (upper-middle photos) in loose clusters from leaf axils, small, inconspicuous, green. Two to five sepals, united at base with yellowish glands on back. Petals absent. **Fruit:** tiny, red, spherical pods, (upper-right photo) similar in size to the green flowers. **Blooms** late July into September. Used as an emetic by Western Keres; by Zuni as an herbal steam with vapor inhaled for headache; Hopi ground seeds, mixed with cornmeal, and made into small dumplings wrapped in corn husks.

WOODBINE
(Thicket Creeper, Western Five-Leafed Ivy)
Grape Family, Vitaceae

Parthenocissus vitacea

A tough vine, clambering to weakly climbing; widespread in canyons and thickets and along moist roadsides; from river bottoms to lower mountains, 4,500–7,500 ft. Vines with few-branched tendrils (lower-left photo) provide anchorage on other plants, fences, or supports. **Leaves** alternate, on long petioles, palmately divided, typically into 5 elliptic to oblanceolate leaflets ca. 1½–3 in. long, all originating from tip of petiole; margins coarsely toothed; turning brilliant red in autumn. Numerous **flowers** in dichotomously branched clusters; small, unopened flower buds (upper-middle photo), greenish white, enclosed by 5 tepals. Open flowers tiny, greenish white, ca. $\frac{1}{16}$–$\frac{1}{8}$ in. across, 5 tepals bending downward, turning upward at their tips; 4 stamens with elongated filaments, ovary red with white tip (upper-right photo). Flowers open in late afternoon. **Fruit:** following fertilization (middle-right photo), fruit matures to a waxy, bluish-black berry ca. $\frac{1}{4}$–$\frac{1}{3}$ in. diameter, containing 3 or 4 seeds (lower-right photo). **Blooms** May and June. The berries are reportedly toxic to humans, and the plant's oxalate crystals may cause skin rash in some (Friends of the Wild Flower Garden, Inc. 2013). However, the Navajo used an infusion of leaves and berries as a lotion for swollen arms and legs, and the berries were used as food. The Jemez used the berry juice mixed with white clay to make a purple paint for skin in ceremonial dances.

CANYON GRAPE

Vitis arizonica

Grape Family, Vitaceae

Much-branched vine in rocky canyons, sometimes weakly climbing into small trees or shrubs, widespread but of local occurrence, 5,000–7,000 ft. **Stems** very slender, tapering rapidly in. diameter from base to apex, angled, bark of older stems becoming dark gray to almost black, separating in small platelets. **Leaves** simple, generally heart shaped to ca. 4 in. long and about as wide, somewhat 3-lobed, apex triangular, margins irregularly toothed. Flower buds greenish, in clusters. **Flowers** whitish green, fertile, in branched clusters 2–4 in. long; 5 tepals with grayish, cottony pedicels (lower-left and middle photos); 4 or 5 sepals, minute; 4 or 5 petals, insignificant, falling at anthesis, stamens recurved. **Fruit** globose to ovate, black with a slight bloom, ca. ⅓–⅜ in. diameter; borne in clusters on red pedicels, usually shorter than leaves (lower-right photo). **Blooms** April to July. Dried fruit eaten like raisins; also pounded, dried, and stored for later use by Apache. Eaten fresh by Isleta and Jemez. Navajo made a cross of the stems as a "love medicine," putting it on top of a basket of cornmeal and flat bread and offering it in courtship.

HOPS
Humulus lupulus var. *neomexicana*

Hemp Family, Cannabinaceae

Twining perennial, somewhat rough to the touch; often in thickets; twining on other plants, fences, or other structures; in mountains throughout the state, 6,000–7,500 ft. **Leaves** opposite, palmately 3–7 lobed, spaces between the upper lobes broad and widely open, petiole shorter than blade; lower surface with yellow, resinous, bitter, aromatic granules. **Flowers** in loose, light-green, typically pendulose, cone-like aggregates (upper-right photo). Monoecious plant with male (staminate) and pistillate (female) flowers separate but on same plant. **Blooms** in July. Apache used boiled hops to flavor wheat flour and potatoes; flowers used to flavor drinks; Navajo used the plant to prepare medicine for bad coughs and colds.

NORTHERN GREEN BOG ORCHID

(Tall Northern Green Orchid)
Orchid Family, Orchidaceae

Platanthera huronensis
(*Orchis huronensis, Habenaria hyperborea*)

Single-stemmed perennial, often in clusters, most common in bright partial shade to full sun on hillside seeps and wet meadows, restricted to ponderosa pine to mixed conifer forest, 8,000–10,500 ft., in more northern mountains. Can be identified on site by its whitish-green to greenish-white color. **Stems** typically 8–28 in. tall. Five or six **leaves** 2–12 in. long, oblong to linear lanceolate, smooth, margin entire, basal leaf rounded at tip, others pointed, gradually reduced to bracts above. Numerous sessile **flowers** in a panicle along upper portions of stem, not showy but sometimes conspicuous; 3 sepals ca. ¼ in. long, greenish white; top sepal, almost rounded or egg shaped, extends forward to form a high, open hood over the column and above the lip petal. Three **petals** ca. ¼ in. long, whitish green with 3 faint green veins along length; spur, slightly curved, rounded at tip. Column (fused portions of the stigma, style, and stamens) longer than wide, extending well beyond sepals and petals. **Blooms** early July to early August.

CANYON BOG ORCHID
(Sparsely Flowered Bog Orchid)
Orchid Family, Orchidaceae

Platanthera sparsiflora
(*Habenaria sparsifolia*)

Perennial, on moist wooded slopes and wet riparian soils of canyons in piñon-juniper woodland and ponderosa pine forest, 7,500–9,000 ft. **Stems** up to 2 ft. tall with 30–100 or more small green flowers. **Leaves** clasping, alternate, linear to elliptic lanceolate, up to 4½ in. long, ¾ in. wide, replaced by floral bracts subtending flowers higher on stem; bracts ca. ¾ in. long at lowest flowers, smaller above. **Flowers** sessile, ca. ½–¾ in. long; borne in narrow, elongated clusters (racemes) along upper stem; greenish white to yellowish green; the petals and the longer, upper sepal form a hood over the top of each flower; lateral sepals usually wrap behind the spur or are held to the side; petals and sepals pale to light green; spur curves downward, ca. ½ in. long. **Blooms** June to September. The common name "sparsely flowered bog orchid" is rather a misnomer, as mature plants often have up to 100 or more green to yellowish-green flowers.

COMMON PLANTAIN
(Broadleaf Plantain)
Plantain Family, Plantaginaceae

Plantago major

Stemless perennial introduced from Europe, common on waste ground; widespread; 4,000–8,000 ft. **Flowering stem** (scape) unbranched, up to 10 in. high. **Leaves** petiolate, in basal rosette from root crowns, ovate to lanceolate or broadly elliptic, to 7 in. long, 4 in. wide, strongly ribbed, edges wavy, smooth to finely toothed. **Flowers** minute, greenish white, in dense terminal spikes covering upper half or more of stem (upper-left photo). **Fruit:** a small elongated capsule, green, turning reddish brown. **Blooms** May to August. Leaves used as food by Acoma and Laguna; very high vitamin A content.

SMOOTH SUMAC
(Scarlet Sumac)
Sumac Family, Anacardiaceae

Rhus glabra

Small tree or shrub, usually 3–10 ft. tall, occurring along streams or rocky canyon bottoms in piñon-juniper woodland up to mixed conifer forest, 5,500–8,000 ft. **Stems** and branches gray brown and smooth. **Leaves** deeply pinnately divided into 13–17 smooth leaflets ca. 3–3½ in. long with longest leaves near the middle; lanceolate to ovate, thin, not leathery, upper surface dark green, whitish beneath. Dioecious plant with male and female flowers on separate plants; female plants shown here. **Female flowers** in dense, pyramidal, terminal clusters 4–6 in. long; of short duration, depending on available moisture; yellowish white to green (upper-left photo). **Fruits** ca. ⅛ in. diameter, bearing one seed, borne in dense clusters, finely hairy; turning red with maturity and remaining so over winter (lower photo). **Blooms** commonly mid-May to July, also at different times throughout summer, depending on habitat and available moisture. Bark eaten by Apache children as a delicacy. Roots chewed by Navajo for sore mouth and tongue; decoction of shredded bark taken for ulcers and venereal diseases. Note: Smooth Sumac is included in both the green and red color groups in this book in order to show the small, rather inconspicuous green flowers, which do not bloom long, compared with the much more prominent, easily visible red fruits, which can be seen for several months.

GLOSSARY

Text

achene: A small, dry, one-seeded, thin-walled fruit that does not split open to release the seed; for example, in sunflowers and all other Asteraceae and in strawberries (the tiny "seeds" on the surface of the fleshy receptacle are actually achenes).

alternate leaves: Leaves arising singly in a left-then-right positioning on the stem; not in pairs or whorls.

annual: Having a life cycle completed in one year or season.

anther: The terminal, sac-like portion of the stamen, containing pollen.

anthesis: The time when a flower expands and opens.

areole: In cacti; a small, light- or dark-colored area or bump from which a cluster of spines grows.

ascending stems or leaves: Growing laterally at first, then angling upward; not erect or spreading.

axil: The upper angle where a leaf meets the stem.

berry: A fleshy fruit with one to many seeds, developed from a single ovary.

biennial: Growing vegetatively the first year and flowering, fruiting, and dying during the second year.

bilaterally symmetrical: Refers to a flower that has identical left and right sides (mirror images) if divided vertically, such as those in the Pea Family and Figwort Family.

blade: The flat portion of a leaf, excluding the petiole.

bract: A modified leaf, often smaller than foliage leaves, appearing petal-like in some plants; often situated at the base of a flower or inflorescence.

bulb: A short, underground stem, the swollen portion consisting mostly of fleshy, food-storing, modified leaves, for example, an onion.

calyx: Collective term for the whorl of sepals around the base of a flower; may consist of tubular, fused sepals or individual sepals, most often green.

carpel: One or more of the units of the pistil in which seeds are borne.

column: An elongated, finger-like structure formed from the union of parts, such as stamens or stamens and pistil (as in orchids and penstemons).

compound leaf: A leaf divided into leaflets.

corolla: Collective term for the petals of a flower; can mean all the individual petals or petals fused to form a tube, bell, or funnel-shaped structure.

cyathium: A cup-like structure enclosing small flowers, such as in *Euphorbia* spp.

deciduous: Shedding leaves seasonally; the shedding of certain parts after a period of growth.

deltoid: Generally triangular in shape, referring mostly to leaves.

dentate: Leaf margin with angular teeth extending at right angles from the leaf edge.

dioecious: A plant having female (pistillate) and male (staminate) flowers on separate plants of the same species.

disk flower: Each of the small tubular flowers making up the radially symmetrical, central portion of the flower head (the disk) in many members of the Aster Family.

entire margin: Leaf edge lacking teeth, serrations, or notches; smooth.

erect stems or leaves: Arranged in an upright position.

flexuous: Not rigid, wavy (referring to stems).

flower: A reproductive complex formed at a branch or stem end, including the receptacle and bearing sepals, petals, stamens, and pistil or some of these.

fruit: A ripened, mature ovary, sometimes including other floral parts that are attached and ripen with it.

guidelines: Lines of dark color on the lower throat of the corolla of insect-pollinated plants.

hemiparasitic plant: One that has chlorophyll and produces some of its nutrition by photosynthesis but depends on parasitism of other living organisms for the remainder.

hemispheric: Shaped like half a sphere or globe.

herb: A plant producing little or no woody tissue; usually dies back at the end of each growing season; may be annual, biennial, or perennial.

herbage: Collective term for all the green parts of a plant together.

hypanthium: An elongated floral tube extending from the apex of the ovary to other floral parts (sepals, petals, stigma, anthers).

imperfect flower: One lacking either stamens or pistils; unisexual.

inflorescence: A flower cluster on a plant or the specific arrangement of flowers on a plant.

involucre: One or more series of bracts (phyllaries) arranged in various patterns to form a cup that holds the flowers within the inflorescence. Present in all Asteraceae; also in some Nyctaginaceae (e.g., *Mirabilis* spp.) and some Caprifoliaceae (e.g., *Lonicera involucrata*).

irregular flower: A bilaterally symmetrical flower, such as penstemons.

joint: Segment of a stem (as in a cactus) or a plant node (as where leaves join the stem).

keel: The lower petal of a flower in the Pea Family.

lanceolate: Lance shaped, much longer than wide and pointed at the end, usually with the widest portion below the middle, as in leaves.

leaflet: One of the leaf-like parts of a compound leaf.

linear: Long, narrow with parallel sides, as in leaves.

lobed: Indented on the edges, with the indentations not reaching the center or base; often used when describing entire leaves or leaflets of pinnatifid leaves.

male flower: A unisexual flower having stamens but lacking a pistil.

monoecious: A plant having both female (pistillate) and male (staminate) organs but in different flowers on the same plant, such as corn.

mycorrhiza (mychorrizae, pl.)**:** A symbiotic, structural, and physiological relationship between plant roots and specific fungi that facilitates absorption of soil nutrients and their transfer into plant roots.

node: The place on a stem from which a leaf or branch originates.

oblanceolate: Similar to lanceolate but with the widest part toward the base.

obovate: More or less egg shaped with the basal end being the narrower, as in leaves or petals; the opposite of ovate.

opposite leaves: Leaves originating in pairs from nodes with one leaf on either side of the stem.

ovate: More or less egg shaped, pointed at the top and broadest near the base or the middle, as in leaves or petals.

palmate leaf: A leaf with three or more divisions or lobes, much like the outspread fingers of a hand.

panicle: A branched, open inflorescence in which the main branches are again branched.

pappus: Thread-like hairs, bristles, scales, or a crown on top of the seed-like fruits of various members of the Asteraceae, such as in dandelions and salsify.

parasite: An organism that derives its nutrition from another living organism.

pedicel: The stalk of each individual flower of a cluster.

pendulose: Hanging downward.

perennial: In reference to a plant that lives for more than two years, usually producing flowers, fruits, and seeds annually.

perfect flower: One with both stamens and pistils present; bisexual.

petal: The basic unit of the corolla; flat, usually broad, and brightly colored or white.

petiole: The stalk-like part of a leaf, the part that attaches it to the stem.

phyllary: The reduced, leaf-like bracts beneath a flower head that comprise the involucre; holds the base of the flowers together in the Asteraceae.

pinnate leaf: A compound leaf with leaflets along the sides of a central stalk (rachis), much like a feather.

pinnatifid: adjective, referring to overall shape of a pinnate leaf.

pistil: The female organ of a flower, composed of an ovary, style and stigma.

pod: A dry fruit that opens at maturity to release its seeds.

pollination: The transfer of pollen from an anther to a stigma by various agents (insects, birds, wind, water, etc.).

raceme: An elongated inflorescence with stalked flowers that arise from the unbranched stalk; maturing from the bottom up, as in delphiniums.

rachis: The main stem, bearing flowers or leaflets.

ray flower: Each of the bilaterally symmetrical flowers around the edge of the central disk in many members of the Asteraceae, or comprising the entire head in some members of the family.

receptacle: The extended portion of the floral axis that bears and supports the flower parts.

recumbent: Prostrate except for the ascending tips at stem ends.

rhizome: A horizontal, underground stem, often enlarged by food storage, distinguished from a root by the presence of nodes and sometimes scale-like leaves.

riparian: Referring to the bank of, or area adjacent to, a natural course of water.

rosette: A crowded cluster of leaves, usually basal, circular, and appearing to grow directly out of the ground, giving rise to flowering stalks.

runner: A horizontal stem that grows above ground and develops leaves, roots, and new plants at nodes or tip; a stolon.

samara: A dry, winged, indehiscent fruit; wing may be long, such as in maples, or small and circular, such as in elms and cow parsnip.

scape: A leafless, flower-bearing stalk.

sepal: The base unit of the calyx; often green, sometimes colored and petal-like, usually smaller than petals (with iris as an exception).

serrated, toothed: Having a saw-toothed edge.

sessile: Without a stalk; referring to a leaf lacking a petiole with the blade attached directly to the stem.

silique: A slender, elongated fruit in the Brassicaceae, more than 3 times as long as it is wide.

simple leaf: A leaf that is not compound.

sp.: Abbreviation for "species," singular.

spatulate: Spatula or spoon shaped, having a broad and rounded apex and narrow base; more pronounced than obovate shape; in leaves or petals.

species (singular and plural): A fundamental category of taxonomic classification, ranking immediately below genus; individuals within a species usually reproduce among themselves and are more closely related to each other than they are to individuals of other species. The species name is the Latin name following the genus; the names of the genus and the species together comprise the plant's scientific name, as in the scientific name of the calypso orchid, *Calypso bulbosa*.

spike: An elongated, unbranched flower cluster in which each flower lacks a stalk; common in many grasses.

spp.: Abbreviation for "species," plural.

spreading stem: One growing horizontally along the ground's surface.

spur: In reference to a flower, a slender, usually hollow projection originating from the petal or sepal.

ssp.: Abbreviation of "subspecies."

stamen: The male organ of a flower, composed of a slender filament topped by an anther; usually several in each flower; produces the pollen.

staminode: A sterile stamen, usually reduced to a filament, sometimes hairy, as in some penstemons.

stem: The main axis of a plant or its branches, responsible for supporting the leaves and flowers.

stigma: The tip of the pistil where pollen lands, germinates, and begins its growth through the style to reach the ovary.

stolon: Horizontal stem that grows on or below the soil surface; rhizome; runner.

style: The narrow, sometimes elongated part of the pistil, connecting ovary and stigma.

tepal: A term used for sepals and petals similar and not easily distinguishable from each other, such as in some Liliaceae.

toothed, serrated: Having a saw-toothed edge.

umbel: An inflorescence in which the individual flower stalks grow from the same point, similar to the ribs of an umbrella; may be compound, with a second set of similar stalks arising from the tips of the first set of stalks. The compact structure may be either flat or domed.

whorl: A circle of three or more leaves, branches, or flower stalks at a node.

Illustrated

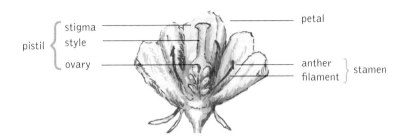

Typical Flower Parts

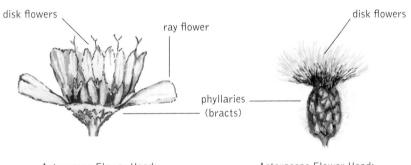

Asteraceae Flower Head:
Disk and Ray Flowers

Asteraceae Flower Head:
Disk Flowers Only

Common Inflorescence Types

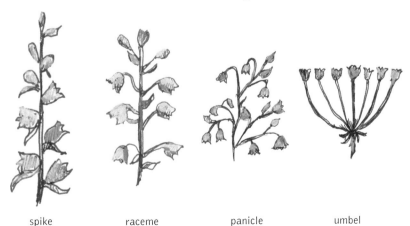

spike   raceme   panicle   umbel

Common Types of Asteraceae Involucres

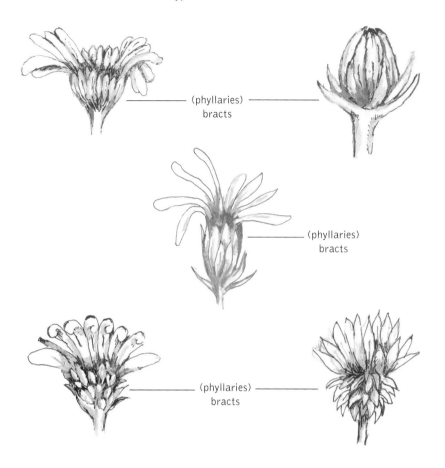

(phyllaries)
bracts

(phyllaries)
bracts

(phyllaries)
bracts

Leaf Attachments and Arrangements on Stem

clasping   stalkless   petiolate   alternate   opposite   whorled
(stalked)

Leaf Types

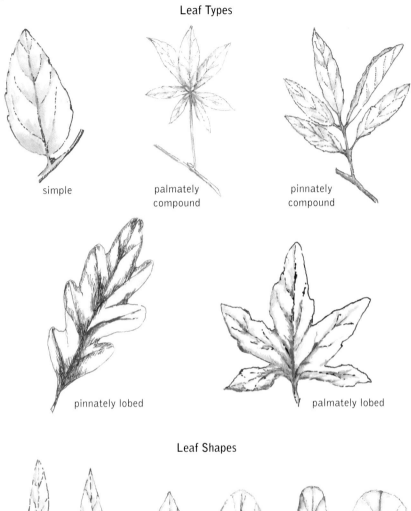

simple

palmately
compound

pinnately
compound

pinnately lobed

palmately lobed

Leaf Shapes

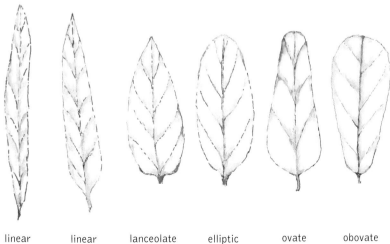

linear

linear
lanceolate

lanceolate

elliptic

ovate

obovate

REFERENCES

References in bold type are the ones that were most often used in the preparation of this text.

WILDFLOWERS (BOOKS AND RESEARCH PUBLICATIONS)

Allred, KW, and RD Ivey. 2012. *Flora Neomexicana III: An Illustrated Identification Manual*, vol. 3. (9 May 2014; www.Lulu.com)

Barkley, TM, ed. 1986. *Flora of the Great Plains*. University of Kansas Press.

Benson, L. 1969. *The Cacti of Arizona*. 3rd ed. University of Arizona Press.

Bookman, SS. 1982. The floral morphology of *Asclepias speciosa* (Asclepiadaceae) in relation to pollination and a clarification in terminology in the genus. *American Journal of Botany* 68(5): 675–679.

Coleman, RA. 2002. *The Wild Orchids of Arizona and New Mexico*. Cornell University Press.

Dodson, C, and WW Dunmire 2007. *Mountain Wildflowers of the Southern Rockies*. University of New Mexico Press.

Dunmire, WW. 1997. *Wild Plants and Native Peoples of the Four Corners*. Museum of New Mexico Press.

———. 2012. *New Mexico's Living Landscapes*. Museum of New Mexico Press.

———, and **GD Tierney. 1995. *Wild Plants of the Pueblo Provinces*. Museum of New Mexico Press.**

Ells, J. 2006. *Rocky Mountain Flora*. The Colorado Mountain Club Press.

Elpel, TJ. 2006. *Botany in a Day: The Patterns Method of Plant Identification*. HOPS Press.

Flora of North America Editorial Committee, eds. 1993–2007. *Flora of North America: North of Mexico*. 27 vols. Flora of North America Editorial Committee.

Heflin, J. 1997. *Pentemons: The Beautiful Beardtongues of New Mexico*. Jackrabbit Press.

Ivey, RD. 2008. *Flowering Plants of New Mexico*. 5th ed. RD Ivey.

Jercinovic, E. 2003. *Wildflowers of the Manzanos*. E Jercinovic.

Julyan, R, and M. Stuever, eds. 2005. *Field Guide to the Sandia Mountains*. University of New Mexico Press.

References

Littlefield, LJ, and PM Burns. 2011. *Wildflowers of the Sandia and Manzano Mountains of Central New Mexico*. Sandia Plant Books.

Martin, WC. 1984. *Spring Wildflowers of New Mexico*. University of New Mexico Press.

——. 1986. *Summer Wildflowers of New Mexico*. University of New Mexico Press.

——. 1988. *Fall Wildflowers of New Mexico*. University of New Mexico Press.

——, and CR Hutchins. 1980. *A Flora of New Mexico*, vol. 1. J. Cramer.

——, and CR Hutchins. 1981. *A Flora of New Mexico*, vol. 2. J. Cramer.

Nelson, RA. 1992. *Handbook of Rocky Mountain Plants*. Rev. RL Williams. Denver Museum of Natural History and Roberts Rinehart Publishers.

Niehaus, TF. 1984. *A Field Guide to Southwestern and Texas Wildflowers*. The Peterson Field Guide Series. Houghton Mifflin Company.

O'Kane, SL, Jr, KN Smith, and KA Arp. 2012. *Physaria iveyana* (Brassicaceae), a new species from the Sandia Mountains, New Mexico. *Phytoneuron* 2012-53: 1–6. (9 May 2014; http://www.phytoneuron.net/PhytoN-Physaria.pdf)

Rickett, HW. 1970. *Wildflowers of the United States*. Vol. 4. *The Southwestern States*. New York Botanic Garden and McGraw-Hill Book Co.

Schiemann, DA. 2005. *Wildflowers of Montana*. Mountain Press Publishing Co.

Sivinski, RC. 2007. *Checklist of Vascular Plants in the Sandia and Manzano Mountains of Central New Mexico*. Museum of Southwestern Biology, University of New Mexico. OccPap-MSB-N10-Sivinski.

Spellenberg, R. 2001. *National Audubon Society Field Guide to North American Wildflowers: Western Region*. Rev. ed. Alfred A. Knopf.

Vines, RA. 1960. *Trees, Shrubs and Woody Vines of the Southwest*. University of Texas Press.

Weniger, D. 1984. *Cacti of Texas and Neighboring States*. University of Texas Press.

Whitson, TD, LC Burrill, SH Dewey, DW Cudney, BE Nelson, RD Lee, and R. Parker. 2002. *Weeds of the West*. 9th ed. Western Society of Weed Science, Western United States Land Grant Universities Cooperative Extension Service, and the University of Wyoming.

WILDFLOWERS (WEBSITES)

Extension Utah State University. 2014. Colorado Columbine. Range Plants of Utah. (31 May 2014; http://extension.usu.edu/rangeplants/htm/colorado-columbine)

Friends of the Wild Flower Garden, Inc. 2013. Plants of the Eloise Butler Wildflower Garden. (10 June 2014; www.friendsofeloisebutler.org/pages/plants/virginia creeper.html)

Jercinovic G. 2003. *Wildflowers of the Manzanos*. NewMexicoFlores.com. (10 May 2014; http://newmexicoflores.com/manzanos.html)

Tom Volk's Fungi. 2010. (10 May 2014; http://tomvolkfungi.net) See especially "Monthly Pages" and "Fungus of the Month, Oct. 2002" for information about the biology and role of mycorrhizal fungi in parasitic nutrition of pinesap and related species.

U.S. Department of Agriculture Natural Resources Conservation Service. 2014. Plants Database. (10 May 2014; http://plants.usda.gov) Information and illustrations of all species of plants in their files, including links to university and museum websites.

Wayne's World: An Online Textbook of Natural History. 2014. (10 May 2014; http://waynesword.palomar.edu/) See especially "Fungus Flowers" (http://waynesword.palomar.edu/pljune97.htm) and "Parasitic Flowering Plants" (http://waynesword.palomar.edu/plnov99.htm), which has similar nutrient source information, including information about orchids.

Wildflowers, Ferns, and Trees of Colorado, New Mexico, Arizona, and Utah. 2014. (10 May 2014; www.swcoloradowildflowers.com) Photographs and technical descriptions of wildflowers common in the Colorado Plateau and adjacent areas.

FLOWERING SHRUBS

Carter, JL. 2012. *Trees and Shrubs of New Mexico.* Mimbres Publishing Co.
———, MA Carter, and DJ Stevens. 2003. *Common Southwestern Native Plants: An Identification Guide.* Mimbres Publishing Co.
Epple, EE, and AO Epple. 1995. *A Field Guide to the Plants of Arizona.* Lew Ann Publishing Co.
Finley, WF, and LJ Nieland. 2013. *Land of Enchantment Wildflowers: A Guide to the Plants of New Mexico.* Texas Tech University Press.
Kearney, TH, and RH Peebles. 1951. *Flowering Plants and Ferns of Arizona.* University of California Press
Martin, WC, and CR Hutchins. 1980, 1981. *A Flora of New Mexico.* 2 vols. J. Cramer.
Vines, RA. 1960. *Trees, Shrubs and Woody Vines of the Southwest.* University of Texas Press.
Weber, WA. 1976. *Rocky Mountain Flora.* 5th ed. University Press of Colorado.
Weniger, D. 1984. *Cacti of Texas and Neighboring States.* University of Texas Press

ETHNOBOTANY AND MEDICINAL, AND OTHER USES OF PLANTS

Kindscher, K. 1992. *Wild Plants of the Prairie: An Ethnobotanical Guide.* University Press of Kansas.
Moerman, DE. 1998. *Native American Ethnobotany.* Timber Press.
Moore, M. 1979. *Medicinal Plants of the Mountain West.* Museum of New Mexico Press.
Tilford, GL. 1997. *Edible and Medicinal Plants of the West.* Mountain Press Publishing Co.

PUEBLO INDIAN LANGUAGES

Sando, JS. 1976. *The Pueblo Indians.* The Indian Historian Press.

Geology

Hunt, CB. 1972. *Geology of Soils.* W. F. Freeman.
Price, LG, ed. 2010. *The Geology of Northern New Mexico's Parks, Monuments and Public Lands.* New Mexico Bureau of Geology and Mineral Resources.

INDEX OF COMMON NAMES

Columbine Blue (Rocky Mountain), 326; Red, 295
Coneflower Cutleaf, 153; Prairie, 348; Short-Rayed, 151
Coralbells, 251
Cosmos, Wild (Southwestern), 223
Cota, 165
Crowfoot, 177
Crownbeard, Golden, 167
Currant Golden, 190; Wolf, 46
Daisy Blackfoot, 20; Coulter's, 15; Cowpen, 167; Easter (Dwarf Townsend's; Easter Stemless), 22; Englemann, 127; Ox-Eye, 19; Paper, 150; Rocky Mountain Townsend (Tall Easter), 260; Showy, 224
Dandelion Burnt-Orange (Orange-Flowered Mountain), 342; Common, 162; Desert, 145
Datura (Sacred), 104
Dayflower, Birdbill, 340
Death Camus, 57
Deer's Ears, 43
Deervetch, Wright's, 206
Delphinium, Ugly, 263
Devil's Claw, 252
Dock, Curly (Curly-Leaf), 350
Dodder, 75
Dogbane, Spreading, 228
Dogwood, Red-Osier, 38
Draba, Twistpod, 197
Dragonhead, 71

Elderberry, Red, 52
Elephant Head, 232
Elk's Lip, 34
Equisetum, 355
Estafiata, 8
Evening Primrose Hooker's, 182; Pink (Cutleaf), 41; Stemless (Tufted), 40
Fairy Candelabra, Northern, 106
False Boneset, 10
False Bugbane, 37
False Flax, Little-Pod, 196
Fendlerbush, 54
Fennel, Dog, 6
Figwort, Mountain, 308
Filaree, Red-Stemmed, 238
Fireweed, 229
Firewheel, 293
Five-Leafed Ivy, Western, 359
Flax, Wild Blue (Prairie), 330
Fleabane Showy (Oregon), 224; Spreading, 320; Trailing, 16
Four o'clock Colorado (Desert; Wild), 271; Mountain, 272; Narrowleaf, 237
Frog's Eyes, 202

Gaillardia, 293
Gaillardia, Yellow, 129
Gaura Scarlet, 300; Small-Flowered, 301
Gayfeather, Dotted, 258
Gentian Green, 43; Fringed, 332; Pleated, 331
Geranium Purple (Fremont), 273; Richardson's, 44
Germander, Cutleaf (Lacy), 73

Gilia Many-Flowered, 339; Scarlet, 315; Trumpet, 337
Globemallow Narrowleaf, 344; Scarlet, 345
Goathead, 180
Goat's Beard, Yellow, 166
Goldeneye, Showy, 137
Goldenrod, 161; Parry's, 147; Rigid, 146
Golden Smoke, 189
Goldenweed, Annual (Slender), 144
Gooseberry, Trumpet, 45
Goosefoot, Fetid, 358
Gourd, Buffalo, 191
Grape Canyon, 360; Oregon, 172
Green Eyes, 125
Greenthread, 165
Greenthread, Stiff, 164
Gromwell Fringed, 173; Wayside, 174
Ground Cherry, Ivy-Leafed, 211
Groundsel Alpine, 156; Cutleaf, 158; Lyrate, 148; Nodding (Bigelow's), 157; Notchleaf (Fendler's), 159; Threadleaf, 160
Gumweed Curlycup, 131; Sharptooth, 130

Harebell, 322
Heal-All, 276
Heliotrope, Bindweed (Phlox Heliotrope), 24
Hellebore, False, 62
Hemlock Poison, 87; Western Water, 86
Heronbill, 238

INDEX OF SCIENTIFIC NAMES

Note: *(syn.)* indicates a synonym

Toxicodendron rydbergii, 117
Tragia ramosa, 356
Tragopogon dubius, 166
Trautvetteria caroliniesis, 37
Trautvetteria grandis (syn.), 37
Tribulus terrestris, 180
Trifolium dasyphyllum, 285
Trifolium hybridum, 248
Typha angustifolia, 353
Typha latifolia, 354

Valeriana arizonica, 254
Veratum californicum, 62
Verbascum thapsus, 188
Verbena bipinnatifida (syn.), 290
Verbena bracteata, 291
Verbena macdougalii, 292
Verbesina encelioides, 167
Vicia americana, 286
Viguiera multiflora (syn.), 137
Viola canadensis, 118
Vitis arizonica, 360

Wyethia arizonica, 168

Xanthium strumarium, 349

Yucca baccata, 1
Yucca baileyi var. intermedia (syn.), 2
Yucca glauca (syn.), 2
Yucca intermedia, 2

Zinnia grandiflora, 169
Zygadenus elegans (syn.), 57

ABOUT THE AUTHORS

Pearl Burns, BS University of New Mexico, is a retired registered nurse, with major avocational interests and activities in the identification and distribution of wildflowers of New Mexico. For decades, she has led wildflower hikes in and around the Sandia Mountains, and in 2005, she coauthored the chapter on wildflowers in *Field Guide to the Sandia Mountains* (University of New Mexico Press). Since retiring, she has pursued that interest full-time, teaching countless wildflower identification courses and leading hikes for the United States Forest Service, the City of Albuquerque's Division of Public Parks and Open Space and Elderhostel/Road Scholar. In 2003, she was honored by the U.S. Forest Service as National Volunteer of the Year for her many years of outstanding volunteer service.

Larry Littlefield, BS Cornell University, MS and PhD University of Minnesota, was a professor of plant pathology at North Dakota State University and Oklahoma State University from 1965 to 2004. He taught plant pathology and mycology and conducted extensive research on the developmental anatomy (both light and electron microscopy) of rust fungi and on other fungal and viral diseases of plants. His research and teaching also took him to Sweden, England, Egypt, Pakistan, and Peru. He retired to New Mexico in 2005 and is an active volunteer at the Sandia Mountain Natural History Center, a joint facility of the New Mexico Museum of Natural History and Science and the Albuquerque Public Schools, and with the U.S. Forest Service, Sandia Ranger District.